D0718149

# The Bedside
# Guardian 2010

# The Bedside Guardian 2010

E D I T E D   B Y   C H R I S   E L L I O T T

**guardianbooks**

Published by Guardian Books 2010

2 4 6 8 10 9 7 5 3 1

Copyright © Guardian News and Media Ltd 2010

Chris Elliott has asserted his right under the Copyright,
Designs and Patents Act 1988 to be identified as the editor of this work

This book is sold subject to the condition that it shall not, by way of trade
or otherwise, be lent, resold, hired out, or otherwise circulated without the
publisher's prior consent in any form of binding or cover other than that in
which it is published and without a similar condition, including this
condition, being imposed on the subsequent purchaser.

First published in Great Britain in 2010 by
Guardian Books
Kings Place, 90 York Way
London N1 9GU

www.guardianbooks.co.uk

A CIP catalogue record for this book
is available from the British Library

ISBN 9780852652183

Designed by Two Associates
Typeset by seagulls.net

Printed and bound in Great Britain by Clays Ltd, St Ives PLC

# Contents

# Foreword

NICK CLEGG

Everyone should read the *Bedside Guardian* – there are few better ways to capture the last year. Essays, letters, columns, obituaries, reports, even a tweet from the editor. The World Cup, the Copenhagen summit, Somalia's civil war, the Greek debt crisis, the Budget, volcanic ash, even Hilary Mantel on the joys of stationery. This was no staid, predictable year. This was 12 months of change, dilemmas and crises. An anthology of such wonderful writing is the best way to make sense of that: bright brushstrokes on a canvas which isn't yet complete.

My highlights? It's the quirky events that stick most in the mind: my middle son's birthday party on the weekend after the election – you try administering Smarties and Ribena to 30 six-year-olds while negotiating a coalition on the phone. Or there was being compared to Churchill and a Nazi by different newspapers within 24 hours. Or, far worse, having to choose between my mother's team and my wife's team for the World Cup final (in a shameless act of fence-sitting I started loyal to my mother, but defected to Miriam at half-time because of Holland's tactics).

But my biggest impression of the last year is quite simply this: the jury's still out. So many of the questions that have dominated this year remain unanswered. Will the world pick up the pieces from Copenhagen and finally agree a meaningful climate change deal? As the banks move back into profit, will we see a different banking system finally emerge, or just the same old mistakes of the past? What will happen to the world economy?

There are two possible responses to an environment of such great uncertainty: you hedge your bets, tread water, wait and see what to do next; or you actively seek to shape events, pushing things along in the direction of your choosing.

In a way, that's the choice we all faced on the two biggest dilemmas in Britain this year: what to do about an uncertain election outcome where no single party had won a slam-dunk victory; and what to do about our economy, especially our sky-high deficit.

Gallons of ink have already been consumed on articles, polemic and analysis about the creation of the new coalition government. People's views have chopped and changed. It's been intriguing to see people who campaigned for years for pluralism in politics condemn this government as an unholy pact. It's been equally intriguing to see people who warned about the cataclysmic effects of a hung parliament now champion the balance and political diversity of coalition politics.

Above all, it's been striking how the heated, anguished views of the Westminster and media elite in London are confounded by the level-headed approach of many people in the country at large. Of course, many people are still making up their minds, but more often I meet people who simply accept this was the only way forward, so let's just give it a chance.

For me, the choices remain as simple now as they did in the hours and days after the election result: first, did we want to pitch the country into yet another draining election campaign within a matter of months rather than seeking to provide a government capable of getting things done? And, second, any new coalition government had to go with the grain of people's expressed preferences in the ballot box, otherwise its legitimacy would be constantly questioned. A so-called coalition of losers would have floundered in weeks.

Then there's the deficit. There's a legitimate debate about the exact pace of deficit reduction. But the need to unburden future generations of this generation's massive debts is surely beyond doubt. There's nothing fair about ducking difficult decisions now and forcing our children to cope with the fallout – decades of debt, higher interest rates and fewer jobs. I didn't come into politics to be a deficit-reducing bean counter. But when the coalition government was formed, it was obvious that the economic firestorm in Greece and Spain would rebound on us too if we didn't act decisively to take control of events. Even our Labour predecessors had plans to make billions of pounds worth of cuts. They simply refused to tell anyone where those savings would come from.

We have set out a five-year plan to get the economy back on a sound footing, spreading the burden as fairly as we can. Not, as the lazy allegation is often made, slashing and burning in the first year, but making an early start in 2010 with bigger, staged reductions over several years ahead. At the same time we will introduce big reforms elsewhere, too, from making politics more transparent and accountable, to restoring hard-won civil liberties, to radically reshaping our public services so they are built around the lives of people, not the needs of bureaucrats. And, from climate change, to financial regulation, to international security and development, we want to create a Britain that can lead the way in answering the big, global questions that will dominate the years ahead.

None of these challenges can be resolved overnight. But if we hold our nerve, if we take the difficult decisions that are needed, I believe we can deliver a fairer, more prosperous and more hopeful future. Future *Bedside Guardian*s will tell us whether we got it right.

# Introduction

CHRIS ELLIOTT

"Every change is a form of liberation," once said Paula Rego, the artist who was made a Dame in the Queen's birthday honours list in June. "My mother used to say a change is always good, even it's for the worse."

Rego's mother probably did not have coalition governments in mind, but she might easily have been presciently remarking on this last year, when the theme of change, for better or worse, was a constant.

Six weeks before the 2010 general election, Simon Hoggart sketched the comings and goings of politicians on College Green, where they went before the TV news cameras. "So they speak very vaguely, and use as few words as possible. The words they use are 'hope', 'future', 'fairness' and 'change'. Especially 'change', a word they can use over and over again in a single speech without evidently having any notion of what it might mean."

It wasn't just the echoes of Barack Obama's successful presidential campaign that put change in the foreground of the British election. The Conservatives' explicit pitch for the "progressive" tag epitomised the appetite for the change message. This year's *Bedside Guardian*, a collection of the best *Guardian* journalism, in print and online, captures some of that mood and rhetoric of change, in the UK election and beyond. By any standards it was an extraordinary election campaign, an extraordinary result and an extraordinary aftermath.

The *Guardian* gave it a kick-start with one of the most apposite April Fool jokes we have ever mounted. Olaf Priol – who else – suggested that a new campaign for Labour was built around Brown's much trumpeted aggression. "Step outside posh boy" was the legend on the fake posters. Such was the paucity of ideas in the Labour camp that the idea was seized on enthusiastically by the hundreds who applied to the *Guardian* for the T-shirts.

Despite a long and at times grinding campaign, the electorate seemed unconvinced that any single party could deliver the necessary "change" to fix things in a world hovering on the edge of a double-dip recession.

Our reporters, commentators and photographers followed the course of an election that ignited with the three televised leaders' debates and a surge in Liberal Democrat support. That support dwindled at the ballot box but nonetheless Lib Dem leader Nick Clegg became the central, critical figure in the political drama that unfolded in the days after the vote – there could hardly be a more apt individual to pen the foreword to this year's *Bedside* book, and for that we thank him.

The last days of Gordon Brown as prime minister and party leader as he stumbled exhaustedly around the country are recorded with exasperation and wit by our writers. Marina Hyde was twice dispatched to Buckingham Palace, first to see Gordon Brown arrive to ask the Queen to dissolve parliament; then, weeks later, to witness Brown's more painful ride to tell her he couldn't form the next government.

Michael White's considered and incisive profile of Brown reflects on a man who is more than the sum of his flaws. Ian Jack provides the narrative for Martin Argles's powerful and poignant last photographs of Gordon Brown, with his family and staff, just minutes before leaving No 10 for the last time; these, two of which are reproduced here, are the telling final images of New Labour's 13 years in power.

Not since the final days of Margaret Thatcher have the political classes, the media and the nation had such a breathless time as in those five days that followed polling day, which culminated in the first coalition government for more than 30 years. (Though one which hardly featured the mix of faces to reflect modern Britain, as Katharine Viner argues.)

The drama of those days was expertly rendered in Andrew Sparrow's Election 2010 live blog, which ran for the duration of the campaign, seemingly without respite. We include here a taste of the blog that became essential reading online. The importance of the web in coverage of the election is also reflected in the readers' live critique of the second televised leaders' debate from Comment is free, and Cif editor Matt Seaton's account of the *Guardian* meeting to discuss the leader line, where Cif readers' comments were read out and pasted on the walls.

After the maelstrom of coalition-making and the rush to cut the deficit it is easy to forget other big election issues, like the threat of the British National party. The very real fears that the recession might result in an upsurge in support for the far right largely evaporated when push came to shove.

To know why we have John Harris's excellent piece of reporting on "the battle for Barking", revealing the fears and concerns of the working classes as they decided how to vote in this traditional Labour stronghold.

But as Marina Hyde discovered as she chatted to tourists outside the Palace, the "Westminster village" can be a far-off place of which people in the outside world often know little, and care even less. The election was a big deal for many of us but the rest of the world got on with the recession, environmental disasters, and just the business of living.

In China, last September, there was an anniversary to celebrate. It was 60 years since the Communist revolution and Tania Branigan talked to those who lived through it, and made it happen.

The following month Alan Rusbridger, the *Guardian*'s editor, used the micro-blogging site Twitter to evoke the spirit of John Wilkes, the 18th-century journalist and fighter for a free press, when the *Guardian* was prevented by a legal instrument known as a "super-injunction" from reporting not only the details of a confidential report about the oil company Trafigura's activities but also the very existence of the injunction or who had obtained it.

Against a journalist's normal instincts and training we ran a story on the front of the newspaper that said almost nothing other than that we had an interesting story we couldn't tell. The Twitterati swarmed and began a campaign to ferret out the information. As the campaign gathered force, Trafigura's name was exposed and the injunction was eventually dropped.

Those hoping for serious change on environmental policy would be buoyed by the global newspaper editorial that opens this collection, but would be left disappointed from December's Copenhagen summit. In a startling account, Mark Lynas, reveals what went on in the room when the Chinese delegation forced a shoddy compromise.

The controversy over leaked emails by climate scientists from the University of East Anglia was another blow to climate campaigners. George Monbiot is blunt and angry in his assessment. He softened his stance later in the year after the publication of inquiries, but the column included here is typically tough and uncompromising, caused a powerful debate within the climate science community, and so demands inclusion.

The lives of the residents along the coasts of the Gulf of Mexico as well as the flora and fauna were shattered when the BP Deepwater rig blew up in April and millions of barrels of oil began pouring into the water. Tim Gautreaux, a Louisiana resident, describes life three months later as he takes stock of the profound damage.

For all the talk of change in Iraq and Afghanistan, the death toll continued in both countries. Mona Mahmood reveals the hand of Iran behind the kidnappers of five Britons in Iraq, four of whom were murdered. Seumas Milne tears into the US claims they have withdrawn from Iraq.

The *Guardian* joined forces with the *New York Times* and *Der Spiegel* to publish astonishing stories and extracts arising out of 92,000 war logs covering US and UK tactical troop actions in Afghanistan that had been leaked to the Wikileaks website.

And far away in Whitehall the inquiry by Sir John Chilcot into the Iraq war rumbles along; with almost no hand-to-hand fighting and few casualties, according to Simon Jenkins.

One of the finest pieces of journalism published in any UK newspaper last year came out of a different, older war. Simon Winchester, who was on the streets of Derry for the *Guardian* on Bloody Sunday in 1972, was back there to see the responses of the people who had waited 38 years for the Saville inquiry to give them the vindication they deserved.

It's a powerful reminder that journalism should first and foremost be about bearing witness.

Throbbing through the year like a migraine that refuses to go away, and is always threatening to explode again, is the economy. Bafflingly, bankers' bonuses are back, as are aggressive takeovers. Nils Pratley looks at the companies that may consume one another, while Larry Elliott takes the fledgling coalition government to task for its determination to cut deeper, wider and without a plan B.

For individuals change comes in forms that are often sudden, painful and unsought. These are the individual stories that catch your throat.

Lionel Shriver penned a moving account of her guilt at her failure to support a friend dying of cancer; Amelia Gentleman's assignment to Dignitas House in Switzerland, where people go, legally, to have advice and support to help them end their lives, delivered another model of compelling reporting.

Of course I hope within the big themes we can also show you that we can enjoy good writing for its own sake or for the sake of a smile – take a bow *Guardian* digester of everything John Crace, tennis blogger Xan Brooks and that horny-handed son of spoil Malcolm Tucker. Or be uplifted by Mark Rice-Oxley talking of his journey through and, thankfully, beyond depression. And for a mildly subversive look at the way the battle for greater diversity is being fought we have Hugh Muir's account of the milkman who learned Gujarati to get on better with his customers.

So there we are; a brief selection of things that have made and marred the year. As ever, it has been painful to face the limits of space, and numerous excellent pieces of journalism have had to be left out – the *Guardian*'s election coverage alone could comfortably fill more than one *Bedside* volume.

It has been a busy year, and what exactly has changed? Well, as Nick Clegg suggests in his foreword, and Jonathan Freedland concludes in his account of 100 days of the coalition that rounds off this collection, it really is too early to say.

# Autumn

# The way we must live now

## GUARDIAN LEADER

All great causes involve a tension between collective belief and individual action. A shared agreement that something must be done is not enough to win the battle if people do nothing. This is especially true of the fight against climate change, which must involve all of humanity over many decades, working together to achieve something that none can see or touch and that can only be measured by scientists: an end to the rapid increase of climate change gases in the atmosphere. Faced with this, even the most generous-spirited of people could be forgiven for feeling daunted – surrendering, perhaps, to the hope that someone else will solve the problem.

Urged to do their bit, individuals may wait instead for governments to act, or engineers to come up with technical fixes, or just give in to the comforting but scientifically unsupported gamble that calamity may be avoided if things go on as they are. Today, the *Guardian* lends its support to a new movement that aims to defy such fatalism. The 10:10 campaign does not claim that climate change can be wished away through a series of small personal measures taken in Britain alone; it fully supports the need for a deal at the Copenhagen summit in December and for great economies such as the US and China to change too. But if the international agreement is to mean anything, the way people live in this country must change. The 10:10 campaign – named after its target of helping people reduce their individual carbon emissions by 10% in 2010 – will put pressure on government to meet its promises, but it will also have an immediate effect. Climate change gases, once in the atmosphere, stay there. The faster emissions fall now, the less will have to be done later.

All calls for individual environmental responsibility tread a tricky path. On the one hand there is a large and committed green movement, represented this week by the climate camp now in place where the Peasants' Revolt once gathered in Blackheath in south-east London. Many of its supporters, for the best of reasons, want human life to change radically and immediately: an end to the global free market, to meat-eating, to air travel, to all coal-produced electricity. They disapprove of mechanisms to bring down carbon emissions such as the European Union's carbon trading scheme; some dislike technological solutions such as carbon capture and storage. The trouble with these ambitions is that they are never likely to be supported by the majority of the population, who, if told that such things are essential to stop climate change, may simply give up trying altogether. But at the other extreme lies an even more unrealistic response: to pretend that all that individuals need to do is make tiny adjustments to their lives – change a light bulb and save the world – while government sorts out the rest at very little cost. The fight is going to be much harder than that. And even if it eventually repays its costs, as Lord Stern has argued, the bills will arrive first and the savings later.

The new campaign hopes to avoid both pitfalls. Individuals have a moral obligation to act which can be met without abandoning the good things about life as it is lived today. Houses can still be heated, but must be insulated too. All sorts of food can still be eaten, but perhaps less meat and less often, and where possible that food should have travelled less far. Walk more, drive less – such things are so obvious that they can seem petty, and yet if enough people and organisations in Britain do them regularly, the effect can be immense. Britain's emissions have fallen since

1990. They must keep on falling sharply: current emissions of over 10 tonnes per capita must drop to two tonnes by 2050. This new campaign will not be enough to achieve that. But it is more than a start; it is the direction Britain must take, if the world as we know it is to survive.

*A version of this editorial, drafted at the* Guardian, *appeared in 56 news-papers in 45 countries*

7 SEPTEMBER 2009

# TV review: Miss Marple's many hats and the voices of 9/11

## NANCY BANKS-SMITH

Another Marple; another hat. This time it is Julia McKenzie wearing a plain tweedy job at a stylish angle – both of them more substantial than the last Marple, Geraldine McEwan, who was (and who wore) a flirty bit of stuff. Watching her Miss Marple, twinkling like sequinned knickers, you were reminded of Bernard Shaw's comment on Leslie Howard playing a suave Professor Higgins: "It's just amazing how wrong Leslie is."

Once TV had found its Poirot in David Suchet, no change seemed plausible or even possible. I was talking to Agatha Christie at some press call (almost certainly at yet another anniversary of *The Mousetrap*), when I saw Robertson Hare being vibrant a few feet away. "There," I said, with the confidence of youth, "is your Poirot." Robertson Hare was a star of the Aldwych farces during which he regularly lost his trousers. He was small and funny and his head seemed to take up an unreasonable amount of his height. You felt that, if you patted his bald head, he would bounce. Christie looked at him steadily, saying nothing for some time (she was a rather disconcerting woman), then said, with less enthusiasm than I expected, "Yes." Conversation, you will have gathered, did not exactly flow. Finding the perfect Poirot took another 20 years.

Miss Marple, on the other hand, has rolled around the board seeking and never quite finding that Marple-shaped hole. Julia McKenzie's Marple is charming, wholesome and, like the script, faithful. (In Miss McEwan's day the killer could easily turn out to be a lesbian.)

*A Pocket Full of Rye* (ITV1) also had positively final last performances from Wendy Richard, who knew perfectly well she was very ill, as the cook, and a ferociously eyebrowed Ken Campbell as the butler. As every skuleboy kno, the butler never does it. Ken Campbell compensated for this dishearteningly minor role by leaping at the camera, roaringly drunk, shouting, "There's something funny going on here! Who the hell are you? Bottoms up, miss!" and getting a highly satisfactory close-up. As McKenzie said with Marplish demureness, "He did not mind too much about scripts." A grand, if maddening, epitaph.

> *Here lies Ken Campbell.*
> *He did not mind too much about scripts.*
> *Better stand well back.*

The cast, like the high tea at Yew Tree Lodge, was lavish. Helen Baxendale, icily regular as the housekeeper, Ben Miles in the unforgiving role of the dull brother and, under a suspicious wig, the unmistakable voice of Prunella Scales.

It was difficult to get to sleep after watching *9/11: Phone Calls from the Tower* (Channel 4). For 100-odd minutes after the first plane struck the first tower, the air was filled with the voices of sons and daughters, fathers and mothers, friends and firemen speaking to each other for the last time. On the 85th floor Jim Gartenburg called his pregnant wife, his best friend and, with astonishing presence of mind, the *New York Times* and a live TV programme: "A fire door has trapped us, debris has fallen around us and part of the core of the building has blown out. But the danger has not increased so please, all family members, take it easy." The daughter he never saw, dark and sparky like him, was shown clambering up a climbing wall.

Take one father and one mother. Bob took a call from his daughter, Melissa. "She was in trouble and she called her father for help and I was 130 miles away." He looks at the tree he planted when she was born. "It was five feet high and skinny as two fingers together." Now it is higher than the house.

Anne found a message from her son blinking on her answerphone: "Mom, its Stephen. I'll be all right and I'll call you." He and his friends, who had decided to stay together, were sharing one mobile phone. Then her husband called and told her not to watch TV. "It was an easy promise to keep. I went out into the back yard and I sat on a five-dollar plastic chair under a tree, preparing myself for what I would need to face." When they told her, she howled like an animal.

The families find the recorded voices comforting.

*Still are thy pleasant voices, thy nightingales, awake.*
*For death he taketh all away but them he cannot take.*

30 September 2009

# Tales of the revolution: sixty years on, veterans of Mao's China remember

## TANIA BRANIGAN

Few could have imagined this day, when communist ideas first began to spread in China in the 1920s. The nationalist leader Chiang Kai-shek's vicious crackdown in Shanghai in 1927 threatened to wipe out the party completely. But communist armed forces established bases in the south and turned from the urban poor to the peasantry as the base of their support. As Chiang Kai-shek continued his campaign against them, they embarked on the Long March in 1934: an astounding journey taking them thousands of miles to a new centre in the north.

Three years later, the two sides were forced into an alliance against a common enemy – the Japanese, who had invaded. By the end of the second world war, full-scale civil war resumed and Communist party membership, and the Red forces, had mushroomed. After three more years of bitter fighting – resulting in at least two million deaths, according to official figures – Mao Zedong proclaimed the creation of the People's Republic of China on 1 October 1949.

The last six decades have seen extraordinary accomplishments, misjudgments and atrocities and remarkable reversals. The party would seize land and hand it to peasant farmers, force them to form communes, then allow them to farm it individually again. The 30 years since reform and opening have seen the undoing of much of the previous 30's work, as "socialism with Chinese characteristics" – a capitalist economy, allied to the existing political system – has transformed the nation Mao made.

## HOU BO, MAO'S PHOTOGRAPHER

Hou Bo should never have got the assignment. Aged just 25, she had picked up a camera after stints as a nurse and teaching peasant farmers to read. But the more experienced photographers were in the provinces and could not reach Beijing in time. So when Chairman Mao stood on the rostrum of Tiananmen Square and proclaimed the creation of the People's Republic to cheering crowds beneath, it was Hou who captured the moment.

Crammed into a tiny space – with her husband, Xu Xiaobing, who was filming – she struggled to compose a shot with her Rolleiflex. "The machine could only take 12 pictures at a time. I didn't have a wide-angle or long lens," she says. Leaning far back over the rails, she realised it was a long way down if she fell.

"It was dangerous – very dangerous. But I was very excited and this photo was very important," she says. "Later, I noticed somebody was hanging on to my shirt [to protect me]. I turned around and had a look. Oh – it was Zhou Enlai." Zhou was, after Mao, one of the defining figures of the revolution; while Mao led the country, Zhou was premier.

The result was the first in a string of iconic shots. Hou became Mao's personal photographer and, over 12 years, produced pictures that burnished his image and shaped the way he is seen even now: on the seashore; pensive before the Yellow river; jovial in a crowd. Many other pictures were not revealed until after his death, judged too intimate or inappropriate to his stature.

She grew to know the chairman well and talks fondly of his love for swimming – sometimes with a lit cigarette in his mouth. Living in party headquarters, she became so close to other leaders that she would confide in them. "They treated us as family members," she says.

Hou had grown up in the communist fold, joining after her family fled invading Japanese troops. It provided her marriage and her career. She met her husband in Yan'an – the revolutionary base – and learned from him how to take pictures.

But the couple's loyalty was no protection against the brutal excesses of the cultural revolution. Both were beaten savagely and exiled to labour camps – separately – in the countryside for years. She is not clear why she was persecuted; millions of others were, too, and hundreds of thousands killed. Like many, she blames those around Mao, not the man himself. "Jiang Qing [Mao's wife, and one of the notorious 'gang of four'] criticised me ... saying I was a fake party member – those sorts of accusations," she recalls. "I joined at the age of 14. These accusations could not stand up. But there was no way out, so I just did the labour work."

Her ordeal ended when the cultural revolution petered out in the mid-1970s. No one told her she could leave, but when even the guards abandoned the fields, she walked away, back to her family. Only in 1977 – a decade after the accusations – was she exonerated.

Frail but articulate, she lives in a comfortable Beijing flat with her husband, now 94, their son and daughter-in-law. Alongside the pictures of Hou and Xu with Mao and other leaders, there is one of their son with the magician David Copperfield. Like their country, the couple have been on a long and strange journey.

"We've had many good experiences, but there have been some mistakes. Ordinary people can understand that."

## SIDNEY RITTENBERG, GI TURNED CADRE

Sidney Rittenberg missed the proclamation of the People's Republic. It was months later that he learned of its creation. "They put me in a cell [where] the windows were boarded up and there was newspaper pasted over the boards on the inside. And one of the papers was for 1 October, the *People's Daily* in big red print," he says.

It was a bittersweet moment.

Rittenberg, who had arrived in China as a US soldier in the early 40s, stayed on and ended up joining the communists at their base in Yan'an in 1946. The young idealist's leftwing beliefs were reinforced by what he saw on his arrival. "Human beings were treated very cheaply. If you had some standing – power, money – you could just wipe people out," he says. "If you asked a country person what he did, he wouldn't say, 'I'm a farmer.' He'd say, 'I suffer.'"

But he saw a sharp contrast between the corruption of Chiang Kai-shek's nationalists, siphoning foreign aid into the black market, and the communists. "I felt it was like living with the early Christians – those kinds of stories; the top leaders lived very frugal lives," he says. He joined them to work on propaganda and monitoring the foreign media – including the *Guardian*.

Despite the apparent puritanism, the Saturday dances and gin rummy sessions in Mao's cave-house were a shock after the earnest conversation of American communists in the US. "People like Zhou Enlai, Zhu De – as you played, they would cuff each other around and tease each other and have great sport," he says. Then he pauses. "Mao liked to play too. But no one cuffed him around." He chuckles.

Rittenberg distinguishes between the man he knew then and the near-emperor of later years – the first, "the best listener I had ever met"; the second, holding forth – though not everyone has such a rosy view of the early days. Political purges had begun long before the party reached Yan'an.

By the time Rittenberg's dreams of a revolution became true, he had been jailed for attempting to wreck it: "I didn't know that

Stalin had personally sent a written message to Mao, asking that I be arrested as chief of an international spy ring."

Despite 16 years in solitary confinement, Rittenberg chose to stay in China when released and was reinstated in official communist circles. He became an enthusiastic advocate of the cultural revolution, only to fall victim himself, leading to his second spell in jail and the persecution of his family.

"No one in his right mind would choose to have that sort of holocaust," he says. But, he added, it made people more critical; less willing to believe what they were told. And he cites the staggering improvements in life expectancy – which has more than doubled – as proof of the last 60 years' worth of achievements. "But could it have been done with less sacrifice?" he asks. "Undoubtedly it could."

## LIU TIANYOU, RED ARMY SOLDIER

She didn't have a name of her own until she was 17. No one had thought she needed or deserved one. She had no mother, no father and no money; she was a girl.

She survived by herding pigs and selling rice liquor on the streets. And when Red Army recruiters in the early 1930s arrived in her hometown in Sichuan province, she enrolled with the name they gave her: Liu Tianyou.

Now, at 95, she lives in a care home for veterans in the former communist base of Yan'an, Shaanxi. Few of her former comrades enjoy this comfort but, as another resident explained, the authorities like them to live there "to do propaganda and education work".

Liu has become something of a celebrity as a communist stalwart. She took part in the Olympic torch relay and though she never met Mao, "Chairman Hu" – as she calls the Chinese president – visited her recently.

When we arrive she is in hospital, recovering from respiratory problems. Even using an oxygen mask, each sentence is a slow, painful struggle – yet she is keen to talk.

"The power of the masses was mighty ... The Red Army attacked despotic gentry and evil landlords, people who exploited our country and exploited individuals ... Everybody was unified. The Red Army never scolded people or beat people up. It never looked down on ordinary people, whether they were rich or poor."

Not all veterans have such rosy memories; others tell of forced recruitment, brutal purges and strategic errors. What all agree on, however, is the improbability of their victory. Vastly outnumbered and outgunned by Chiang Kai-shek's Kuomintang, many fought with spears, clubs and wooden "guns" until they could capture Kuomintang weapons. The lucky had cloth shoes; others wore grass sandals.

Liu was there for the hardest part of all: the Long March. Driven out of their southern bases by the nationalists, the communists trekked for 8,000 miles in desperate conditions to their new base in Yan'an. Their extraordinarily circuitous route reflected uncertainty about their ultimate destination, as well as the need to avoid hostile forces. Only a fifth of them completed the journey: barely 40,000. Others deserted, fell in battle or starved along the way. Yet this ignominious retreat became enshrined as a glorious victory; the guts of survivors made it a founding myth.

The bitterest time, Liu recalls, was crossing the grasslands and the snow-covered mountains. Many froze to death. Desperate for nourishment, the troops stripped bark from the trees to eat and boiled up their leather belts.

"The soldiers before her had eaten all the grass; she had to eat the grass's roots," her son tells us.

Yet Liu remembers her soldiering days with relish. "The Kuomintang wanted to wipe out the communists. Aiya! The Red

Army had such strong power. How could you finish them off? Wherever you went, the Red Army was there. The Red Army is wily!"

She takes as much delight in the republic she helped to found: "China is a great country now. The whole world knows it," she says.

12 OCTOBER 2009, 9.05PM

# arusbridger at Twitter.com

## ALAN RUSBRIDGER

Now Guardian prevented from reporting parliament for unreportable reasons. Did John Wilkes live in vain? http://tinyurl.com/yhjxo38

*Link is to David Leigh report, below*

13 OCTOBER 2009

# Gag on *Guardian* reporting parliament

## DAVID LEIGH

The *Guardian* has been prevented from reporting parliamentary proceedings on legal grounds which appear to call into question privileges guaranteeing free speech established under the 1688 Bill of Rights.

Yesterday's published Commons order papers contain a question to be answered by a minister later this week. The *Guardian* is prevented from identifying the MP who has asked the question, what the question is, which minister might answer it, or where the question is to be found.

The *Guardian* is also forbidden from telling its readers why the paper is prevented – for the first time in memory – from reporting parliament. Legal obstacles, which cannot be identified, involve proceedings, which cannot be mentioned, on behalf of a client who must remain secret.

The only fact the *Guardian* can report is that the case involves the London solicitors Carter-Ruck, who specialise in suing the media for clients, who include individuals or global corporations.

Last night the *Guardian* vowed urgently to go to court to overturn the gag on its reporting. The editor, Alan Rusbridger, said: "The media laws in this country increasingly place newspapers in a Kafkaesque world in which we cannot tell the public anything about information which is being suppressed, nor the proceedings which suppress it. It is doubly menacing when those restraints include the reporting of parliament itself."

The media lawyer Geoffrey Robertson QC said last night Lord Denning ruled in the 1970s that "whatever comments are made in parliament" can be reported in newspapers without fear of contempt.

He said: "Four rebel MPs asked questions giving the identity of 'Colonel B', granted anonymity by a judge on grounds of 'national security'. The director of public prosecutions threatened the press might be prosecuted for contempt, but most published."

The right to report parliament was the subject of many struggles in the 18th century, with the MP and journalist John Wilkes fighting every authority – up to the king – over the right to keep the public informed. After Wilkes's battle, wrote the historian

Robert Hargreaves, "it gradually became accepted that the public had a constitutional right to know what their elected representatives were up to."

15 OCTOBER 2009

# A potent mix of old media and the Twittersphere

### ALAN RUSBRIDGER

One day – if it's not happening already – they will teach Trafigura in business schools. This will be the scenario for aspiring MBAs. You are in charge of a large but comfortably anonymous trading company based in London and have a tiresome PR problem. Three thousand miles away are 30,000 Africans in one of the poorest countries in the world claiming to have been injured by your company dumping toxic sludge. You are being hit by one of the biggest lawsuits in history. Worse, you now have a bunch of journalists on your case.

What to do? The business school textbooks will advocate a mix of carrot and stick. In charge of your carrot you hire Lord (Tim) Bell, who once performed a similar role on behalf of Mrs Thatcher. He will be in charge of attempts to reposition positive public perceptions of the Trafigura brand. He might, for instance, suggest you become an official sponsor of the British Lions tour of South Africa and an arts prize. And in charge of your stick you hire Britain's most notorious firm of libel lawyers, Messrs Carter-Ruck, who like to boast of their reputation for applying chloroform over the noses of troublesome editors.

For a while all goes well, especially on the stick front. Carter-Ruck spray threatening letters around newsrooms from Oslo to Abidjan. They launch an action against the BBC. And they persuade a judge to suppress a confidential but embarrassing document which has fallen into journalists' hands. A new term is coined: "super-injunctions", whereby the existence of court proceedings and court orders are themselves secret.

Nice work, large cheques all round. But the plan began to unravel rather rapidly on Monday when it transpired that an MP, Paul Farrelly, had tabled a question about the injunction and the awkward document in parliament. That was bad enough, what with the nuisance of 300-odd years of precedent affirming the right of the press to report whatever MPs say or do. There was a tiresomely teasing story on the *Guardian* front page. And then there was Twitter.

It took one tweet on Monday evening as I left the office to light the virtual touch paper. At five past nine I tapped: "Now *Guardian* prevented from reporting parliament for unreportable reasons. Did John Wilkes live in vain?" Twitter's detractors are used to sneering that nothing of value can be said in 140 characters. My 104 characters did just fine.

By the time I got home, after stopping off for a meal with friends, the Twittersphere had gone into meltdown. Twitterers had sleuthed down Farrelly's question, published the relevant links and were now seriously on the case. By midday on Tuesday, "Trafigura" was one of the most searched terms in Europe, helped along by re-tweets by Stephen Fry and his 830,000-odd followers.

Many tweeters were just registering support or outrage. Others were beavering away to see if they could find suppressed information on the far reaches of the web. One or two legal experts uncovered the Parliamentary Papers Act 1840, wondering if that would help? Common #hashtags were quickly developed, making the material easily discoverable.

By lunchtime – an hour before we were due in court – Trafigura threw in the towel. The textbook stuff – elaborate carrot, expensive stick – had been blown away by a newspaper together with the mass collaboration of strangers on the web. Trafigura thought it was buying silence. A combination of old media – the *Guardian* – and new – Twitter – turned attempted obscurity into mass notoriety.

So this week's Trafigura fiasco ought to be taught to aspiring MBAs and would-be journalists. They might nod in passing to the memory of John Wilkes, the scabrous hack and MP who risked his life to win the right to report parliament. An 18th-century version of crowd-sourcing played its part in that, too.

16 OCTOBER 2009

# Why there was nothing "human" about Jan Moir's Gately column

CHARLIE BROOKER

The funeral of Stephen Gately has not yet taken place. The man hasn't been buried yet. Nevertheless, Jan Moir of the *Daily Mail* has already managed to dance on his grave. For money.

It has been 20 minutes since I've read her now-notorious column, and I'm still struggling to absorb the sheer scope of its hateful idiocy. It's like gazing through a horrid little window into an awesome universe of pure blockheaded spite. Spiralling galaxies of ignorance roll majestically against a backdrop of what looks like dark prejudice, dotted hither and thither with winking stars of snide innuendo.

On the *Mail* website, it was headlined: "Why there was nothing 'natural' about Stephen Gately's death." Since the official post-mortem clearly ascribed the singer's death to natural causes, that headline contains a fairly bold claim. Still, who am I to judge? I'm no expert when it comes to interpreting autopsy findings, unlike Moir. Presumably she's a leading expert in forensic science, paid huge sums of money to fly around the world lecturing coroners on her latest findings. Or maybe she just wants to gay-bash a dead man? Tragically, the only way to find out is to read the rest of her article.

She begins by jabbering a bit about untimely celebrity deaths, especially those whose lives are "shadowed by dark appetites or fractured by private vice". Not just Heath Ledger and Michael Jackson. No: she's eagerly looking forward to other premature snuffings.

"Robbie, Amy, Kate, Whitney, Britney; we all know who they are. And we are not being ghoulish to anticipate, or to be mentally braced for, their bad end: a long night, a mysterious stranger, an odd set of circumstances that herald a sudden death."

Fair enough. I'm sure we all agree there's nothing "ghoulish" whatsoever about eagerly imagining the hypothetical death of someone you've marked out as a potential cadaver on account of your ill-informed presumptions about their lifestyle. All she's doing is running a detailed celebrity-death sweepstake in her head. That's not ghoulish, that's fun. For my part, I've just put a tenner on Moir choking to death on her own bile by the year 2012. See? Fun!

Having casually prophesied the death of Robbie Williams and co, Moir moves on to her main point: that Gately's death strikes her as a bit fishy. "All the official reports point to a natural death, with no suspicious circumstances ... But, hang on a minute. Something is terribly wrong with the way this incident has been shaped and spun into nothing more than an unfortunate mishap on a holiday weekend, like a broken teacup in the rented cottage."

That's odd. I don't recall anyone equating the death with "an unfortunate mishap on a holiday weekend". I was only aware of shocked expressions of grief from those who knew or admired him, people who'd probably be moved to tears by Moir likening the tragedy to "a broken teacup in the rented cottage". But never mind that – "shaped and spun" by whom, precisely? The coroner?

Incredibly, yes. Moir genuinely believes the coroner got it wrong: "Healthy and fit 33-year-old men do not just climb into their pyjamas and go to sleep on the sofa, never to wake up again. Whatever the cause of death is, it is not, by any yardstick, a natural one."

At this point, I dare to challenge the renowned international forensic pathologist Jan Moir, because I personally know of two other men (one in his 20s, one in his early 30s), who died in precisely this way. According to the charity Cardiac Risk in the Young (c-r-y.org.uk), "Twelve apparently fit and healthy young people die in the UK from undiagnosed heart conditions" every single week. That's a lot of broken teacups, eh Jan?

Still, if his death wasn't natural "by any yardstick", what did kill him? Moir knows: it was his lifestyle. Because Gately was, y'know ... homosexual. Having lanced this boil, Moir lets the pus drip out all over her fingers as she continues to type. "The circumstances surrounding his death are more than a little sleazy," she declares. "Cowles and Gately took a young Bulgarian man back to their apartment. It is not disrespectful to assume that a game of canasta ... was not what was on the cards ... What happened afterwards is anyone's guess."

Don't hold back, Jan. Have a guess. Draw us a picture. You specialise in celebrity death fantasies, after all.

"His mother is still insisting that her son died from a previously undetected heart condition that has plagued the family." Yes. That poor, blinkered woman, "insisting" in the face of official medical evidence that absolutely agrees with her.

Anyway, having cast aspersions over a tragic death, doubted a coroner and insulted a grieving mother, Moir's piece builds to its climax: "Another real sadness about Gately's death is that it strikes another blow to the happy-ever-after myth of civil partnerships ... Gay activists are always calling for tolerance and understanding about same-sex relationships, arguing that they are just the same as heterosexual marriages ... in many cases this may be true. Yet the recent death of Kevin McGee, the former husband of Little Britain star Matt Lucas, and now the dubious events of Gately's last night raise troubling questions about what happened."

Way to spread the pain around, Jan. Way to link two unrelated tragedies, Jan. Way to gay-bash, Jan.

Jan's paper, the *Daily Mail*, absolutely adores it when people flock to Ofcom to complain about something offensive, especially when it's something they've only learned about second-hand via an inflammatory article in a newspaper. So it would undoubtedly be delighted if, having read this, you paid a visit to the Press Complaints Commission website to lodge a complaint about Moir's article on the basis that it breaches sections 1, 5 and 12 of its code of practice.

18 NOVEMBER 2009

# Ludwig Minelli: why suicide is a "marvellous opportunity"

AMELIA GENTLEMAN

Ludwig Minelli is explaining the best techniques for an efficient suicide when the doorbell goes and he pauses to answer via an intercom.

It is already dark outside his cluttered, dimly lit conservatory, and heavy rain is beating at the glass roof. "Would you excuse me for a moment?" he says, frowning at the interruption. "A taxi driver tells me that Greek persons are coming and they want to speak with me."

Ten minutes later he re-emerges, shaking out his black anorak which is glistening with rain. "It's absurd," he says, with an embarrassed laugh.

"A Greek lady and her uncle, knowing not a single word of German and no English, have come to Zurich." Standing on his doorstep in the pouring rain, the Greek woman has somehow made it clear that she would like him to help her to die.

Such peculiar intrusions happen every month or so because Minelli, 76, is now famous around the world as the founder of Dignitas, the not-for-profit assisted suicide organisation that has helped 1,032 people to die since 1998. He tells anecdotes, with black humour, of other unexpected visitors who arrive, hoping to die. A few months ago, as he was driving home, he saw a German taxi parked at the side of the road, the driver asking a passer-by for directions. "I stopped because I knew there could only be one person they were looking for," he says. Inside there was a woman in her 90s who had taken a 200-mile taxi ride from Munich and who told him: "I am now here."

Another time there was a young man from Germany, only 20 but profoundly depressed, who rang him and said: "I am in front of your house. I want to die, immediately."

"I do not like these incidents," Minelli says. "It is not very agreeable either for me or for the people looking for help." He has sent the Greek woman away, telling her he cannot help her since she has made no appointment, but he is dismayed at the suffering that has driven her to travel from Athens to seek out his home in a suburban village outside Zurich, and mutters: "Deplorable."

There are established procedures that must be followed in order to receive Minelli's assistance in securing a swift death with a 15mg dose of a lethal drug. Merely turning up on his doorstep is not the correct way.

First, you need to become a member of Dignitas; anyone can join if they pay an annual fee of 80 Swiss francs (£47). When you are ready to die, you need to send in copies of your medical records, a letter explaining why things have become intolerable and £1,860. These files are dispatched to one of Dignitas's affiliated doctors, who considers on the basis of the medical history whether or not he would be ready to write a prescription for the fatal dose. If he agrees in principle, then a "green light" is given to the member, and they can contact staff at the Dignitas headquarters, who will schedule a date and offer advice on hotels. Once they arrive in Zurich, the individual must pay £620 for two appointments with the doctor (to check their records and prescribe the drugs) and a further £1,860 to pay for two Dignitas staff members to organise and witness the death. Those who cannot afford the fees may pay less.

Since Swiss law allows assisted suicide, but not euthanasia (the difference being that the person who wants to die must actively take the dose himself), the act of voluntarily drinking the drug, mixed with 60ml of water, and the subsequent death is videoed by the Dignitas companions, who stay behind to deal with the police and the undertakers in the hours that follow. For those unable to lift the glass to their lips, there is a machine that will administer it, once they press a button.

In the months leading up to the death, Minelli and his colleagues repeatedly question whether the individual really wants to die, and set out alternatives to suicide. "It is quite simple. As long as we are able to help them in the direction of life, we help them in the direction of life," he says. When this fails, "We are ready to help them in the other direction."

The vast majority of people who visit Dignitas are the terminally ill or those with an incurable, progressive disease. "Usually, if the person has terminal cancer, motor neuron disease or multiple sclerosis and they are telling us 'I don't like to live some weeks or months until the terrible end,' then it is quite clear and we have no difficulty in saying yes," Minelli says.

Then there are those people who are just tired of life. With life expectancy growing and medical sophistication improving, people are increasingly worried about whether they will be "condemned to linger on," Minelli says, "forced to end their lives in an institution. Our members say: with our pets, when they are old and in pain, we help them. Why am I not entitled to go to the vet? Why haven't I such an opportunity? We hear this often."

But it is not always as simple as he suggests. Minelli's vision goes beyond helping the infirm to shorten a painful end; his views are much more radical. He believes the right to choose to die is a fundamental human right and, in theory, he is willing to help anyone.

News that the conductor Sir Edward Downes, 85, travelled this summer to Dignitas to die together with his wife Joan, 74, who had terminal liver and pancreatic cancer, prompted questions over why he had been allowed to die too – when he was virtually blind and increasingly deaf, but not himself terminally ill. The same questions were asked when Daniel James, a 23-year-old rugby player, paralysed during a training accident, was helped to die.

Minelli offers dry cinnamon-and-nutmeg biscuits and an unusual Chinese tea – white monkey paw – which he has meticulously prepared, sticking a thermometer into the kettle, heating the water to precisely 70C, setting a digital alarm for five minutes to allow the tea to brew before decanting it into a vacuum flask. Then he sets out his vision like this: everyone should have the right to end their life, not just the terminally ill, but anyone who wants to, and he passes no moral judgment on their wishes. "We don't discuss moral questions. What moral? Which moral? Catholic? Muslim? Buddhist? We are just working on the atheist basis of self-determination," he says.

Section 115 of the Swiss criminal code says that anyone who acts on selfish motives to assist someone to kill themselves can be punished with up to five years in jail. The law has been interpreted by Dignitas and other assisted suicide organisations as meaning that assisted suicide is not illegal as long as there is no selfish intent (such as helping an aunt to die in order to get her inheritance).

But the Swiss medical regulations inhibit Minelli's more radical ideas, prohibiting doctors from prescribing drugs to healthy people, and restricting involvement in assisted suicide for the mentally ill – making it practically impossible for Dignitas to help people who are profoundly depressed to die. This is a prohibition that Minelli is fighting.

So far there have been no prosecutions following any of the suicides he has helped organise (for people from more than 60 countries, 132 from Britain) but Minelli is involved in a handful of legal battles with the Swiss government, determined to clarify the law which governs suicide.

"We have a lot of members [who have had] depression for years and years and years. They say, 'We have tried so many treatments and they haven't worked.' If they tell you, 'I have been depressed for 15 years and I don't intend to be so for another 15 years,' who should say no to that?" In extremis, he will offer advice on how to end one's life efficiently at home.

Three firmly held beliefs lie beneath this practice. First, his conviction that once you give someone the freedom to talk about suicide this reduces their desire to go ahead with it. Second, he believes that even the offer, in the abstract, of an assisted suicide gives someone who is in pain a lot of relief – they know that their future no longer rests on a decision between enduring "the hell of their own suffering or attempting a high-risk suicide by themselves". His research shows that 80% of those who get the green light to go ahead with an assisted suicide do not go through with it.

Third, he argues that providing a service to help people kill themselves properly will reduce the large number of catastrophically failed suicides. He is appalled by the prevalence of botched suicides, committed in isolation by desperate people who do not have the expertise necessary to succeed. He points out that it is now very difficult to kill oneself by overdosing on tablets – instead they ruin the functioning of their liver. Jumping from a building, throwing oneself beneath a train, and trying to use a gun also tend not to be very effective, he points out, frequently leaving the individual alive but in a terrible state physically. These failed suicide attempts end up putting a heavy burden on a nation's health service, he says, another motivation for his organisation's work.

"If we want to reduce the number of suicides and suicide attempts, we should break the taboo of suicide. We should not say suicide should not happen, we should say suicide is a marvellous opportunity given to man to withdraw them from a situation that is unbearable for them," he argues.

His fondness for describing suicide as a "marvellous opportunity" is very irritating to conservative Swiss officials who object to the country's new image as a suicide tourism destination. (Minelli brushes off the suggestion that his work has damaged the nation's reputation, with a typically acid aside: "Switzerland was already famous for tax-evasion tourism.")

The Swiss government last month announced that it would consult on whether to ban, or call for greater regulation of, assisted suicide. On a more personal level, one of Minelli's opponents in the public prosecutor's office has told him that there will eventually be a "biological solution" to the problem of Dignitas, hinting that he hopes Minelli will drop dead.

Minelli courts controversy with some of his more inflammatory comments. Condemning the Swiss government's campaigns to regulate the arrival of suicidal foreigners, he remarks: "In the second world war they closed the borders to Jews and those Jews who wanted to come here were repelled, and were murdered in concentration camps. And now we have people looking to end their lives in Switzerland and they are sent back and forced to live on. What is the difference? What is more cruel?"

His decision to found Dignitas, leaving behind a career as a human rights lawyer, has its roots in a childhood memory of witnessing his dying grandmother begging her doctor in vain to help her end things. The experience inspired an attachment to the concept of a good death.

"Death is the end of our life. After a good life, we should have a good death. A good death is death without pain, where you can say, 'I had a good life, and I can now go to the other side,'" he says. "Nowadays, death is exported to institutions, to hospitals. Death has become a lonely occasion."

People who travel to Switzerland to die with Dignitas are encouraged to come with family and friends, who stay with them as they drink the lethal dose; one person brought 12 friends with him. Dignitas staff are happy to give advice on good restaurants for a final meal, nearby cinemas and excursions to the mountains, for the preceding days, but they observe that usually members are keen just to get on with dying.

Minelli says he is never present at the deaths. Instead, Beatrice Bucher, a paid member of Dignitas staff who now works in the head office but has been a companion at more than 20 deaths, describes the process. She has a quietly compassionate tone, soothing and sympathetic, and believes strongly that she is performing an important role in society. "They need to know that they can go home at any time. I'm constantly asking if this is what they want. I have to be clear that this is really the moment," she says. On more than one occasion she has helped people return home who have changed their mind. "One woman still calls me to say thank you," she says.

Bucher has to judge when the time is right for both the person who wants to die, and their relatives. "Once I had a mother – not so old, in her 50s – who was really ill. She came with her daughter who was perhaps 25. The mother was very firm that she would go quickly and that it was not a problem. She told the daughter that she was not to cry and made her go and stand in the kitchen. I had to explain that this is not the way, you should not tell your daughter she cannot cry," she says. Staff also suggest that relatives stay to witness the death, because they believe this helps with the mourning process.

People are encouraged to lie down, because if they die sitting up at the table, their mouth drops open and their body slumps, and it is harder for the family to watch the process. "Then we install the film in the video camera, but I am always asking 'Do you need more time?' Usually they are calm. Most of them are in a lot of pain and they know that this drink will end it forever."

The 15g of white powder is mixed with water and drunk from a small glass. Bucher advises people to say anything they need to say, their final words, before they drink, because after there is not much time – usually just between one to three minutes before they sleep, fall into a coma and then die. "Some people say thank you and tell their family they love them, that they have had a really good life and that they are grateful that they can die," she says.

She warns them that the drink will be bitter, and some people choose to neutralise the taste with a chocolate. "They feel good. There is no pain. It's like before an operation – they feel woozy," she says.

"Another time, there was a mother who clearly did not have a good relationship with her two daughters who were with her. It was very strained. But after she drank, she took them in her arms and said, 'I love you, you are my best ones,'" Bucher says, still moved by the memory. "Then she died. They said it was the first time she had hugged them like that. That was a good moment for me – it was not too late for her to show how she felt."

As soon as the person dies, the undertakers and police are called.

In a side room, there is a television for the police to watch the video, so they can file a report. Upstairs, there is a washing machine, and a box with some folded clothes and shoes belonging to recently dead people, ready to be dispatched to the Red Cross.

Minelli has delegated much of the organisation of Dignitas to his staff of 10 part-time workers. The Dignitas office, in a street near his home, 20 minutes drive from the Pfaffikon apartment, is very office-like – no sofas or handkerchiefs. He checks the files, and notes that one English person is booked in to die this week, but otherwise there is an unexpected lull in appointments. Bucher puts it down to the Indian summer most of Europe has experienced, and predicts that things will get a bit busier in the run-up to Christmas.

"We have had good weather for the last few weeks, so people don't call us so much," she says.

Minelli meets people here occasionally to discuss their desire to die, but mostly his work is concentrated on the court cases and campaigning. Back at his house, where he lives alone, he describes with enthusiasm a new technique for painless death he is experimenting with; one which uses a chemical that is easily available without the need for a doctor's prescription. He requests that we do not publish details of the chemical or the technique, to prevent it becoming more widely used. The method can be administered easily by staff, and using this he could circumvent using doctors altogether. He struggles with hanging on to doctors, just as he struggles with keeping apartments; most are nervous about co-operating with Dignitas for fear of losing their licence.

Costs from the various legal battles come to around £100,000 every year, money which is raised through the annual membership fee and periodic appeals to supporters for funds. Minelli says he does not pay himself a salary, and remarks, "I have made a lot of debt in order to maintain Dignitas."

An estranged colleague, Soraya Wernli, who worked for several years helping with the suicides, lost faith in the organisation and told the police around five years ago that Minelli was making money from death and the fear of it, and criticised him for running "a production line concerned only with profits". Police investigations found nothing suspicious.

Minelli's novelist daughter Michele, who has arrived to visit her father, remarks that she and her sister will have no inheritance when her father dies because everything has been spent on his campaigning work. She was wounded by Wernli's allegations, more sensitive to criticism of her father than he is on his own behalf. ("He doesn't mind people throwing tomatoes at him," she says.) Disturbed by the claims, she offered to help him gather feedback from the relatives of people who have died, and now she is responsible for sending out forms and compiling responses. The overwhelmingly positive replies have reassured her, and she collects a few from the pile of new post and spreads them out over the worn red-checked tablecloth.

One person from Britain who recently came to witness a relative's death describes the process as a "calm day filled with the deepest sorrow I have ever felt", before thanking Dignitas for its assistance. Another person who also travelled earlier in the autumn from Britain says the experience was "a time of sadness, naturally, but also of peace, calmness, spiritual comfort in a relaxed, compassionate, unhurried atmosphere". "Long may you continue your good work," another writes.

The doorbell rings again and it is the Greek woman back again with her uncle and a translator who she has managed to find somewhere in the city. This time, Minelli invites her in; they sit in the main room out of sight but her anguished voice can be heard clearly. "Mr Minelli! Mr Minelli! Mr Minelli!" she keeps interrupting him, angry, as he tries to explain that she needs to bring him a complete medical history before her case can be considered.

As it becomes clear that he will not help her to die, she begins shouting: "Ach, Mr Minelli! Ach, Mr Minelli!"

He remains calm, explaining once again that she must come fully equipped with her medical records so that a doctor can consider whether to prescribe a drug. After almost an hour or so they leave, promising to return from Greece with more documents in the spring. Minelli explains that she suffers from paranoid schizophrenia and is determined to die. Whether he will be able to help depends on whether a Greek psychiatrist can write a letter that says she is capable of rational thought. He is despondent at the desperate steps that people are forced to take in their search for a painless death, steps which he compares with the measures women once had to take if they wanted an abortion.

He hopes that she will reconsider, and happily recounts stories of other applicants who have been persuaded to change their minds. When the depressed young German man arrived on his doorstep some years ago, demanding to die immediately, Minelli felt sorry for him, took him in, and spent a day or so explaining why suicide was not the answer. On the third morning, when the young man said once again that he wanted to die, Minelli took a new approach, telling him: "If you really want to die, there are three options. There is hanging, but it is very risky: if you are found too early you will live on, but as an idiot because the blood will have stopped flowing to your brain. You can go to the Swiss glacier, wearing light clothes, and you will die of cold, but if you are found too early you will lose your legs. Or you can stop eating and just drink tea and water."

"He said, 'Yahoo! I will die by starvation.' He was completely happy. It was a 180-degree change," Minelli says. They drove together to a bathing resort 30km away, and they spent the afternoon swimming together.

"We came back here at midnight and looked through my telescope up at Jupiter with its four Galilean moons and Saturn. He was delighted. We discussed cosmology and astronomy and I sent him to bed." The man went home to Germany, where Minelli put him in touch with a psychiatrist. His crisis passed and the two remain in occasional contact.

"As an amateur of astronomy, I know life is a speciality that is known only on earth and is something that is very rare and so we have to care as much as we can for life," Minelli says. "But we must also accept that a feeling human being must have the opportunity to say: 'This has been it. I have had now enough and I will now stop.'"

25 NOVEMBER 2009

# We must not become the deniers over the climate email scandal

GEORGE MONBIOT

I have seldom felt so alone. Confronted with crisis, most of the environmentalists I know have gone into denial. The emails hacked from the Climatic Research Unit (CRU) at the University of East Anglia, they say, are a storm in a teacup, no big deal, exaggerated out of all recognition. It is true that climate change deniers have made wild claims which the material can't possibly support (the end of global warming, the death of climate science). But it is also true that the emails are very damaging.

The response of the greens and most of the scientists I know is profoundly ironic, as we spend so much of our time confronting other people's denial. Pretending that this isn't a real crisis isn't going to make it go away. Nor is an attempt to justify the emails with technicalities. We'll be able to get past this only by grasping reality, apologising where appropriate and demonstrating that it cannot happen again.

It is true that much of what has been revealed could be explained as the usual cut and thrust of the peer review process, exacerbated by the extraordinary pressure the scientists were facing from a denial industry determined to crush them. One of the most damaging emails was sent by the head of the climatic research unit, Phil Jones. He wrote: "I can't see either of these papers being in the next IPCC report. Kevin and I will keep them out somehow – even if we have to redefine what the peer review literature is!"

One of these papers, which was published in the journal *Climate Research*, turned out to be so badly flawed that the scandal resulted in the resignation of the editor-in-chief. Jones knew that any incorrect papers by sceptical scientists would be picked up and amplified by climate change deniers funded by the fossil fuel industry, who often use all sorts of dirty tricks to advance their cause.

Even so, his message looks awful. It gives the impression of confirming a potent meme circulated by those who campaign against taking action on climate change: that the IPCC process is biased. However good the detailed explanations may be, most people aren't going to follow or understand them. Jones's statement, on the other hand, is stark and easy to grasp.

In this case you could argue that technically he has done nothing wrong. But a fat lot of good that will do. Think of the MPs' expenses scandal: complaints about stolen data, denials and huffy responses achieved nothing at all. Most of the MPs could demonstrate that technically they were innocent: their expenses had been approved by the Commons office. It didn't change public perceptions one jot. The only responses that have helped to restore public trust in parliament are humility, openness and promises of reform.

When it comes to his handling of Freedom of Information requests, Professor Jones might struggle even to use a technical defence. If you take the wording literally, in one case he appears to be suggesting that emails subject to a request be deleted, which means that he seems to be advocating potentially criminal activity. Even if no other message had been hacked, this would be sufficient to ensure his resignation as head of the unit.

I feel desperately sorry for him: he must be walking through hell. But there is no helping it; he has to go, and the longer he leaves it, the worse it will get. He has a few days left in which to make an honourable exit. Otherwise, like the former Speaker of the House of Commons, Michael Martin, he will linger on until his remaining credibility vanishes, inflicting continuing damage to climate science.

Some people say that I am romanticising science, that it is never as open and honest as the Popperian ideal. Perhaps. But I know that opaqueness and secrecy are the enemies of science. There is a word for the apparent repeated attempts to prevent disclosure revealed in these emails: unscientific.

The crisis has been exacerbated by the university's handling of it, which has been a total train wreck: a textbook example of how not to respond. RealClimate reports that "We were made aware of the existence of this archive last Tuesday morning when the hackers attempted to upload it to RealClimate, and we notified CRU of their possible security breach later that day." In other words, the university knew what was coming three days before the story broke. As far as I can tell, it sat like a rabbit in the headlights, waiting for disaster to strike.

When the emails hit the news on Friday morning, the university appeared completely unprepared. There was no statement, no position, no one to interview. Reporters kept being fobbed off while CRU's opponents landed blow upon blow on it. When a journalist I know finally managed to track down Phil Jones, he snapped "no comment" and put down the phone. This response is generally taken by the media to mean "guilty as charged". When I got hold of him on Saturday, his answer was to send me a PDF file called "WMO statement on the status of the global climate in 1999". Had I a couple of hours to spare I might have been able to work out what the heck this had to do with the current crisis, but he offered no explanation.

By then he should have been touring the TV studios for 36 hours, confronting his critics, making his case and apologising for his mistakes. Instead, he had disappeared off the face of the

Earth. Now, far too late, he has given an interview to the Press Association, which has done nothing to change the story.

The handling of this crisis suggests that nothing has been learnt by climate scientists in this country from 20 years of assaults on their discipline. They appear to have no idea what they're up against or how to confront it. Their opponents might be scumbags, but their media strategy is exemplary.

The greatest tragedy here is that despite many years of outright fabrication, fraud and deceit on the part of the climate change denial industry, documented in James Hoggan and Richard Littlemore's brilliant new book *Climate Cover-up*, it is now the climate scientists who look bad. By comparison to his opponents, Phil Jones is pure as the driven snow. Hoggan and Littlemore have shown how fossil fuel industries have employed "experts" to lie, cheat and manipulate on their behalf. The revelations in their book are 100 times graver than anything contained in these emails.

But the deniers' campaign of lies, grotesque as it is, does not justify secrecy and suppression on the part of climate scientists. Far from it: it means that they must distinguish themselves from their opponents in every way. No one has been as badly let down by the revelations in these emails as those of us who have championed the science. We should be the first to demand that it is unimpeachable, not the last.

# Winter

# George Michael: "I'm surprised I've survived my own dysfunction"

## SIMON HATTENSTONE

As I reach George Michael's house, a huge Land Rover draws up and a man in shades gets out. At the same time, two women jump out of a little car across the road and run up to him, panting and shaking. They are middle-aged, German and seem to have been waiting a long time – hours, possibly days. "Would you please have a photograph taken with us?" they say. George Michael obliges with a ready smile. It's cold and windy. "Would you please sign these?" They produce various George Michael paraphernalia. He obliges, but the smile is not quite so effusive. "I have to go inside now, ladies," he says, "thank you." As we retreat, the panting women tell him they feel a little dizzy and overcome, and that this has been the greatest day in their lives. "We've heard the new Christmas single," says one, "and it's brilliant." "Yes, brilliant," echoes the other. "Even better than Last Christmas."

As he closes the door, Michael tells me it's lucky I was there otherwise he'd have told them to piss off. Really? "No. What can you do, especially if they come from abroad? You can't be nasty." One of the many grandfather clocks in the house chimes six times. They seem more like stalkers than fans, I say. Michael smiles. He knows all about stalkers. "There's one woman, she broke into my house seven times. The police did nothing. And I saw her down the road one day wearing my clothes." Outside, he says, two paparazzi employed by a tabloid are permanently stationed for mishaps.

Imagine being George Michael. How crazy must that be? It's not just the stalker-fans, it's the whole shebang. You're a pop star who 20 years ago was absolutely massive, global. And, however little you do, your fame refuses to diminish. So you wait five years, possibly more, to put out a new record – enough time for the world to forget you existed – and still your public hangs on anxiously. You watch *EastEnders*, one of your favourite soaps, and discover that a new baby has been named after you. You watch the TV sitcom *Arrested Development* and find another character named after you. You turn on *The X Factor*, and the contestants are singing your songs. You open the papers and, under the headline "George's hairless whisper", discover that you are going bald.

And then there's Michael's own contribution to his fame – or infamy. However private he professes to be (and in many ways he is), there is some strange little trait, be it recklessness or obstinacy, bad timing or principle, that ensures he grabs more headlines than he was looking for. So when he criticises Rupert Murdoch, he calls him "the devil"; when he falls out with his record company, he goes on strike; and when he finally tells the world about his sexuality in 1998, it is via a public toilet, humiliating arrest and the most conspicuous outing ever.

Let's not forget the music. Georgios Kyriacos Panayiotou was born in 1963 to a Greek Cypriot restaurateur father and an English dancer mother. He grew up in north London, close to where he lives today. Michael emerged in 1982 as the sexier half of pop duo Wham! – with big hair, fake tan, great loopy earrings and a shuttlecock down his shorts, he had a sexuality that appealed equally to girls and boys. Wham! had a series of huge hits, including Club Tropicana, Young Guns (Go For It) and Wham Rap! (Enjoy What You Do?), but by 1986 they had split up. And that should have been that. Only Michael went solo, and became even bigger. The cheesy, hedonistic disco morphed into melancholy smoocheramas (Careless Whisper, his first solo hit, reached number one in 1984), soulful ballads (Father Figure, Jesus To A Child) and white funk classics (Faith, I Want Your Sex).

Even when he was struck by disaster, he turned it to his advantage. In 1998, he was arrested for "engaging in a lewd act" after a sting by the Beverly Hills cops, and sentenced to 80 hours of community service. It would have extinguished most careers, but Michael went on television, explained himself in a brilliantly unapologetic TV interview, and wrote Outside, a cheeky song about al fresco sex – "I'd service the community, but I already have"; the video featured urinals with silver disco balls and kissing policemen.

Since then, he has released only one album of original material – 2004's *Patience* – but still his public waits on him. So much so that when he releases a DVD of his recent world tour and new Christmas single, as he is about to, it is big news.

Michael is greeted by his two labradors and goes downstairs to light the fire. Meanwhile, I have a good snoop around. The first thing you notice is a large Harland Miller painting of an imaginary Penguin classic called *Incurable Romantic Seeks Dirty Filthy Whore*. It says everything you need to know about Michael. On another wall is a Picasso cartoon. The house is full of lilies and roses. In the lounge, there are a couple of cushions on the sofa – one says GEORGE, the other KENNY. He lives here with his boyfriend Kenny Goss. On a table lies the biggest book I've ever seen – a hardback about Michelangelo, large enough to sleep on.

He calls me down when the fire is lit, and offers a glass of wine. Only he can't find a corkscrew. "You can see how often I drink." I last interviewed Michael four years ago. He was emerging from a horrific decade in which he said he felt that he was cursed. So many people close to him had died – his mother, his boyfriend, even the puppy he bought to replace his elderly dog drowned. "You said I looked pinched then," he says. He's got a good memory for slights.

He looks better today, bigger and stronger. "I was probably more stoned in those days. I was existing on a balance of Starbucks and weed," he says while rolling a joint. A bag of grass and half a dozen pills sit on the table in front of him.

What are the pills for? "Mind your own business. No, some of them are vitamin, some are anti-smoking and some are for my back." In the bad old days, he reckons he was smoking around 25 spliffs a day, and was worried he'd do permanent damage to his voice. "I probably do about seven or eight a day now." It was a relief to discover that he could sing as well as ever on the world tour. His voice sounds in great nick – more mature, a little deeper, richer. "I've not used it as regularly as a professional usually uses his voice. It must be a case of don't use it that much and it stays. I'm very proud of the live DVD."

Last time I saw him, he had creative block. Not any more. Most days, he says, he's in the studio. There's so much he's doing, he doesn't know where to start. Like what? Suddenly he comes over all coy. "I've got some great stuff, and I don't know whether I should release it or hold on to it. It uses my supposed infamy on my own terms." Tell me more. "I can't." The tiniest hint? "I can't tell you. Let's just say my foreseeable future in musical terms is fairly schizophrenic." What kind of music is it? "Can't tell you."

Perhaps this is the strangest thing about Michael – the disjunction between what he regards as public and private. For many years, he was so embarrassed about his sexuality that his private self was hermetically sealed. He has said it took him so long to come out because he didn't want to upset his mother. But now, having been outed, or having outed himself, in such an uncompromising manner, it's as if nothing can embarrass him any more.

This is me – like it or lump it. His private self has become wholly public. You sense he would regard it as an act of hypocrisy not to answer questions about drugs or sex. Meanwhile, his public self – most obviously his music – has become private, virtually a no-go area. To ask too much about the music becomes an act of intrusion, voyeurism even.

We retreat to the safe ground of sex, drugs, gossip and conspiracy theories. Michael seems to have become more paranoid over the years, partly with good reason and partly, perhaps, because of all the dope. So, to the people out to get him. First, there's Murdoch. Why? "Well, I'm the only person who mentions Murdoch in a negative context. The last person to go against him was Dennis Potter, and that was how many years ago? And if he hadn't died, he would have been dead soon after, after what he said." He's joking. Sort of.

The tabloids might be out to get him, but he doesn't help matters by giving them such great scoops. He lost his driving licence in 2007 after he was found slumped at his steering wheel. Ah, he says, this is another thing he wants to clear up. "For all the doctored pictures, every single breathalyser test I've taken in my life has read 0.0, and I've never failed a sobriety test." He stops. "I always preface this with, 'I deserved to lose my licence, I needed to lose my licence.'" Yes, he had taken drugs, but he was not stoned. "I had a problem with sleeping pills for about a year and a half, and I fucked up really badly. I got in the car twice when I'd forgotten I'd already downed something to try to get me to sleep. It doesn't matter that it wasn't deliberate – ultimately, I did it a second time, and I could have killed somebody. But the fact remains I was never accused of driving under the influence. I got done for exhaustion and sleeping pills."

He used to tell people that the worst thing about the stories in the papers was that 90% of them were true. Now, he says, hardly any are – they take advantage because they know he can't face suing.

The most worrying report was that when he was arrested cottaging on Hampstead Heath last year, he was charged with possession of crack cocaine. He shrugs dismissively.

Is he smoking crack? "No."

Has he ever? "No!" He starts again. "I mean, I've done different things at different times that I shouldn't have done, once or twice, you know." I say I'd hate to think of him on crack. "Of course. Of course. Nobody wants to regularly smoke crack." I'm feeling more parental by the second. It's hard not to worry about Michael – for all his paranoia, recklessness and self-absorption, he exudes intelligence, warmth and generosity. "Look me in the eye," I say. "Were you smoking crack?"

"Was I? On that occasion? Yeah."

"When was the last time you smoked it?"

"I'm not going to tell you that. But I am going to tell you, whatever I do, I did 105 really good performances, and none of my musicians can ever say they've seen me wasted."

He's rolling another joint. A few months ago he was involved in a terrible accident with a lorry. "He came into my lane, and I had nowhere to go and ended up being battered between him and the central reservation, and I have to say it's fucking amazing that I'm alive."

The accident made him reassess things. "If that juggernaut had killed me, I think I'd be perfectly happy with the amount of quality music I have left in the world. My ego is sated." Michael has always been interesting about ego – recognising that too much is dangerous, but with too little he would not have achieved what he has. "I watch people who are not driven by creativity any more, and I think how dull it must be to produce the same kind of thing. If you don't feel you're reaching something new, then don't do it." He says he thinks albums are passé, that you have to work in a different way today for a market that listens to music by the song. "What I want now is a little more integration in terms of who I actually am. I'm 10-12 years into life as an out gay man and I'm a different person. I think there are things about my journey that might be useful to other people, and coming up with a hit record on its own doesn't seem to be enough any more." He comes over all coy again and says he can't give away anything else.

What's a typical day in the life of George Michael? The common perception is that he gets up late in the afternoon, gets stoned and goes cruising. Rubbish, he says. "The handful of times a year it's bloody warm enough, I'll do it. I'll do it on a nice summer evening. Quite often there are campfires up there. It's a much nicer place to get some quick and honest sex than standing in a bar, E'd off your tits shouting at somebody and hoping they want the same thing as you do in bed. DyaknowhatImean?"

Why does he like to cruise when he could get any man he wanted? He seems astonished by the question. "I do get anyone I want. But I like a bit of everything. I have friends up there, I have a laugh."

Michael has always liked men his own age or older. Yet another story last year claimed he had been caught on the heath with an elderly Bernard Manning lookalike. Was it true? "The poor bastard. His only crime was being the least fortunate-looking person to come off the heath after me. They chased him down. Poor man had never met me ..."

Back to a typical day in the life. "I normally get up about 10am, my PA will bring me a Starbucks, I'll have a look at my emails. At the moment I've got nothing that pressurised other than keeping an eye on the video they're making for the Christmas single. Then, if I'm in the mood, I'll come up to the office in Highgate, do some work, writing, backing tracks or whatever. Come home. Kenny will be here, the dogs are here. Maybe eat locally, hang out, and then probably go off and have a shag or have someone come here and have a shag." He laughs – he's exaggerating. "It's not typical – that's probably a couple times a week."

Is he talking about shagging Kenny? "Too personal, man." But, of course, with Michael there is the compulsion to answer. "If it was shagging with Kenny, I wouldn't have to invite him round, would I?" He pauses, worried he might give the wrong impression. "Kenny gets his, believe me." There have been rumours that they have split up, but again Michael says this is nonsense. "He's probably upstairs now."

Over the past few years, a number of stars have said they fear for Michael – notably Elton John, one of his heroes. He smiles. "Elton lives on that. He will not be happy until I bang on his door in the middle of the night saying, 'Please, please, help me, Elton. Take me to rehab.' It's not going to happen. You know what I heard last week? That Bono ... Oh for God's sake ..." He's choking on his laughter. "Geri [Halliwell] told Kenny that Bono, having spoken to Elton, had approached Geri to say, 'What can we do for George?' This is what I have to deal with because I don't want to be part of that social clique. All I'd have to do to stop it is hang out in London, so people realise I don't look close to death."

So Bono could save him? "As if Bono gives a shit what I do with my private life ... Elton just needs to shut his mouth and get on with his own life. Look, if people choose to believe that I'm sitting here in my ivory tower, Howard Hughesing myself with long fingernails and loads of drugs, then I can't do anything about that, can I?"

There are photos on the mantelpiece – Kenny, his sister, his parents. There is nobody famous apart from his old Wham! partner Andrew Ridgeley, who retired from the business many years ago. "He spends half his time pissed out of his head in Cornwall. He really enjoys his life."

I ask for a tour of the house. "No," he says, "That's just too Oprah!" OK, he says, he'll show me the back garden because they've just had it done up. It goes on for ever. There's a swimming pool with a cleaner-robot paddling along the bottom, exotic Japanese trees and a steam room. Michael laughs when he shows me this. "It wasn't planned like this. But it actually looks like a cottage – even the entrance looks like a public toilet!" At times, he says, his house is a prison. "Mind you, if you're going to live in a prison, it might as well be a good one."

He talks about the recent tour and the DVD, and says, for him, it represents the culmination of one phase of his career. Again, he's not prepared to say where the new one starts, or with what. There might be an element of campaigning. "Just the politics of being me and being buffeted around in the media between liberals and homophobes puts me in a position to use some of that experience." People certainly like his honesty. "Well, that always helps. A bit of humour and a bit of honesty."

He knows he's not there yet. While he'll defend his right to take drugs to the last, he's equally aware they slow him down. "The best answer for me is to keep busy. If I'm busy I don't sit around puffing." He received a massive advance from HarperCollins for his autobiography, but he is going to have to give it back – he says the time isn't right, adding with an embarrassed grin that when he signed the deal he didn't realise Murdoch owned the publishing house. Before he can write well about himself, he thinks he has some progress to make. "There are things I need to resolve. And I think I'll be a much better writer when I've got through those things. But it's great to know that at 46 I'm still very much a changing person."

Does he like the way he's changed? "Well, yeah, thank Christ. Most visible traces of self-loathing have gone." He's beginning to regard himself as a survivor, and enjoys the feeling. "I'm surprised that I've survived my own dysfunction, really."

The funny thing is, he says, everything that has happened to him in recent years has made him feel more normal. When he was regarded as pop's Mr Perfect, he felt a fraud – knowing that so many people were envious left him uneasy. And, somehow, being a flawed hero, or even antihero, makes life easier to cope with.

"People want to see me as tragic with all the cottaging and drug-taking ... those things are not what most people aspire to, and I think it removes people's envy to see your weaknesses." He stops. "I don't even see them as weaknesses any more. It's just who I am."

9 December 2009

# A very British inquiry, like a private chat in a Whitehall club

SIMON JENKINS

The Chilcot inquiry yesterday met its first "hostile" witness, Sir John Scarlett, former head of MI6. Mastermind of Saddam's threat of weapons of mass destruction and thus architect of Tony Blair's case for the Iraq war, he entered the inquisition room like a small, well-bred bull, ready for battle. Within seconds he was wandering round the ring, lost and searching for a matador. The inquiry appeared to have gone on strike.

Scarlett duly droned for a third of his allotted time on the structure of the joint intelligence committee. The inquiry members looked to the ceiling, gazed at their feet, even seemed to fall asleep. Scarlett teased them with tales of dossiers and spin, with murmurs of American pressure, aluminium tubes and the clear impression that weapons inspectors were spies. They barely noticed. He failed to mention Alastair Campbell or Tony Blair. He did all he could to cause a fight, but he failed. He walked out unmarked. Chilcot is an inquiry with much to prove.

For two weeks, the investigation into the alleged failures of the 2003 invasion of Iraq has dealt with processes and procedures. One elegant mandarin after another has paraded, well-rehearsed, before it. Rarely do more than a few onlookers grace the airless room, overwhelmed by infantile government security. At one session a group of bemused tourists declared it "at least better than the House of Lords". This may be merely a prologue to the star turn, Blair, who is not due until next year. But Scarlett was the star's apprentice, and the place was for once packed and expectant.

When pressed on being told to "firm up" the intelligence of weapons of mass destruction in 2002, Scarlett was left to declare blandly that that is what he did. When asked if there was any coercion from America, he said no.

When asked if perhaps the September dossier, and its 45-minutes warning, was confusing, he said probably. When asked if he might have disapproved of Blair's "without doubt" interpretation of it, he said maybe.

I never thought I would cry "send for a lawyer" but the inquiry desperately lacks a skilled cross-examiner, someone who at least knows the word supplementary. The inquiry's two historians, Sir Martin Gilbert and Sir Laurence Freedman, appear to be researching their next book. Lady Prashar is interested only in "clearing things up". The diplomat Sir Roderic Lyne occasionally leaps to inquisitorial life, but not when faced by the head of MI6. This was like a private conversation in a Whitehall club.

For all that, a picture is starting to emerge from Chilcot. It is of 2002 and an ever more lonely Blair, desperate to be "a serious player" on the world stage. He is trapped between what his Washington ambassador, Sir Christopher Meyer, eulogised as his "enormously close relationship" with George Bush, and British lawyers telling him an invasion would be illegal, British generals saying an occupation would be a shambles and cabinet colleagues thinking him mad. (I hope we hear from some of them.)

The inquiry so far has been dominated by two themes, the chaos of the American occupation of Baghdad, and the zeal of the Foreign Office to drive a stake through Blair's heart at the nearest crossroads, for destroying Britain's reputation in the diplomats' beloved Middle East. Rarely can Whitehall's finest have turned so savagely on a recent boss. The FCO's chief, Sir Peter Ricketts, was blunt: "We quite clearly distanced ourselves from talk about regime change," which Blair had mooted as early as 1998. His colleague, Sir William Patey, said that when Bush came to power, "we heard the drumbeats from Washington ... and our policy was to stay away from that part of the spectrum. It had no basis in law." The illegality of the invasion is a leitmotif, yielding Chilcot's one inadvertent scoop, a leak of a letter submitted by the then attorney general, Lord Goldsmith, to Blair in 2002. This declared that the invasion had "no legal basis for military action ... As things stand you obviously cannot do it." When Blair ignored the letter and banned Goldsmith from cabinet, the attorney general reportedly threatened to resign and famously lost three stone in weight. Just two weeks before the invasion, Goldsmith was still warning the cabinet, as well as the chief of the defence staff, Admiral Lord Boyce, that British soldiers could be "arraigned before the international criminal court" if they went to war. This led Boyce to demand "unequivocal advice" that the war was legal. Goldsmith duly changed his mind. The then lord chancellor, Lord Falconer, has publicly dismissed the spin put on the letter as "totally false". Since he and Goldsmith cannot both be right, their cross-examination in the new year should be the next test of Chilcot's muscle. They should be forced to appear together.

Meyer has been the undoubted star of the show so far. In a startling but unnoticed revelation, he mentioned that Blair refused even to use his good offices with Bush to lobby for relief from tariffs on Britain's special steel or seek domestic slots for Sir Richard Branson's Virgin planes. Blair was hugely popular but his clout in Washington was exhausted. Thanks to him the pre-Iraq phase was an awful episode in British diplomacy. No wonder the Foreign Office wants history to free it of blame.

More serious was the frustration clearly faced by the army. Admiral Lord Boyce told the inquiry that he was banned by the defence secretary, Geoff Hoon, from actively preparing for invasion since it might suggest Britain was not serious about seeking the abortive UN resolution. In the understatement of the inquiry, Boyce said he found this ban, just months from a putative invasion, "very frustrating". He could not even talk to his own head of logistics. Boyce added that he found the whole American approach "anorexic", largely because of "dysfunctionality" between departments in Washington. He himself had sometimes to act as go-between. This led to the Americans being desperately understaffed on the ground when trouble began in late 2003. While the lack of post-invasion planning is hardly news – there is a shelf of memoirs on it – Whitehall's desperation to put its warning of chaos on the Chilcot record is palpable.

The FCO's Iraq expert, Edward Chaplin, spoke of neocon Washington's "real blind spot", indeed its "touching faith", that there would be "dancing in the streets after the invasion ... all sweetness and light". Major General Tim Cross, stationed in Baghdad, said he told Blair that post-war planning was "chaotic", but Blair just stared. On his arrival in the city after the invasion, Cross told of his "amazement" at the shambles that greeted him. Entire government departments were being run from single tables in Saddam's palace corridor, those in charge changing by the week.

The purpose of this inquiry remains obscure. Its tales are familiar to those who have followed the war, and such interest as exists comes largely from hearing the old tales from the horses' mouths. Sir John Chilcot treats witnesses like a therapist with a nervous patient. The absence, at least so far, of any Iraqis, Americans, foreigners of any sort or even British politicians has become glaring. If this is to be a first rough draft of history, it is so far a highly partial one.

Chilcot emphatically rejects being cast as a court, let alone a foretaste of a Nuremberg trial. It is a far cry from the scrutiny of America's Capitol Hill or the milder forensic thrust of a Hutton or a Butler. This appears as a very British inquest, an intrusion into the private grief, or perhaps the self-styled triumph, of one man, Tony Blair.

But who knows? Perhaps still waters yet run deep.

9 DECEMBER 2009

# The Danish text: rich nations accused of Copenhagen power grab

## JOHN VIDAL

The UN Copenhagen climate talks were in disarray last night after developing countries reacted furiously to leaked documents that show world leaders will next week be asked to sign an agreement that hands more power to rich countries and sidelines the UN's role in all future climate change negotiations.

Observers said that the appearance of the secretly agreed negotiating text so late in proceedings made a mockery of the two-year slog of international meetings that has led to the Copenhagen summit.

Controversially, the 13-page document proposes that financial support for developing countries to develop clean technologies and adapt to climate change should be contingent on their taking action to de-carbonise their economies. In essence: no action, no money.

The poor countries argue that this stance undermines the principle that money pledged by the developed world should be seen as compensation for the damage done by the carbon dioxide pollution that they have released.

The document is also being interpreted by developing countries as setting unequal limits on per capita carbon emissions for developed and developing countries in 2050, meaning that people in rich countries would be permitted to emit nearly twice as much under the proposals.

It also indicates that airlines and international shipping could be forced to make unspecified emissions cuts by 2020 and make "financial contributions" to a global climate fund, an independent body that would distribute the money raised, most likely for adaptation.

The so-called Danish text, a secret draft agreement worked on by a group known as "the circle of commitment" but understood to include the UK, US and Denmark, has only been shown to a handful of countries since it was finalised this week.

The agreement, leaked to the *Guardian*, is a departure from the Kyoto protocol's principle which states that rich nations, which have emitted the bulk of the $CO_2$, should take on firm and binding commitments to reduce greenhouse gases, while the poorer nations are not compelled to act. Developing countries believe that the Danish draft text hands effective control of climate change finance to the World Bank and that it would abandon the Kyoto protocol, the only legally binding treaty that the world has on emissions reductions.

The text says that international public finance support for developing countries should only be provided "on the basis of appropriate increases in mitigation and adaptation efforts by developing countries".

It does make clear, however, that this money should be in addition to existing overseas aid budgets.

The G77-plus-China group of developing countries said the document threatened the talks.

"This text is a very serious development and very unfortunate. It is a major violation that threatens the success of the Copenhagen negotiations," said Lumumba Di-Aping, the Sudanese ambassador to the US and lead negotiator for the G77 group. "The Danish text destroys both the Kyoto protocol and the UN framework convention on climate change itself. It sets new obligations for developing countries. It does away with two years of negotiations. It superimposes a solution on developing countries."

The Danish delegation refused to comment on the draft but a UK diplomat last night played down the leak, saying the text was nearly two weeks old. "It would be natural to have all kinds of texts, different texts, circulating at this stage. I would expect a lot of texts doing the rounds."

The official insisted that developing countries had to commit to taking some actions, but he said, "it would not be fair for them to be held to the same standards as developed countries".

Developing countries that have seen the text are understood to be furious that it is being promoted by rich countries without their knowledge and without discussion in the negotiations. "It is being done in secret. Clearly the intention is to get [Barack]

Obama and the leaders of other rich countries to muscle it through when they arrive next week," said one developing-world diplomat, who asked to remain nameless.

Simon Hughes, the Liberal Democrat spokesman for energy and climate change, said that rich countries had to take responsibility for their past actions. "Unless the talks in Copenhagen have the objective of protecting the poorest and most vulnerable countries from the worst effects of the climate crisis, there will not be a deal and there should not a deal."

23 DECEMBER 2009

# How do I know China wrecked the climate deal? I was in the room

## MARK LYNAS

Copenhagen was a disaster. That much is agreed. But the truth about what actually happened is in danger of being lost amid the spin and inevitable mutual recriminations. The truth is this: China wrecked the talks, intentionally humiliated Barack Obama, and insisted on an awful "deal" so western leaders would walk away carrying the blame. How do I know this? Because I was in the room and saw it happen.

China's strategy was simple: block the open negotiations for two weeks, and then ensure that the closed-door deal made it look as if the west had failed the world's poor once again. And sure enough, the aid agencies, civil society movements and environmental groups all took the bait. The failure was "the inevitable result of rich countries refusing adequately and fairly to shoulder their overwhelming responsibility," said Christian Aid. "Rich countries have bullied developing nations," fumed Friends of the Earth International.

All very predictable, but the complete opposite of the truth. Even George Monbiot, writing in yesterday's *Guardian*, made the mistake of singly blaming Obama. But I saw Obama fighting desperately to salvage a deal, and the Chinese delegate saying "no", over and over again. Monbiot even approvingly quoted the Sudanese delegate Lumumba Di-Aping, who denounced the Copenhagen accord as "a suicide pact, an incineration pact, in order to maintain the economic dominance of a few countries".

Sudan behaves at the talks as a puppet of China; one of a number of countries that relieves the Chinese delegation of having to fight its battles in open sessions. It was a perfect stitch-up. China gutted the deal behind the scenes, and then left its proxies to savage it in public.

Here's what actually went on late last Friday night, as heads of state from two dozen countries met behind closed doors. Obama was at the table for several hours, sitting between Gordon Brown and the Ethiopian prime minister, Meles Zenawi. The Danish prime minister chaired, and on his right sat Ban Ki-moon, secretary-general of the UN. Probably only about 50 or 60 people, including the heads of state, were in the room. I was attached to one of the delegations, whose head of state was also present for most of the time.

What I saw was profoundly shocking. The Chinese premier, Wen Jiabao, did not deign to attend the meetings personally, instead sending a second-tier official in the country's foreign ministry to sit opposite Obama himself. The diplomatic snub was obvious and brutal, as was the practical implication: several times during the session, the world's most powerful heads of state were forced to wait around as the Chinese delegate went off to make telephone calls to his "superiors".

To those who would blame Obama and rich countries in general, know this: it was China's representative who insisted that industrialised country targets, previously agreed as an 80% cut by 2050, be taken out of the deal. "Why can't we even mention our own targets?" demanded a furious Angela Merkel. Australia's prime minister, Kevin Rudd, was annoyed enough to bang his microphone. Brazil's representative too pointed out the illogic of China's position. Why should rich countries not announce even this unilateral cut? The Chinese delegate said no, and I watched, aghast, as Merkel threw up her hands in despair and conceded the point. Now we know why – because China bet, correctly, that Obama would get the blame for the Copenhagen accord's lack of ambition.

China, backed at times by India, then proceeded to take out all the numbers that mattered. A 2020 peaking year in global emissions, essential to restrain temperatures to 2C, was removed and replaced by woolly language suggesting that emissions should peak "as soon as possible". The long-term target, of global 50% cuts by 2050, was also excised. No one else, perhaps with the exceptions of India and Saudi Arabia, wanted this to happen. I am certain that had the Chinese not been in the room, we would have left Copenhagen with a deal that had environmentalists popping champagne corks in every corner of the world.

How did China manage to pull off this coup? First, it was in an extremely strong negotiating position. China didn't need a deal. As one developing-country foreign minister said to me: "The Athenians had nothing to offer to the Spartans." On the other hand, western leaders in particular – but also presidents Lula of Brazil, Zuma of South Africa, Calderon of Mexico and many others – were desperate for a positive outcome.

Obama needed a strong deal perhaps more than anyone. Above all, he needed to be able to demonstrate to the Senate that he could deliver China in any global climate regulation framework, so conservative senators could not argue that US carbon cuts would further advantage Chinese industry. With midterm elections looming, Obama and his staff also knew that Copenhagen would be probably their only opportunity to go to climate change talks with a strong mandate. This further strengthened China's negotiating hand, as did the complete lack of civil society political pressure on either China or India. Campaign groups never blame developing countries for failure; this is an iron rule that is never broken. The Indians, in particular, have become past masters at co-opting the language of equity ("equal rights to the atmosphere") in the service of planetary suicide – and leftish campaigners and commentators are hoist with their own petard.

With the deal gutted, the heads of state session concluded with a final battle as the Chinese delegate insisted on removing the 1.5C target so beloved of the small island states and low-lying nations who have most to lose from rising seas. President Nasheed of the Maldives, supported by Brown, fought valiantly to save this crucial number. "How can you ask my country to go extinct?" demanded Nasheed. The Chinese delegate feigned great offence – and the number stayed, but surrounded by language which makes it all but meaningless. The deed was done.

All this demands the question: what is China's game? Why did China, in the words of a UK-based analyst who also spent hours in heads of state meetings, "not only reject targets for itself, but also refuse to allow any other country to take on binding targets?" The analyst, who has attended climate conferences for more than 15 years, concludes that China wants to weaken the climate regulation regime now "in order to avoid the risk that it might be called on to be more ambitious in a few years' time".

This does not mean China is not serious about global warming. It is strong in both the wind and solar industries. But China's growth, and growing global political and economic dominance, is based largely on cheap coal. China knows it is becoming an uncontested superpower; indeed its newfound muscular confidence was on striking display in Copenhagen. Its coal-based economy doubles every decade, and its power increases commensurately. Its leadership will not alter this magic formula unless they absolutely have to.

Copenhagen was much worse than just another bad deal, because it illustrated a profound shift in global geopolitics. This is fast becoming China's century, yet its leadership has displayed that multilateral environmental governance is not only not a priority, but is viewed as a hindrance to the new superpower's freedom of action. I left Copenhagen more despondent than I have felt in a long time. After all the hope and all the hype, the mobilisation of thousands, a wave of optimism crashed against the rock of global power politics, fell back, and drained away.

31 DECEMBER 2009

# The hand of Iran behind Britons' Baghdad kidnapping

MONA MAHMOOD

The five British men kidnapped in Iraq were taken in an operation led and masterminded by Iran's Revolutionary Guard, according to evidence uncovered during an extensive investigation by the *Guardian*.

The men – including Peter Moore, who was released yesterday after more than two years in captivity – were taken to Iran within a day of their kidnap from a government ministry building in Baghdad in 2007, several senior sources in Iraq and Iran have told the *Guardian*.

They were incarcerated in prisons run by the al-Quds force, a unit that specialises in foreign operations on behalf of the Iranian government.

One of the kidnappers has told this paper that three of the Britons – Jason Creswell, Jason Swindlehurst and Alec Maclachlan – were subsequently killed after the British government refused to take ransom demands seriously.

Last night it emerged that part of the deal that led to the release of Moore involved the handing over of a young Shia cleric, Qais al-Khazali, a leading figure in the Righteous League, which emerged in 2006 and stayed largely in the shadows as a proxy of the Iranian Revolutionary Guard's elite unit, the al-Quds forces. Khazali was last night handed over by the US military for release by the Iraqi government.

The year-long *Guardian* investigation can also reveal that Moore was targeted because he was installing a system that would show how a vast amount of international aid was diverted to Iran's militia groups in Iraq. The bodyguards' bodies were eventually traded for the release of Iraqi prisoners, and they had probably been dead for at least 18 months before three of their bodies were handed over earlier this year.

Moore, 37, a computer expert from Lincoln, and the four security guards were taken on 29 May 2007 from the Iraqi ministry of finance's technology centre in Baghdad. He had been a contractor working to install sophisticated software in the ministry to track down billions of dollars in international aid and oil revenues.

A group of up to 100 men entered the building and took the Britons, racing off into Baghdad traffic in a fleet of Toyota Land Cruisers. A sixth man – who the *Guardian* can reveal was Peter Donkin – was left by the kidnappers after he managed to hide under floorboards.

A former Iranian Revolutionary Guard member, speaking to this paper under condition of anonymity, said the extraordinary kidnap was masterminded by Iran. The man, a former major who worked for 14 years inside the Iranian organisation and claims to have taken part in kidnap operations himself, believes the hostages were held in two al-Quds camps in Iran – one known as Qasser Shiereen military camp, close to the Iraqi border crossing with Mehran, and a second camp known as the Tehran Pars, located near a salt lake north-east of Qom.

"It was an Iranian kidnap, led by the Revolutionary Guard, carried out by the al-Quds force," he said. "My contact works for al-Quds. He took part in the planning of the kidnap and he watched the kidnapping as it was taking place. He told me that they spent two days at the Qasser Shiereen camp. They then took them deep inside Iran."

This claim is backed up by a serving Iraqi minister with close links to Iran. "This was an IRG [Iranian Revolutionary Guard] operation," he said. "You don't think for a moment that those militia groups from Sadr City could have carried out a high-level kidnapping like this one."

A former intelligence chief at the Iraqi ministry of defence has also described to the *Guardian* how intelligence operatives followed the kidnappers as they took the hostages from a mosque in Baghdad's Sadr City to the Iranian border. "They were hooded and handcuffed, then the cars drove off in a new direction – they were headed towards the Iranian border," the intelligence chief said.

While the hostages were in Iran the kidnappers made sure those who took care of them were Iraqi nationals. "At all times they were surrounded by Iraqi voices. Everything was done to make sure they had no idea they were in Iran," said an Iranian source with knowledge of the kidnap.

A *Guardian* report in July revealed evidence that Iraqi officials colluded in the kidnap of the five, and that one motive was to prevent millions of dollars of aid money from being tracked – including an estimated $18bn that had gone missing.

A former senior Iraqi intelligence chief claims the project Moore was working on would have laid bare exactly where all Iraq's money was going. He claims there was an Iranian link to the alleged financial cover-up. The Foreign Office said last night: "We have no evidence that the British hostages, including Peter Moore, were held in Iran. We are not in a position to say with any certainty where they were held during each and every single day."'

19 January 2010

# Takeovers are a brutal game that sells Britain short

NILS PRATLEY

Once upon a time the City used to pretend that the takeover game was about dispatching lazy and incompetent managements. The process might be brutal but in the long run we were all supposed to be richer as talented executives were entrusted with bigger empires. Nice theory, but it is complete nonsense. Cadbury is just the latest company to fall victim to the modern version of the takeover business, where the desire for short-term profits trumps long-term investment.

Consider the relative performances of the two companies. Cadbury had a rocky patch a few years ago but had been turning out sparkling numbers for the past 18 months. Kraft, on the other hand, has found the label "low-growth conglomerate" impossible to shake off. That is because the description is basically correct: Kraft is a sprawling company that has been a disappointment to its investors for the past five years. Yet Cadbury's assets have ended up in the hands of inferior managers. That is not the result the system is meant to deliver.

Why did it happen? Look at the people who will deliver Cadbury to Kraft – the shareholders. It's no good blaming the hedge funds, which had consumed 25% of Cadbury by the time the board rolled over and accepted 850p a share. Those hedge funds were only able to buy a quarter of Cadbury because other investors had sold shares to them in recent weeks, generally at below 800p. The desire to bank a profit on an asset trading at 550p last summer was too great – turning down a 45% return over five months can kill a career.

Yet many of the same Cadbury investors must know Kraft has got a bargain. Even at the close of a five-month battle, Kraft could boast that buying Cadbury for £11.9bn will be "accretive" to its own earnings from the second year. In other words, Kraft expects this deal to start paying for itself by the end of 2011. That is not a surprise. As Cadbury's defence document showed, a bidder would have had to pay 900p-plus even to get close to past takeover valuations in the confectionery industry. A few Cadbury loyalists – Standard Life Investments and Legal & General – had accepted this point.

Can anything be done to protect valuable, but vulnerable, UK companies such as Cadbury in future? "All things being equal it is easier to take over a company here than anywhere else in the world," Lord Myners, the City minister, declared during the battle of Bournville. He's right. We know that Cadbury-style deals would not happen in France or Germany and that US companies often run off to Delaware to adopt a variety of poison-pill defences. True, Anheuser-Busch, brewer of Budweiser, the American national beer, is now in Belgian hands, but that's one that got through the net.

So how about giving committed long-term UK investors, such as L&G, a bigger voice during takeovers – enhanced voting rights, in the jargon? There is no guarantee such a system would have saved Cadbury but it might have improved its chances.

In the end, the only surefire method is to put up the shutters sometimes and declare the public interest to be paramount. That's what we used to do. In 1988, the Tory trade minister Lord Young, hardly an instinctive protectionist, referred to the Monopolies Commission a bid for Rank Hovis McDougall from the Australian group Goodman Fielder Wattie. The grounds were the "possible effects on competition, especially in the market for bread, arising out of the financing of the proposed acquisition". In retrospect, Young's actions look like shameless political interference.

Lord Mandelson, two decades on, might struggle to mount a public interest case for saving the maker of Curly Wurlys. But he would face less difficulty in defending, say, Pilkington, Boots, Npower, P&O Ports, Powergen or BAA, all of which have fallen to foreign bidders. Too late now, of course, but the argument that the UK is better off for its open-doors policy is hard to sustain.

France and Germany, quicker out of the recession than the UK, are not noticeably suffering from a grave misallocation of capital. Their companies tend to be more competitive internationally for a simple reason: their managements are not afraid to invest because they are not constantly feeding the City's appetite for special dividends, instant profits and deals. The idea that the takeover train delivers greater productivity and long-term wealth is now a bad joke.

27 JANUARY 2010

# Haiti earthquake: death of a daughter

RORY CARROLL

Fabienne Cherisma spent her life assessing margins. She was just 15 but had a knack for knowing what would sell on the family's knick-knack stall, and for how much. In Port-au-Prince's raucous, hardscrabble market it was a gift that helped keep her parents and five siblings on the right side of the survival line.

"My daughter was a sales lady. A good one," said her father, Osam. "Whatever she bought she was always able to sell it on for a bit more." A few cents extra profit meant an extra spoon of rice for dinner in the family's one-room shack.

His daughter spent mornings in stores and other markets hunting bargains – pots, soap, combs, zips, bras – and then hawked them with a mark-up from the family's patch of concrete near Grand Rue, an open-air market where traders shout over the throb of generators and flies hover over steaming garbage.

Fabienne spent her afternoons at school, excelling at maths, French and science. "She was very intelligent," Osam said. "Her head was full of knowledge." Despite her nose for commerce her ambition was to become a nurse.

Haiti's 12 January earthquake changed Fabienne's usual calculations. The family home escaped unscathed, and within days the market resumed, but mobs were looting nearby stores. Human ant-trails carrying food, electrical goods and furniture passed her stall.

Amid the devastation, Fabienne spotted an opportunity, and last Tuesday she joined the throng. Most looters were male but the girl in the pink mini-skirt emerged from the melee with two plastic chairs and three framed pictures.

She was scrambling back over collapsed rooftops, just a few streets from her stall, when police in fluorescent yellow vests began shooting in the air. A bullet to the head felled Fabienne. She collapsed on to one of the paintings, blood trickling from the wound.

"People ran past saying a little girl was shot. My girl," said her father. He ran to the scene. His daughter was dead. Someone had gone through her pockets. The chairs she had carried had disappeared.

He had not picked up Fabienne up since she was a toddler, but Osam, lean and muscular like most Haitian men, swung her body over his shoulder and took her home. His wife, Amante, collapsed. Just days earlier the family had celebrated surviving the quake but now death had visited after all. "She was my baby," she said.

It was unclear whether police, who have executed looters, intentionally shot the girl. Her family said the shooting was deliberate and that three head wounds proved she was shot twice more at point blank range.

That claim was impossible to verify. When asked, police in the area shrugged and said they knew nothing. "It's not like it's easy keeping track of bodies," said one sergeant. Osam insisted his daughter was no looter, that she set out with $70 (£43) – the family's entire cash reserve – to buy chairs, having estimated she could sell them for $75. The framed pictures must have been a spontaneous purchase. If so she would have been a lone shopper amid a tumult of scavengers.

With morgues overflowing, and earthquake fatalities being bull-dozed into mass graves, the Cherismas took their daughter's body out of the city. With a borrowed $70 they rented a private bus, and drove for four hours to relatives in Zorange. They buried her in a Catholic ceremony and placed a white cross over the grave.

In Port-au-Prince there are few mementoes of the teenager's existence: a pair of grubby white training shoes; a brown school uniform in a red bucket that serves as a chair, table and container.

The one photo of her, in which she smiles, is lost. So is her birth certificate. There is no police investigation and the death is not registered. Officially, it is as if the teenager never was.

The question is not whether Fabienne will be remembered as a victim of the earthquake but whether, outside her family, she will be remembered at all.

Her sister Amanda, 13, more shy and withdrawn, said she would miss Fabienne's jokes, banter with customers, and advice on what to charge: "She said you have to know what is not too little, not too much. You have to get it just right."

18 FEBRUARY 2010

# Obituary: Cy Grant, singer, actor and writer

GUS JOHN

Cy Grant, who has died aged 90, was among the first set of RAF officers from the West Indies and qualified as a barrister, but such is the allure of television that he will be chiefly remembered as a singer, actor and broadcaster. In 1957, he began to make daily appearances on the BBC's *Tonight* programme, bringing levity to current affairs by giving a calypso rendition of the news, often using texts written by Bernard Levin. Cy's ability to compose tunes spontaneously and fit the news into verse was highly commended and won him the admiration of viewers nationwide. For the first time, the country was seeing a black face on TV on a regular basis. Nevertheless, Cy gave up the position in 1960, fearing that he would be considered capable of nothing else.

He acted on stage and screen, but was disillusioned with the obstacles that black actors faced in getting parts that matched their abilities. He once told me: "We suffered the indignity of seeing white actors blackening themselves and giving themselves bulbous lips to play black parts, reinforcing the caricature of us as black people, a caricature which casting directors, artistic directors and playwrights themselves refused to allow us to escape."

Cy spent his entire life in Britain combating such marginalisation. He saw this as a redemptive mission, appealing to white Britain to sweep away notions of cultural supremacy. He held a mirror up to British society and painstakingly interpreted it, as he groped towards actively reshaping it and striving to humanise it.

Born in Beterverwagting, a village in British Guiana (now Guyana), after the end of the first world war, Cy had two brothers and four sisters. His mother was a talented pianist and he grew up surrounded by music, playing the guitar and singing folk songs. He excelled at school and was keen to study law, but his parents lacked the funds.

After working as a civil servant, Cy left for Britain and joined the RAF in 1941, one of roughly 400 men recruited from the Caribbean after the huge losses in the Battle of Britain. He trained as a navigator and in 1943 was shot down in the Battle of the Ruhr, landing in Holland. Joost Klootwijk, the young son of a Dutch farmer, looked on as his parents tried to help the airman. The boy was moved by the novelty of a uniformed black RAF officer crash-landing near his home. The Gestapo identified Cy as "a member of the Royal Air Force of indeterminate race" and he was held as a prisoner of war for two years. Cy later used that phrase for the title of his book about his war service. Klootwijk's subsequent research enabled his son, Hans, to write a book about Cy's crew, *Lancaster W4827: Failed to Return*.

Although he qualified as a barrister in 1950, he struggled to get work. In his own words, "this was Britain in peacetime and I was no longer useful". He became a recognisable voice on radio, singing folk songs, and recorded several albums. He also hosted his own TV series, *For Members Only*, in the mid-50s, interviewing a variety of guests and playing the guitar. In 1956, he appeared in *A Man from the Sun*, a television drama written by John Elliot about the experience of Caribbean migrants to Britain after the second world war. He voiced a character for Gerry Anderson's *Captain Scarlet and the Mysterons* and also appeared in an episode of *The Persuaders*, opposite Roger Moore.

Cy successfully auditioned for Laurence Olivier and had stage appearances for Olivier's Festival of Britain company in London and New York. In 1965, he was acclaimed as Othello at the Phoenix theatre, in Leicester. The next year he starred in *Cindy Ella* with Cleo Laine at the Garrick theatre, in London. He also appeared in the films *Shaft in Africa* (1973) and *At the Earth's Core* (1976).

Frustrated with many of the roles he was offered, he determined to take on the theatre establishment on his own terms. In order to launch black artistic talent, in 1973 he founded Drum Arts Centre, in London, with the Zimbabwean actor John Mapondera and others, including me. Drum collaborated with Steve Carter of New York's Negro Ensemble theatre and staged a number of productions, including *Bread* by Mustapha Matura and *The Gods Are Not to Blame* by Ola Rotimi.

Two major influences in Cy's life, which helped determine the direction of his artistic expression and his later writing, were the poet, politician, philosopher and architect of negritude, Aimé Césaire, and a Chinese text, the *Tao Te Ching*. He produced and performed Césaire's epic poem *Notebook of a Return to the Native Land* as a one-man show, touring Britain for more than two years. He was later to say of Césaire: "His revolt against Europe is what worked on me in a subliminal yet positive way. It wasn't just a revolt against racism, colonialism and the excesses of European culture, but a call for a return to our native human values, to recognise that nature is alive and bounteous and that we should not abuse her."

In his book, *Blackness and the Dreaming Soul* (2007), Cy argued that white society must first discover new ways of seeing itself, in order that it might comprehend and value the "otherness" of its indigenous black citizens. In his essay *The Way of the West* (2008), he argued that the black man, having reclaimed his authentic history and recovered his lost soul, must not fall into the trap of aspiring to assimilate into the so-called civilised values of his former oppressors.

Criticising the notion of Black History Month, Cy argued: "Before we decide upon a calendar of socially relevant events, we would do well to look again at who and what we are and begin to know, like Césaire, that 'the tree of our hands is for all'."

In his last years, Cy wrote copiously and did everything with a new urgency, especially after he became ill. He particularly wanted to see his war memoirs, essays and poems form part of the curriculums in schools and universities.

He is survived by his wife, Dorith, whom he married in 1956, their two daughters and a son from an earlier marriage, and his sister, Valerie.

# Spring

3 March 2010

# Michael Foot, 1913-2010: the unlikely Machiavelli

IAN AITKEN

It used to be said of Michael Foot by less principled colleagues that he might be a good chap, but he wasn't really fit for office. "Poor old Michael," they would say condescendingly, "he may be able to make a good speech, but he couldn't run a whelk stall, let alone a department of state."

That verdict seemed to be sustained by his generally dishevelled appearance, his taste for talking enthusiastically about Byron, Keats and Shelley, and his clear conviction that books mattered at least as much as politics. But it had to be abandoned PDQ when he finally achieved office under Wilson and Callaghan from 1974, with its two elections. That government's tiny majority was gradually whittled away in byelections, eventually forcing it to survive by doing more-or-less shabby deals, first with the Liberals, then with the Scottish Nationalists, and ultimately with the Ulster Unionists. The man who brokered those deals was the supposedly pure Michael, as leader of the Commons.

In fact it was Foot, newly revealed as a latter-day Machiavelli, who kept the Callaghan government tottering on until its final demise in 1979. It was defeated by a majority of one vote at the end of perhaps the most dramatic Commons debate since the 1940s, and it was Foot's job to wind up that debate against a background of almost hysterical tension.

He rose to the occasion by delivering one of the funniest speeches I have ever heard delivered from the dispatch box. In spite of the frenzy just minutes before the crucial division, he managed to make both sides of the packed house rock with laughter. It was a remarkable achievement.

If he had not agreed to stand for the leadership of the Labour party to succeed Callaghan, he might well have been remembered for that stint as a top cabinet minister. But alas, he became leader just as the party was plunging into a period of hate-filled sectarianism that made it virtually unelectable. By the time General Leopoldo Galtieri invaded the Falkland Islands, thus turning Margaret Thatcher into a modern Britannia, the next election was in effect lost.

There are many inside and outside the Labour party who believe that Labour MPs, on the last occasion when they would have had the exclusive right to elect a leader, would have done better to have chosen Denis Healey. He was the more abrasive character, and might have given Mrs Thatcher a rougher time as prime minister. But it was precisely his abrasiveness that ensured he didn't become leader. Many MPs who weren't on the left nevertheless feared that Healey would split the party from top to bottom.

In the end, of course, the party did split, when the Gang of Four marched out to form the SDP. Foot failed to prevent the exodus, although he tried desperately to dissuade Shirley Williams from leaving. He saw her as the most appealing of the four, and pleaded with her repeatedly to stay. To his profound regret, she left with the rest.

His relations with the most senior of the Gang of Four, Roy Jenkins, had never been good, although they shared a love of books. But he was frankly scornful of the arrogance of David Owen. Once, responding to an aggressive intervention by Owen, he quoted Zsa Zsa Gabor: "In my experience, men who are macho usually aren't mucho."

Out of office, and eventually out of parliament (he flatly refused to go to the Lords), he churned out a succession of delightful books of essays about people he had known and places he had been to. And he developed a broad new range of friendships with civilised Tories. The most notable of these was Ian Gilmour, a former cabinet minister sacked by Thatcher as a "wet". The basis of their friendship was Byron.

Throughout his life he delighted in his large and remarkable family. In particular, he cherished his very leftwing nephew Paul Foot, who warmly returned his love. Paul once brought him a bottle of Bollinger for his birthday. Pressing it into his uncle's hands, he declared: "There – now you really are a Bollinger Bolshevik."

But the deepest love of his life was his beautiful wife, the film producer Jill Craigie. I suspect he never quite got over the fact that he, asthmatic and with chronic eczema, had managed to land someone quite so lovely. But there was no doubting her love for him, which was total. They remained devoted to each other until her unexpected death in 1999.

In spite of that, however, she nearly managed to kill the both of them in a horrendous car accident in 1963. They survived, with the surprising side effect that Michael's asthma was cured. I remember writing a hurried and anguished obituary of him for the *Daily Express* that night. Little did I think that it would be half a century before it was needed.

6 MARCH 2010

# The joys of stationery

### HILARY MANTEL

When narratives fracture, when words fail, I take consolation from the part of my life that always works: the stationery order. The mail-order stationery people supply every need from royal blue Quink to a dazzling variety of portable hard drives.

Their operation is error-free, sleek and timely. In fact, it's more than timely: it's eerie. I have only to call out to my spouse: "Let's be devils and get bubble wrap," and a man with a van is pulling up outside. Where I live – in the remote fastness of Woking – the morning post comes at three, my parcels go to the right number but another street, and on one occasion, when a hapless person tried to send me a present, Amazon denied that my address existed.

So this speedy stationery service looks spooky. Maybe they've implanted a chip in my brain, and soon I'll only need to think about my order, and coloured lights will flash at their HQ, and the laden vehicle will be screaming in my direction. I can sit and read the stationery catalogue for hours on end, marking its pages with the very Post-it notes it has previously sold me in 12-pad packs. I often wish I could review it: it's crisp and perfectly achieved, and what it lacks in originality it makes up for in the graceful, coded compression of what it offers the dazzled reader.

If you think there's little on offer but paperclips, think again: you can buy biscuits, buckets and bayonet-fitting bulbs. Sometimes I fantasise that all my furniture has been destroyed in a cataclysm, and I have to start again with only the stationery catalogue. My entire house would become an office, which would be an overt recognition of the existing state of affairs. Sustained by a giant jar of Fairtrade instant coffee, I could spend whole days putting up Kwik-Rak shelving and assembling "modular reception seating" into long, worm-shaped sofas. They don't sell beds – so much for office romance – but who would want to rest if you could spend the night printing out masterpieces at your ergonomic melamine workstation, and weighing them at dawn on a "solar parcel scale", which takes up to 20 kilos and comes with a three-year warranty?

Writers displace their anxiety on to the tools of the trade. It's better to say that you haven't got the right pencil than to say you can't write, or to blame your computer for losing your chapter than face up to your feeling that it's better lost. It's not just writers who muddle up the tools with the job. The reading public also fetishises the kit.

We have all heard the tale of the author who is asked: "How do you write?" and answers in an exquisitely modulated Nabokovian-Woolfian-Dostoevskian discourse, only to be floored by the flat supplementary: "I meant, Mac or PC?" There is persistent confusion between writing and writing things down, a confusion between the workings of the writing mind and the weight of the paper scribbled over. "How many words do you do per day?" people ask, as if the product unwinds in a flowing, ceaseless stream of uncriticised, unrevised narrative, and as if the difference between good and bad writers is that the good ones have no need to do it again. Almost the opposite is true; the better you are, the more ambitious and exploratory, the more often you will go astray on the way to getting it even approximately halfway right.

So while it's on its way to going right, you take comfort in buying new notebooks. Buying them in foreign cities is a good way of carrying away a souvenir. That said, *le vrai moleskine* and its mythology irritate me. Chatwin, Hemingway: has the earth ever held two greater posers? The magic has surely gone out of the little black tablet now that you can buy it everywhere, and in pastel pink, and even get it from Amazon – if they believe your address exists. The trouble with the Moleskine is that you can't easily pick it apart. This may have its advantages for glamorous itinerants, who tend to be of careless habit and do not have my access to self-assembly beech- and maple-effect storage solutions – though, as some cabinets run on castors, I don't see what stopped them filing as they travelled. But surely the whole point of a notebook is to pull it apart, and distribute pieces among your various projects? There is a serious issue here. Perforation is vital – more vital than vodka, more essential to a novel's success than a spellchecker and an agent.

I often sense the disappointment when trusting beginners ask me how to go about it, and I tell them it's all about ring binders. But I can only shake my head and say what I know: comrades, the hard-spined notebook is death to free thought. Pocket-size or desk-size, it drives the narrative in one direction, one only, and its relentless linearity oppresses you, so you seal off your narrative options early.

True, you can cross out. You can have a black page to show for your hour's work. Moleskine's website shows a page from a Sartre novel that is almost all crossing-out. But deletion implies you have gone wrong, whereas perhaps you are not going wrong, just generating material in an order the sense of which has yet to emerge. What you need is not to obliterate errors, but to swap them around a bit; then, often enough, they start to look less like errors than like the wellspring of new hope. For myself, the only way I know how to make a book is to construct it like a collage: a bit of dialogue here, a scrap of narrative, an isolated description of a common object, an elaborate running metaphor which threads between the sequences and holds different narrative lines together.

7 JANUARY 2010

Jonathan Ross presents the media waiting outside his house with cups of tea, after announcing he will leave the BBC. GRAEME ROBERTSON

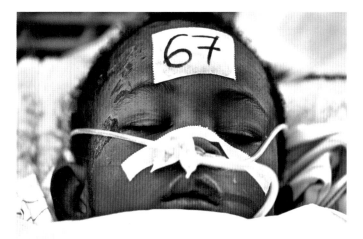

16 JANUARY 2010

Jean Chandula, 3, is treated in a hospital in Port-au-Prince, Haiti, four days after the island was struck by a massive earthquake. DAVID LEVENE

16 JANUARY 2010
A man walks past a barrow laden with dead bodies alongside a cemetery in Port-au-Prince, Haiti. DAVID LEVENE

14 APRIL 2010

Gordon Brown has breakfast at his constituency home in North
Queensferry in the second week of the election campaign. MARTIN ARGLES

15 APRIL 2010

Peter Mandelson dances with Hanna Rita-Mackenzie at the Tower
Ballroom in Blackpool. GRAEME ROBERTSON

You must be able to loop back on yourself, and to be able to arrange the elements of which your story consists in an order that is entirely flexible. In the end you must make a decision, but why not postpone it till the last possible point? Because once you have made the commitment, what you have written starts to look right. It gains a brutal ascendancy over you. It's easy to revise sentence by sentence, but very difficult to recognise and accept, at some late stage, that the whole structure of a book went wrong because you let your stationery boss you about.

But these days, you'll say, doesn't everybody write on screen? True, but you can still, by premature decision-making about how you store your text, set up for yourself the equivalent of the hard-spined notebook. Files are not flexible unless their maker is. The good news about the computer is its endless scope for procrastinative fussing. Is this a nice font? Shall I rename all my files? Learn some new software?

At twilight, though, when the day's work is on pause, swivelling in my executive chair (variable seat height and de luxe lumbar support), I never reminisce about dear old WordStar 2000 back in the 1980s. I think instead about other trades I might have pursued, with different and privileged stationery: that pink tape, for instance, that barristers use to tie up their bundles.

Do they still, at the Treasury, use treasury tags? Could I use one? The shades of evening make me mourn lost paper sizes; when did you last see a ream of foolscap? The late author David Hughes once sent me a few sheets, and I'm keeping them carefully, for when I have a long, thin story to write.

13 MARCH 2010

# The battle for Barking

## JOHN HARRIS

The tube heads east, through Whitechapel, Stepney Green, Mile End, Bow Road. Canary Wharf is there in the near distance, but seems like another world. The train passes through post-industrial remains – rusty gasometers, empty canals – and blocks of flats, from inter-war mansion blocks to the great leviathans put up in the 60s. Finally, the landscape opens out into a grey plateau, and you're there: most of the way to Essex, into the borough of Barking and Dagenham.

As arranged, Nick Griffin's bodyguard calls me at 1.30pm, and picks me up at Dagenham Heathway station – whereupon we drive to the home of Richard Barnbrook, one of the British National party's leading Barking councillors and their solitary member of the London Assembly. An English flag and a Union Jack fly either side of the front door; inside, the lounge is dominated by two big glass tanks populated by Chinese water dragons and other exotic reptiles.

And there he is, like a Bond villain relocated to the set of the Royle Family: Nick Griffin, 51, here for the day before resuming his current job in Strasbourg and Brussels as the MEP for England's north-west. He is personable, if a little nervous. Depending on your point of view, the scene's fine details suggest either the banality of evil, or the comfortingly Pooter-esque tastes of the house's owner: a matter not just of the reptiles, but of Barnbrook's insistence that everyone, his leader included, walks around in their stocking feet, and the fact that he makes a point of offering Griffin a soft drink: "Do you want an apple juice, Nick?"

"Oh, I'd love an apple juice."

Eventually, we make our way to the Thames View estate, a blighted housing development cut off from the rest of the borough by the cacophonous A13. Seemingly for my benefit and that of a BNP volunteer making a campaign video, Griffin, Barnbrook and another five or six BNP members – at least two of whom are wearing secret-service-type earpieces – approach the few members of the public who are braving the rain, and talk to them about the more difficult aspects of their lives.

In Shannon's Bakery, 60-year-old Shannon Slattery tells them about her daughter, who lives with her four-year-old son in a grim, privately rented flat full of pigeon droppings that have apparently made the boy chronically ill. They're on the council waiting list, "but every time, she's, like, number 200 or 300". She and her husband Derek now vote BNP: "They talk straight – they stand up for the English." All this is explained while a few black school kids jostle at the counter for cakes, and Barnbrook makes awkward small talk with them: "You going to take some exercise after that? You don't want to get big round the middle."

Once a dependable Labour stronghold, Barking and Dagenham is now represented by two MPs who could not be more different: the left's favourite, Jon Cruddas; and Margaret Hodge, New Labourite, and minister at the Department for Culture, Media and Sport. They have one thing in common: a long, grinding fight against the British National party. Since 2006, the BNP has had 12 councillors here – nine of whom are in Hodge's Barking constituency – and come May it could make it to 26 seats and be handed control of the borough. Meanwhile, Hodge is in the early stages of a general election battle against the far right's most recognisable and infamous face: Nick Griffin.

Modern politicians don't talk about such issues much, but the underlying problems here are simple enough. Local life used to revolve around the massive Ford car works, which once employed 50,000, but is now home to a diesel engine plant staffed by only 2,000. Back then, the borough was also a byword for plentiful council housing.

Margaret Thatcher's Right-to-Buy scheme changed things for ever, though only once former tenants sold up and moved on. As that happened, thousands of ex-council houses contributed to the cheapest rental market in London, drawing more and more of the economic migrants who now keep so much of the city running. The borough was thus transformed from a largely white community where abundant accommodation ensured that extended families lived within doors of each other, to a multi-coloured milieu in which people at the sharp end had to compete for scarce supplies of just about everything: decent jobs, adequate schools and, most of all, somewhere to live. The result: a tinderbox, where issues get reduced to race and nationality.

One Saturday in January, I follow a crowd of Labour party people on one of Hodge's Days Of Action: six or so hours of door-to-door calls. She flits between packs of canvassers, talking to the public when required, noting down their sources of anger and concern, endlessly talking about the BNP's fascist pedigree. To some people now in the habit of voting for them, this is news.

At the entrance to one of the Becontree Estate's cul-de-sacs, we meet Jackie Morrell, who clocks her MP – and starts shouting. "All the trouble we have down here, and the council do fuck all. We have trouble from black people, but they call us racist: music all hours of the night at one house. At another they chuck dog shit over the fence."

Morrell is 42: a trained chef, currently unemployed. She lives in a one-bedroom flat with her mother. She's on the housing waiting list, but way down the queue. She votes BNP. "The reason I go for them is because they go for a lot of my policies."

Such as? "Stop the immigrants. You've got to shut the floodgates."

"You're fed up with us lot, then?" Hodge says, and out come a few of her stock lines: "The borough's changing. But we can make it work. It doesn't have to be bad."

Hodge is 65. Born in Egypt, she came to Britain with her Jewish parents, who were refugees from Nazi-occupied Austria. Her father Hans founded the firm that eventually became Stemcor, the world's largest independent steel trading business, in which she owns a major stake. Having served time as the leader of Islington Council, she became the MP for Barking in 1994. Back then, according to local Labour insiders, she and the local party struck a deal whereby she saw to her Westminster commitments and they focused their attention on the council. In this telling of the story, it was assumed that Labour rule would extend into eternity, so there was little neighbourhood campaigning, leaving the door open for the BNP when local affairs turned troublesome.

So I wonder: how much responsibility does she feel about her party being asleep on the job?

"Oh, of course ... I share the responsibility. When I was first the MP in Barking, we were a safe constituency and people felt they could weigh the votes in without bothering ... And that included me. I kick myself that I didn't hear the alarm bells. I wish I'd been tougher."

Some of the big failures, she acknowledges, happened at the heart of government. "We failed to realise the importance of the quality of life on council estates and the importance of affordable housing ... I think we got that wrong. From 2001, I was saying, 'Housing is the key issue.' I showed all the decision-makers in the party my research" – she means people right at the top – "and they all thought it was very interesting. Did it change what they did? No."

A month later, sitting in a pub on the Thames View estate drinking a pint of light ale and bitter, Nick Griffin tells me that Hodge is an easy target: "far more unpopular than Jon Cruddas", "fantastically wealthy" and the embodiment of the ties that bind politics and big business. Could he win? "I'm not particularly fussed: I'd love to be an MP, certainly. I'd like to represent this place. I've been coming down to Barking – in fact, this estate specifically – since I was 17."

That was with the National Front, presumably?

He goes quiet. "The NF, yeah."

His plan, he tells me, is to draw media hostility away from other BNP candidates – particularly for the borough council – and thus allow them a relatively clear run. "The flak will only potentially damage my chances here. So in terms of the benefits for the party, and especially our drive to take the council, well, that's the real prize. It really is."

When I ask what the BNP might do with local power, he outlines a "sons and daughters" housing policy, and a few measures – from the teaching of "British values" in schools to unspecified work through local youth clubs – that would aim at "integrating" outsiders into his party's understanding of British life. He mentions "integration" at least twice, so I remind him that, despite being forced to admit non-white members, his party's constitution still says they are "wholly opposed to any form of racial integration between British and non-European peoples". The two don't sit comfortably together, do they? "They don't sit particularly well. But this is practical politics as opposed to, um, ideological perfection."

A church "coffee afternoon" hosted by Hodge in Bastable Avenue, Barking. Around 30 locals have shown up, mostly pensioners, none of whom votes BNP or says they're minded to. The exchanges with

Hodge are stilted and sedate, until she mentions immigration and the room explodes.

"We've gone stark raving mad," shouts one man. "We take in more people than anywhere else in Europe."

"You can't even get on the bus," offers a woman at the same table.

Nearby, another voice bemoans the predicament of his son. "Generations after generations of my family have been here. Even if you build new flats, what chance has he got?"

In 2006, just before the BNP won all those council seats, Hodge caused outrage by claiming that eight out of 10 people in Barking were thinking about voting for them. The response of Labour councillor Liam Smith was not untypical: "We have had people saying they're considering voting BNP because they feel that once the Labour minister says something, it must be right." The BNP sent her a bunch of flowers.

"It made me unpopular with people who didn't like me anyway," Hodge says. "It gave them something to latch on to. But I think the idea that it was, in any way, the reason why 12 BNP councillors succeeded in the borough elections is ... fatuous."

A year later, she sparked another uproar when she argued that the system for allocating council houses should be changed to favour local people, arguing for policies whereby "the legitimate sense of entitlement felt by the indigenous family overrides the legitimate need demonstrated by the new migrants". Last month, via an article in the *Daily Mail*, she pushed the same point again. As her critics see it, this is desperate stuff: a proposal that blurs into the BNP's policies, and thus makes their drive for respectability all the easier.

"One of the mistakes we made in the past was refusing to tackle some of the issues which draw people to the extreme right," Hodge says. "If we don't capture that terrain with our purpose and our values, we leave it to the BNP. And then you get what I get on the doorstep, all the time: 'Everything the BNP say, I agree with.' They're impelled by racism, right? I'm driven by fairness."

The *Sun*'s headline, seizing on what she also said about benefits, was "Minister: Ban Dole For Migrants", which can't have done wonders for community relations. "Well, I can't control the headlines. What I won't have is, 'Don't enter this territory – it's territory for the extreme right'. I won't have that. We've got to capture it for us."

In the pub with Nick Griffin, I bring up the reluctance of pensioners round here to vote BNP, based on their memories of the second world war, and his party's history of neo-Nazism. "We have things there, sure, yeah," he says, though reminders of his own backstory are either denied or dodged. For example: yes, he led a National Front march to the Cenotaph in 1986 – alongside people who were Sieg Heiling, according to reports – with a banner that said, "No more brothers' wars", but that was "about the first world war".

When I ask where he now stands on what he once called "nonsense about gas chambers" – surely given even more charge because of Hodge's family history – he pleads the same defence he tried on *Question Time*: "I genuinely cannot tell you what I used to believe, and why I've changed my mind ... three times a month I go through France and Belgium, where you're accessible also to the German courts, and even to say why I've changed my mind and become more mainstream would lay me open to a communist magistrate."

The subject is batted between us fruitlessly for a few minutes, before we get to the BNP's campaigning in Barking and its apparent habit of telling lies. Late last year, it falsely claimed Hodge had a personal financial interest in plans – since cancelled – to build a new prison in the borough. "That was an error for which I wasn't responsible. I didn't even see it before it was printed. The moment I saw it, we pulled it."

Griffin returns to his theory that recent changes in Britain's racial make-up have been the product of a politically motivated conspiracy dreamed up by a Labour government run by "Marxist cranks", before arriving at a denouement, of a sort. "Let me put all this another way. The middle-class Guardianistas have this concept that the working class are basically happy. They're OK, until along come these wicked people to stir them up. And it's basically a way of saying that because these people are working class, they're stupid and they can't make up their own minds."

But when it comes to patronising judgments of his beloved white working class, Griffin himself isn't wholly in the clear. I read him what he said to two reporters masquerading as French fascists about the white people of London, caught on camera in 1997 by ITV's *The Cook Report*: "The people who have the brains and ability got out years ago, one way or another. The people who are left are either the 15% of the population who are happy to put up with it, they're so decadent they actually like it, or they're too stupid to do anything about it. They will vote BNP, but you can't build a movement on those people."

"I wasn't talking about this part of London. We were talking about the likes of Brixton and Hackney. People here have still got fight in them."

That still implies a pretty dim view of white people in Brixton and Hackney. "It's not a dim view. I feel very sorry for them. But we can't organise in a place like that. They're good, decent people. But to organise something, you have to have people who've got an unusual flair and spark."

I repeat his words: "They're too stupid to do anything about it." Is he minded to take that back?

"Yes. Yes. I was probably extremely drunk. And I was talking to a Frenchman who didn't speak very good English, so it had to be simplified."

In early March, I meet Hodge again in her Westminster office and ask what she thinks would happen if the BNP took control of the council.

"I think Barking and Dagenham would become a no-go area for the rest of the country. That's the thing that scares me most. Would you buy a house there if you knew there was a BNP council? I think we'd get unrest and violence in the street that we haven't seen yet, because it would put race at the heart of what the borough was about."

If Labour is to hold on to the council, it faces problems. In a drive to revive the local party, Hodge says, 13 of Labour's 36 councillors have been deselected and replaced with "people who see themselves entirely as campaigning in the community". Her Labour adversaries see it as an act of war against her opponents on the council; in the midst of local rancour, another seven Labour councillors have resigned, and some are threatening to run as independents. Might that split the vote and let in BNP candidates?

"I'm not worried about that. The thing that bothers me is the Christian party." The latter are a new outfit who want to "honour Christ in politics" by putting up candidates for parliament and the council, and are going for the votes of Barking's black churchgoers. She has pleaded with them to stand their people down, to no avail: as they see it, her views on abortion, gay rights and stem cell research are just as salient as the great fascist menace.

Inevitably, the BNP campaign against her is not pretty. In leaflets she is portrayed as a witch-like figure in high-heels ("and fat," she reminds me), handing out goodies to stereotyped immigrants drawn according to the usual far-right rules: bug-eyes, goofy teeth. Bob Bailey, leader of the BNP group on the local council, has described her thus: "Poisonous bitch. Lives in Islington. A multi-millionairess and a foreigner to boot."

Though Griffin hasn't mentioned her Jewishness, she claims his people bring it up on the doorstep, via her maiden name, Oppenheimer. By way of a response, he claims the issue is "irrelevant", and the idea of the BNP playing it up is "a classic Labour smear ... there's plenty of things to hit Margaret Hodge with without getting into red herrings and anti-semitism". Of late, his party has been trying to shed its history of the latter, in order to court Jewish votes and pursue its loathing of Islam, though Griffin obviously has no end of form. What about his infamous pamphlet *Who Are The Mindbenders?*, aimed at exposing "Jewish influence and control in Britain's news and information industry"? "That was a long, long time ago. Under my leadership, the BNP's got Jewish councillors" – it has one, in Epping Forest – "and Jewish members." The pamphlet, I remind him, came out in 1997: not that long ago at all. "It is in political terms," he says.

Back in Westminster, the bell rings for a House of Commons vote on some arcane matter of constitutional reform. Hodge runs off to the lobbies, with her mind presumably on much more important things. "I feel totally passionate, in a way that I've never felt about an election before," she says. "I want to expel them, so Barking and Dagenham in 2010 will be seen as the point where we started to see the decline of this wave of fascism. That would be great, wouldn't it?"

Belligerent optimism is her message, though as I walk to Westminster tube station, it's hard to shake off a creeping feeling of unease. Eight weeks remain: at the far end of the District Line, the morning of 7 May may yet feel like the start of a long, splitting headache.

20 MARCH 2010

# When my best friend was diagnosed with cancer I doted on her. At first

## LIONEL SHRIVER

I met Terri in the early 1980s at an arts camp in Connecticut. We were both in the metalsmithing workshop, and this sharply featured, appealingly surly Armenian taught me some new tricks. Her speciality was rivets and other "cold connections", an apt expression in her case. She was a wilful, stubborn woman, more fiercely so than I first realised; 25 years later, I'd discover just how defiant my closest girlfriend could be, even in the face of the undeniable.

Terri was full of the contradictions that always captivate me in people: inclined to bear grudges but incredibly generous (often rocking up with gifts for no reason – why, I still have half a dozen pairs of her shoes). Harsh but warm. Prone to depression but with a knack for festivity. I conjure her scowling down the pavement and rolling in laughter with equal ease. She was tortured and brooding; she was terribly kind. And she was a serious artist in the best sense: not pretentious, but determined to craft interesting work well.

Back in Queens, where we both lived in our mid-20s, we found common cause in our improbable aspirations. She wanted to become a famous artist, I a famous novelist – but Terri had then sold next to nothing and I'd not published more than my phone number. It was a big, indifferent world out there, and an ally was crucial. We'd conspire over a six-pack in my tiny one-bedroom flat, jovially certain that we'd still be best friends when we were "cancerous old bags". It was a running gag. We thought it was funny.

Beware the jokes of your heedless, immortal youth. Fast-forward through two and a half decades, during which Terri and I survived abusive boyfriends, marital problems, professional setbacks, my expatriation to the UK and her exile to New Jersey, Terri's painful endometriosis and four failed IVF treatments, as well as, of course, each other. During my regular summer migration to New York, in 2005, Terri shared her perplexity that she'd been running a low-grade fever for weeks. I said it sounded like a tenacious virus. But shortly thereafter she rang from hospital.

She was being tested for a range of ailments, the most far-fetched of these a rare disease called mesothelioma. Thus it was quite a shock when the doctors confirmed that peritoneal mesothelioma was exactly what she had – almost certainly caused by exposure to the asbestos that laced metalsmithing materials when she was in art school. Her husband Paul reported grimly that the average survival rate for this ravaging cancer was a single year.

Terri was only 50, and the timing was tragic for other reasons, too. From frustration, malaise and exactingly high standards, through most of her career she had underproduced. Yet in recent years something had loosened up, and her output had accelerated. Better still, she was at last imbuing her creations with the feeling they'd sometimes lacked, the most moving of which was an elegy to her unavailing IVF treatments. She was finally pulling in big commissions, one of which was about to go on display at the V&A. At the same time, her brooding demeanour had brightened; she'd grown more outgoing, energetic and relaxed. Almost ... happy. Well, so much for that.

On the heels of her diagnosis, I was doting. I'm not tooting my own horn. I suspect being a paragon at the very start of a loved one's illness is pretty much the form. We're on the phone daily. We stop by regularly, and bring freshly baked scones. We follow every medical twist and turn. And we're inclined to rash promises. With a flinch, I recall declaring before Terri's surgery that I'd be willing to move into their house in New Jersey for weeks at a time! I'd be at her beck and call, running errands, preparing meals and filling prescriptions.

Useful tip: if someone close to you falls gravely ill, at the outset, in the first flush of anguish and desperation to help? Watch the mouth.

For the timing of Terri's cancer was terrible for me as well. A month after her diagnosis, I was intending to return home to London, where a host of professional commitments could not (or so it seemed) be reneged upon. Although for most of my literary career I'd scribbled in obscurity, my prospects were suddenly looking up. My seventh novel had inexplicably hit the bestseller list in the UK, and subsequently won the Orange prize earlier that summer. (I still have the droll good-luck package Terri and Paul delivered when I made the shortlist: orange marmalade, orange candles, orange oil.) For the first time, I faced a smorgasbord of opportunities – festival gigs, bookstore appearances, feature assignments – and I was in the middle of a new book.

So, however reluctantly, I flew back to London. After Terri's surgery, Paul phoned with the lowdown: the surgeons had discovered a patch of aggressive "sarcomatoid" cells, which meant Terri's prognosis was bleak.

I will give myself this grudging credit: I did fly back to visit Terri for Thanksgiving that November, and for a while I kept in faithful touch, ringing weekly and following every grisly detail of her punishing chemotherapy. But this is not a boast about what a wonderful friend I was in Terri's time of need. This is a mea culpa.

Little by little, I'd notice that it had been a fortnight since I'd rung New Jersey. I'd kick myself. But some book review would be due that afternoon, so I'd vow to ring tomorrow. Time and again some immediate task would seem more urgent, and I'd tell myself that I should ring Terri when I'm settled and concentrated. Watch out whenever you "tell yourself" anything; it's the red flag of self-deceit. Long hours of being "settled and concentrated" mysteriously failed to manifest themselves.

I stuck a Post-it note on the edge of my desk: "RING TERRI!" Over the months, the note faded, much like my resolve. On the too-rare occasions I acted on the reminder, I had to put a mental gun to my head. But why? This was one of my closest friends, and she was dying. While she was still on this Earth, why was I not battling to maximise every moment? Surely the problem should have been my ringing too often, whizzing back to the States too many times, making a pest of myself.

Granted, our conversations were sometimes awkward. My own life had never gone more swimmingly, while Terri's was circling the drain. I was embarrassed. I found myself editing from our discussions anything I'd done that was exciting or fun. When I returned from an author's tour of Sweden, I portrayed the trip as a drag. This sort of cover-up reliably backfired. So apparently I felt sorry for myself – for going to Sweden! When Terri could rarely leave the house.

I make no apologies for this, since this is what novelists do: at some midpoint in Terri's decline, I decided that my next novel would draw on this encounter with cancer. At least I had the humanity to refrain from taking notes during our phone calls, thus relinquishing many a "telling detail" and much "great material". Consequently, I had to do an enormous amount of research on mesothelioma later, and this is what I do apologise for: not having done all those web searches on her treatments – the surgery, the drugs, the side-effects – when Terri was still suffering through them. Now, I'm mortified to have Googled "mesothelioma" only once the search was for a book.

When I returned to the US that second summer, Terri had alarmingly deteriorated. Thin to start with, she'd lost weight. She was gaunt and weak, her skin tinged a dark, unsettling orange: a chemo tan. It was obvious where this was headed. But whenever anyone acted as if she wasn't going to make it, Terri grew enraged. She resented the "sentimental" testimonials her friends and relatives recited at her bedside; she thought they were delivering a death sentence. Though she wouldn't have put it that way. I wonder if throughout her illness I ever heard her say the word "death" aloud.

Thus on one count only could I blame Terri herself for my increasingly deficient friendship. Her refusal to admit she was dying meant we couldn't ever talk about the elephant in the room. Pretending that the treatments were working and she was going to come through this injected an artifice in our relationship at odds with the confidences we'd shared for 25 years. Days I did visit, afternoons I did ring, we'd end up talking, lamely, about recipes. Indeed, on a brief trip in November 2006, I visited Terri in New Jersey; it was the last time I'd ever see her, and I knew this instinctively at the time. Yet we spent an appalling proportion of that final visit talking about mashed potatoes.

When her husband rang me in London a few days later with the news, he was consumed with a steely rage. Obviously Paul was angry that he'd lost his wife. But he was also angry at other people. Oh, he expressed his disgust in general terms, as a disillusionment with the human race, a good-riddance to our whole species. But I knew what he meant. Paul's fury was aimed at Terri's friends and family, who had almost universally made themselves scarce for months. His fury was also aimed at me.

I thought I deserved it. I had visited, some. I had rung up, some. But not nearly often enough, and in truth one of my best friends perishing before my eyes had instilled a deep aversion, an instinctive avoidance, a desperation to flee.

It would be a far better thing if I were a lone shithead amid an ocean of altruists. And surely some folks really do step up to the plate when a friend or relative falls mortally ill – wonderful people who keep popping by with casseroles to the very last day. I have a new admiration for such stalwarts, as well as a new appreciation for the Christian duty to "visit the sick". Yet I fear this suddenly-remembering-somewhere-you-gotta-be is a common failing of our time. In fearing and avoiding death, we fear and avoid the dying.

I'll risk sounding preachy, since I've paid for my sermon with a regret that never leaves me. Most of us will experience the afflictions of our nearest and dearest perhaps multiple times before we're faced with a deadly diagnosis of our own. So be mindful. Disease is frightening. It's unpleasant. It reminds us of everything we try not to think about on our own accounts. A biological instinct to steer clear of contagion can kick in even with diseases like cancer that we understand rationally aren't communicable. So the urge to avoid sick people runs very deep. Notice it. Then overcome it. There will always be something you'd rather do than confront the agony, anxiety and exile of serious illness, and these alternative endeavours seem terribly pressing in the moment: replacing the printer cartridge, catching up on urgent work-related email. But nothing is more pressing than someone you love who's suffering, and whose continuing existence you can no longer take for granted. So never vow to ring "tomorrow" – pick up the bloody phone.

22 MARCH 2010

# To understand Britain's economic plight, consider the giant panda

ADITYA CHAKRABORTTY

When you watch Alistair Darling's Budget tomorrow, don't think about the growth forecasts and tax rises, and don't – unless you enjoy feeling anxious – spend too long pondering the size of the public debt. No, consider for a moment how the British economy resembles a giant panda.

Granted, the similarities aren't immediately striking. Giant pandas have deformed bones they pass off as opposable thumbs, subsist on un-nutritious bamboo, and are so undersexed that those in captivity are shown panda porn to encourage mating (examples can be found online, but we both know that's not why your office pays for broadband). The British economy boasts none of these attributes – and yet, as the *Financial Times*'s trade editor Alan Beattie points out in his book *False Economy*, the panda is an example of a phenomenon that economists know very well, and which helps account for the mess the UK is currently in: "path dependency".

This is the notion that chance decisions made way back can lock a person, industry or entire country into an inefficient course they would never subsequently have chosen. Or, as Beattie rather cruelly puts it: "The giant panda's problem is that it went down an evolutionary cul-de-sac and has now found it too late to reverse."

What economies call path dependency is entirely man-made. Take the keyboard I am using to write this. The QWERTY layout was not designed to make typing faster – precisely the opposite. As Paul David, the godfather of path-dependency theory, points out, the keys on mid-19th-century versions of the typewriter would jam if struck too fast – so the most frequently used letters were spaced apart to slow down typists. The mechanics at Remington then promoted the letter R to the top, and thus, assembled on one row, were all the keys needed by any salesman hoping to woo customers by quickly pecking out the brand name: TYPE WRITER.

Even after the mechanical problems were sorted out, the QWERTY keyboard still became the standard among manufacturers and customers. A bunch of chance factors thus combined to make an uncomfortable and inefficient keyboard the industry norm.

And that, in a nutshell, is how path dependency works. Other economists have argued that Betamax was a technically superior format to VHS – it's just that video stores stocked more of the latter, so customers bought VHS recorders. The theory applies to geography too: when William Hewlett and David Packard came out of Stanford University in the Great Depression, they decided to set up shop nearby in what was then called Santa Clara County. Easy access to engineering graduates, and to supplies, drew in more and more technology entrepreneurs so that, by the mid-70s, Santa Clara had become better known as Silicon Valley.

All of which brings us back to this week's Budget. Because while the arguments around what the chancellor should do tomorrow have focused on spending cuts – when to make them, how big they should be – it's clear that what any government really has to do, in successive budgets, is sort out the UK's own path-dependency situation: the economy's dominance by the City of London.

During this decade's long boom, Cityphilia didn't look like much of a problem – at least, not to those sat in Whitehall. After all, financial services contributed well over a quarter of all corporation tax and, in the final bubbletastic months before the credit crunch, accounted for nearly 50% of the quarterly growth in national income. As chancellor, Gordon Brown would regularly tell the banks they had made Britain "a new world leader". Which is precisely why the policy-makers didn't want to ask too many questions about what investment bankers were up to.

Brown is not a natural Cityphile, and there was no conspiracy to elevate the City above all other industries (path dependency doesn't work like that). But the effect was the same: manufacturers like a weak pound as it makes their goods cheaper abroad, while the City prefers a strong pound that holds down inflation. The bankers' argument came to look like economic good sense, with the result that more than a million manufacturing jobs were lost in the decade after Tony Blair took power.

Only now, in the wake of the biggest banking crisis since 1929, does it seem that this economic policy has led the UK down a panda-like cul-de-sac. Academics at the Centre for Research on Socio-Cultural Change at Manchester University recently totted up what more than a decade of betting everything on the banking sector, while allowing other industries to be hollowed out, had yielded. They found that London and the south-east had over 40% of all jobs in Britain's world-beating finance industry; the north-east and Wales had less than 6% of all finance jobs between them. Did these hollowed-out industrial regions have much in the way of other new, private-sector jobs? No: they are now largely reliant on the state to provide new employment.

Economies aren't like pandas, of course: they can change path. But it takes a long time and a lot of effort. Alistair Darling can't do any more tomorrow than push the UK a little bit in the right direction – say, by announcing a new green investment bank to help fund companies and jobs outside the City and north of the Watford Gap. The real test of his Budget, however, will be whether he even tries.

25 MARCH 2010

# How China's internet generation broke the silence

TANIA BRANIGAN

One cold but sunny autumn day, a young white-collar worker in Shanghai received an anxious phone call from his family. The authorities were requisitioning their farmland for development.

Wang Shuai believed the scheme was illegal, but officials refused to discuss it. He tried journalists, but they thought his story both too common and too sensitive. That was when he turned to the internet.

"It was the choice of having no choice," he said. "But I had read complaints about injustices on the net before and I knew some cases had worked out. There were reports like officials who used public money for holidays; when they appeared, the nation began investigating."

The authorities had launched an "anti-drought initiative" which included chopping down fruit trees – conveniently allowing them to slash compensation to families turfed off the land.

"Great tactics for fighting drought in Ningbao village!" Wang headlined his post. Underneath, he added pictures of the tree stumps.

It would indeed grab attention; but not quite as he had expected. Wang's story exemplifies the growing power of the internet in China: the airing of grievances, the ability to reach a wider audience, the use of satire to discuss serious topics.

While China has the world's most sophisticated internet censorship system, it also has almost 400 million internet users – at least some of whom are challenging those restraints with increasing boldness. Controls mean that almost everyone self-censors to some degree. But some have used the variations and gaps in the system to stake out spaces where they can find or share viewpoints that are not officially sanctioned.

In fact, the internet is arguably more important than in other countries since the mainstream media is still more firmly controlled. The Chinese have even invented a word – *wangmin* ("netizen") – that captures this sense of the internet as a space for social and political discussion.

It is also a space for enjoyment.

"The internet community is diverse, lively, and contentious, full of fun and dynamism," said Guobin Yang, author of *The Power of the Internet: Citizen Activism in China*. "This aspect of Chinese internet culture is not well understood by the general public in the west. It is capturing more and more things, good or bad, political or non-political, and then weaving them into all sorts of new creatures – new languages, new relationships, new images ... despite and perhaps because of political control."

Users are increasingly creative in the ways they elude restraints – perhaps using analogies to discuss topics – and increasingly open in their mockery of them. Deleted sites have "been harmonised", in reference to President Hu Jintao's calls for a "harmonious" society. Censors are referred to as "river crabs", because in Chinese those two words together form a homophone for "harmony".

Heavy-handed propaganda is ridiculed. Take the reaction to last month's Chinese new year gala on the state broadcaster, which featured a paean to the Communist party using the Uighur word *yakexi*, or good; this, months after vicious inter-ethnic violence tore through Xinjiang, home of the Uighur minority.

"Now the nation has abolished the agricultural tax ... Ah! The Chinese Communist party central committee's policies are *yakexi*," the singers enthused.

Within hours, the word *yakexi* was popping up all over the internet. Han Han, the country's most popular blogger, launched a contest for the best rewrite of the lyrics. Others wrote about the "yake lizard" – *xi* is a homophone for lizard – which "enjoys arse-licking" and survives only in China, North Korea and Cuba.

Because they are outspoken, articulate and keen to engage with the outside world, the numbers of the liberal, socially aware users prepared to poke fun at those in power are easy to overestimate.

"Maybe there are much less than 100,000 people concerned about those issues and maybe only 2,000 who are active," suggested Ai Weiwei, a leading artist and vociferous social critic with 25,000 Twitter followers.

Most of these will use software such as virtual private networks and proxies to evade the Great Firewall – allowing them to read articles or debates outlawed at home, or to post controversial material on blog platforms hosted overseas.

Like their counterparts around the world, the majority of China's internet users have little interest in seeking such debates: they want entertainment, shopping and other services.

And even among those who want to debate current affairs, there are plenty of pro-government voices, sometimes paid – known as the "50 cent party" – but sometimes acting independently.

Yet between the highly motivated and the largely uninterested poles lie many more who are not overtly politicised but whose attention is piqued by a story, or who suddenly find a means to be heard, like Wang or Tang Xiaozhao.

Tang is a Shanghai businesswoman in her 30s and began to blog on opera in 2005. She had decided Chinese politics were "too cruel" to worry about, but what she read online reignited her interest and soon she was writing on current affairs. When articles were deleted, she opened blogs at other sites. She learned to use homophones to evade the censors.

Then she posted Charter 08 – a groundbreaking call for reforms which angered officials and led to its co-author being jailed for 11 years. Each time she put it up, censors quickly deleted it – but not before perhaps a few hundred users had had a chance to read it, she noted. Instead of intimidating her, the repeated disappearance of her articles spurred her into signing the charter herself – and, later, into blogging about her resulting brush with police. Last year, no fewer than nine of her blogs were closed down.

"We cannot see what we want to and cannot speak as we like. But if 10 people speak and they are censored, five of them will keep talking. And China is a huge country. There will be new people who want to speak," she said.

As the reaction to Charter 08 shows, the government is genuinely alarmed by the internet.

It fears both that it will be used to organise real-world action, and that it will spread unsuitable political and social influences, such as pornography. Many citizens share at least some of these concerns; studies have shown that support for government controls on content is higher in China than elsewhere.

Yet officials permit a far wider range of discussion on the internet than in other media.

"[The authorities] are becoming increasingly sophisticated in how they handle dissent," said Phelim Kine, Asia researcher at Human Rights Watch. "They have realised they do not need to round up everyone making rude jokes about someone's son online."

The authorities can track the public mood and monitor individuals or groups. Netizens can help officials to push forward an argument in the face of opposition from other interest groups or even countries. And for higher authorities, it can be a useful way of keeping local cadres in check.

But many officials do not relish such scrutiny, as Wang Shuai discovered. Authorities from his hometown in Henan sent police

750 miles to Shanghai to detain him for defamation – a criminal and civil offence in China. He was taken back in shackles and held for eight days, until he confessed to libelling local officials. Then he was bailed.

"I thought using the net would help to protect me; I thought it was harder to track me down. When they came to me I was shocked," said Wang.

Angered, he wrote another post. This time, a newspaper journalist spotted it. The resulting article spread rapidly, with readers piling in to denounce Wang's treatment, which they saw as emblematic of official injustices.

Eventually, in spring last year, the provincial police head apologised and Wang received compensation. The authorities abandoned the development project. Without the mainstream press, his story might not have garnered much attention. But without the internet to publish it initially, and then amplify the effect of the news article, he believes he would never have received the apology and compensation.

Many in the west see it as self-evident that an increased flow of information will make officials more accountable and encourage people to challenge them.

Yet studies of the internet's impact in China are inconclusive. One found that people with access to unofficial information and the internet actually held a more favourable view of inequalities and the party's justification of them.

Another showed that blog posts on subjects such as political reform and freedom of expression were increasingly frequent, even when controlling for the rise in bloggers.

Certainly, users like Tang believe the internet is slowly changing society. She admits to being petrified when police summoned her for informal questioning. "But the influence of that experience is now very small," she said. And she continues to blog.

As long as the government fears the net, it will attempt to tame it. But, said an experienced industry source, it faces hundreds of millions of users with their own ideas and feelings and ambitions. "With so many brains, how can you control them? Nobody can win this battle," she said.

1 APRIL 2010

# Labour's election strategy: bring on no-nonsense hard man Gordon Brown

OLAF PRIOL

In an audacious election strategy, Labour is set to embrace Gordon Brown's reputation for anger and physical aggression, presenting the prime minister as a hard man, unafraid of confrontation, who is willing to take on David Cameron in "a bare-knuckle fistfight for the future of Britain", the *Guardian* has learned.

Following months of allegations about Brown's explosive outbursts and bullying, Downing Street will seize the initiative this week with a national billboard campaign portraying him as "a sort of Dirty Harry figure", in the words of a senior aide. One poster shows a glowering Brown alongside the caption "Step outside, posh boy", while another asks: "Do you want some of this?"

Brown aides had worried that his reputation for volatility might torpedo Labour's hopes of re-election, but recent internal polls suggest that, on the contrary, stories of Brown's testosterone-fuelled eruptions have been almost entirely responsible for a recent recovery in the party's popularity. As a result, the aide said, Labour was "going all in", staking the election on the hope that voters will be drawn to an alpha-male personality who "is prepared to pummel, punch or even headbutt the British economy into a new era of jobs and prosperity".

Strategists are even understood to be considering engineering a high-profile incident of violence on the campaign trail, and are in urgent consultations on the matter with John Prescott, whose public image improved in 2001 after he punched an egg-throwing protester.

Possible confrontations under discussion include pushing Andrew Marr out of the way while passing him on a staircase, or thumping the back of Jeremy Paxman's chair so hard that he flinches in shock.

One tactic being discussed involves provoking a physical confrontation at one of the three ground-breaking TV debates between the candidates. In this scenario, Brown, instead of responding to a point made by Cameron, would walk over from his microphone with an exaggerated silent display of self-control, bring his face to within an inch of the Tory leader's, and in a subdued voice, ask "what did you just say?" before delivering a single well-aimed blow to his opponent's face, followed by a head-lock if required.

The bloodied and bruised Cameron could then be whisked to a nearby hospital, where a previously briefed team of doctors and nurses would demonstrate the efficiency and compassion of the NHS under a Labour government.

Saatchi & Saatchi, the agency behind the poster campaign, are also considering reworked posters from classic movies, casting Brown as The Gordfather, the Terminator, and Mr Brown from *Reservoir Dogs*, or perhaps linking him to Omar Little, the merciless killer in the TV series *The Wire*, in order to burnish the prime minister's "gangsta" credentials. Another set of designs appropriates the Conservative anti-Brown poster campaign, employing adapted slogans such as: "I took billions from pensions. Wanna make something of it?"

The Brown team has been buoyed by focus group results suggesting an outbreak of physical fighting could re-engage an electorate increasingly apathetic about politics. They also hope they can exploit the so-called "Putin effect", and are said to be exploring opportunities for Brown to be photographed killing a wild animal, though advisers have recommended that weather, and other considerations, mean Brown should not remove his shirt.

Labour further hopes to "harness the power of internet folksourcing", the aide explained, encouraging supporters to design their own posters, which could be showcased online. The "design your own poster" initiative has caught the imagination of Downing Street strategists, the aide said, because it is cheap above all, nothing could possibly go wrong with it.

For their part, Conservative strategists are said to be troubled by internal research suggesting that several members of the shadow cabinet – including Cameron and George Osborne – would in fact not "come here and say that" if challenged by Brown, instead turning pale and running away, or arranging for an older brother to wait outside the Houses of Parliament to attack him when he is least expecting it.

3 APRIL 2010

# Put the pope in the dock

GEOFFREY ROBERTSON

Well may the pope defy "the petty gossip of dominant opinion". But the Holy See can no longer ignore international law, which now counts the widespread or systematic sexual abuse of children as a crime against humanity. The anomalous claim of the Vatican to be a state – and of the pope to be a head of state and hence immune from legal action – cannot stand up to scrutiny.

The truly shocking finding of Judge Murphy's commission in Ireland was not merely that sexual abuse was "endemic" in boys' institutions but that the church hierarchy protected the perpetrators and, despite knowledge of their propensity to reoffend, allowed them to take up new positions teaching other children after their victims had been sworn to secrecy.

This conduct, of course, amounted to the criminal offence of aiding and abetting sex with minors. In legal actions against Catholic archdioceses in the US it has been alleged that the same conduct reflected Vatican policy as approved by Cardinal Ratzinger (as the pope then was) as late as November 2002. Sexual assaults were regarded as sins that were subject to church tribunals, and guilty priests were sent on a "pious pilgrimage" while oaths of confidentiality were extracted from their victims.

In the US, 11,750 allegations of child sex abuse have so far featured in actions settled by archdioceses – in Los Angeles for $660m and in Boston for $100m. But some dioceses have gone into bankruptcy and some claimants want higher level accountability – two reasons to sue the pope in person. In 2005 a test case in Texas failed because the Vatican sought and obtained the intercession of President Bush, who agreed to claim sovereign (ie head of state) immunity on the pope's behalf. Bush lawyer John B Bellinger III certified that Pope Benedict XVI was immune from suit "as the head of a foreign state".

Bellinger is now notorious for his defence of Bush administration torture policies. His opinion on papal immunity is even more questionable. It hinges on the assumption that the Vatican, or its metaphysical emanation, the Holy See, is a state. But the papal states were extinguished by invasion in 1870 and the Vatican was created by fascist Italy in 1929 when Mussolini endowed this tiny enclave – 0.17 of a square mile containing 900 Catholic bureaucrats – with "sovereignty in the international field ... in conformity with its traditions and the exigencies of its mission in the world".

The notion that statehood can be created by another country's unilateral declaration is risible: Iran could make Qom a state overnight, or the UK could launch Canterbury on to the international stage. But it did not take long for Catholic countries to support the pretensions of the Holy See, sending ambassadors and receiving papal nuncios in return. Even the UK maintains an apostolic mission.

The UN at its inception refused membership to the Vatican but has allowed it a unique "observer status", permitting it to become signatory to treaties such as the law of the sea and (ironically) the convention on the rights of the child, and to speak and vote at UN conferences where it promotes its controversial dogmas on abortion, contraception and homosexuality. This has involved the UN in blatant discrimination on grounds of religion: other faiths are unofficially represented, if at all, by NGOs. But it has encouraged the Vatican to claim statehood – and immunity from liability.

This claim could be challenged successfully in the UK and in the European court of human rights. But in any event, head of state immunity provides no protection for the pope in the international criminal court (see its current indictment of President Bashir). The ICC Statute definition of a crime against humanity includes rape and sexual slavery and other similarly inhumane acts causing harm to mental or physical health, committed against civilians on a widespread or systematic scale, if condoned by a government or a de facto authority. It has been held to cover the recruitment of children as soldiers or sex slaves. If acts of sexual abuse by priests are not isolated or sporadic, but part of a wide practice both known to and unpunished by their de facto authority then they fall within the temporal jurisdiction of the ICC – if that practice continued after July 2002, when the court was established.

Pope Benedict has recently been credited with reforming the system to require the reporting of priests to civil authorities, although initially he blamed the scandal on "gay culture". His admonition last week to the Irish church repeatedly emphasised that heaven still awaits the penitent paedophile priest. The Holy See may deserve respect for offering the prospect of redemption to sinners, but it must be clear that in law the pope does so as a spiritual adviser, and not as an immune sovereign.

7 April 2010

# Playwrights' XI would know how to bowl a good line

## FRANK KEATING

Timely, somehow, that a new cricket season coincides with the Old Vic's revival this weekend of Tom Stoppard's *The Real Thing* – and we can only presume there will be neither nip, tuck nor alteration to the famous cricket bat speech in Act 2 Scene 5: "It's a wooden club sprung like a dance floor. If you get it right, the ball will travel 200 yards in four seconds, and all you've done is give it a knock like knocking the top off a bottle of stout, and it makes a noise like a trout taking a fly. But if you don't get it right, then the ball will travel about 10 feet and you will drop the bat and dance about shouting 'Ouch!' with your hands stuck into your armpits."

By nice fluke, a few weeks after first hearing that Stoppard speech in 1982, I interviewed Peter Gibbs, one-time Derbyshire opening batsman then beginning to make a name for himself as a film and television playwright (it was good to enjoy *Arthur's Hallowed Ground*, Gibbs's 1984 homage to Derby's legendary groundsman Walter Goodyear, on Film 4 last week). In that long ago piece Gibbs had been, in real life, even more metaphysical than Stoppard in explaining how a single stroke had determined his retirement from county cricket.

"I'd hit my 12th century in Derbyshire's match at Edgbaston when, of a sudden, sublime revelation took over. I hit Lance Gibbs off the back foot through midwicket, an old-fashioned attacking shot, one of the most difficult imaginable, and I played it to absolute perfection, consummate, transcendental, flawless. Yet back in the pavilion, the moment taunted, tormented me. I knew I'd probably never recapture such a supreme sensation again, never ever play such a shot as that – while somebody like Barry Richards was strolling out and doing it without a thought on any day of the week." Gibbs called it a day there and then.

Gibbs, still Derby's fabled stonewall stodge, can open our Playwrights' innings with Stoppard as wicketkeeper-bat. Half a century ago, I played with Tom for the *Bristol Evening World* side; a non-stop natterer, he'd keep us slips in fits. At numbers three and four we send in cricket's two Nobel lit laureates, Pinter and Beckett. The former's masterpiece *No Man's Land* featured Spooner, Briggs, Hirst and Foster, and in *The Birthday Party* the scary brainwashing scene includes the unanswerable question, "Who watered the wicket in Melbourne?" (Which, by the way, the Germans translated as "Who pissed on the Australian gate?")

I played against Pinter's Gaeties XI a few times; Harold fancied himself as an all-rounder, but he can't have been as good as Beckett, whose last report in 1922 from Portora Royal School read: "A very attractive bat and a good medium-paced bowler with a sharp break-back." I read the other day that actor John Alderton, a fine Estragon in *Waiting For Godot* at the National in 1987, had been given a note by Beckett to imagine the parts of Vladimir and Estragon as "batsmen numbers five and six fretfully waiting to begin their innings at a Test Match at Lord's".

Our own un-nervous middle-order can be made up of the classy cricket-loving triumvirate of Simon Gray, David Hare and Ronald Harwood, each worth a ton of stylish runs. The peppery Gray once bragged to me how, in his youth, he had commandingly swept the googly of one-time England leg-spinner Ian Peebles for a one-bounce boundary backward of square: "My sheer impudence stays with me – and the look Peebles gave me, of utter loathing, still makes me tremble with joy."

I was delighted to see the rave notices last week for cricket-nut actor and writer Michael Simkins in Alan Ayckbourn's new London revival *Taking Steps*. Simkins' Scarborough Theatre XI boast many unbeaten seasons – although he denies ever advertising in the *Stage*: "Iago wanted. Must bowl accurate off-breaks." At nine and 10 we field those two incorrigible jester-dramatists Peter Tinniswood and Jack Rosenthal, the latter who wove a whole beguiling play, *P'tang Yang Kipperbang*, around the radio commentaries of John Arlott.

At No 11 is tearaway pace bowler, Forest of Dean demon Dennis Potter. Not only was Dennis coached in the back garden by daughter Sarah – who opened the bowling for the England women's team – he'd swear that great-grandad Potter clean bowled WG for a duck at the Coleford fete two summers running.

7 April 2010

# Apocalypse Now as the Brownmobile races to the palace

MARINA HYDE

Only the British can combine the raw materials of a queen, a prime minister, an election and a 775-room palace and from them create an occasion with all the pomp-soaked drama of a man clocking in and out of a car park.

This glorious reverse alchemy was at play outside Buckingham Palace yesterday, as Gordon Brown made his historic – and historically uneventful – journey to see Her Majesty. Tourists congregating for the changing of the guard were about to discover that ritual was not the only quaint pageant of British public life on offer. In fact, one set of trumpets and horses relieving another set of trumpets and horses appeared easier to compute than serried ranks of photographers waiting for a car to whoosh by them.

"So why is Gordon Brown coming here?" wondered a man from New Jersey. "Is he in trouble for something?" There are a few unrelated beheading offences he's appealing against, but today he is calling an election so he has to ask the Queen if she will dissolve parliament. "Do you think she's going to say yes?"

It would certainly have enlivened the day had Her Majesty declined the request, though in the end she "very kindly agreed", as Brown put it. A relief for the PM, then, but for those accidental election tourists whose experience of British establishment culture might have led them to expect that Helen Mirren would shortly appear on the balcony to make a formal announcement, the occasion tended towards the anticlimactically opaque.

Pointlessly, there were more helicopters than a Vietnam movie. Yet despite the fact that Sky News now act as though their "Skycopter" were a vital part of the fabric of national life, the only important chopper was the one ferrying the Queen from Windsor Castle, and which may or may not be codenamed ERwolf. That craft whirred into view at 9.50am – cutting it fine for a 10 o'clock meeting, but you know what? That's the way Her Majesty rolls. Handbag luggage only and someone else to stick the kettle on.

Then again, it was never her presence that was going to be in doubt. Given Brown's trigger-shy reputation, there was always the chance that he might get cold feet at some point on the two-minute journey from Downing Street, and force his driver to perform a handbrake turn on the Mall while he screamed out of the window at bemused passersby: "June the third! It was never not going to be June the third!"

Fortunately the occasion still delivered on bemusement. "Gordon Brow-en?" repeated a quizzical Finn and a couple from Texas, rolling the name around their mouths like that of a particularly obscure Qin dynasty philosopher. The struggle to get a positive ID wasn't helped by photographers practising the shot snapping any passing vehicle, causing many of the tourists immediately behind them to follow suit, and some behind those to scuttle after the departing vehicle in the hope of at least getting its momentous rear view. It was the sort of domino effect that could easily have seen a palace plumber anointed prime minister.

"Was that Gordon Brown?" a breathless woman demanded of a police officer as a dirty silver people carrier trundled out of the gate to a barrage of clicks.

"No," he sighed.

The big dramas? Well, it looked as though Plod might feel moved to deploy a stronger weapon than sighing when a sharp-suited chap from Ladbrokes set up his bookie's blackboard in front of the palace gates.

But it turns out that even for the Met, arresting someone under the Prevention of Terrorism Act for possession of election odds in the vicinity of Buckingham Palace is a satirical point too far. It is, however, deemed necessary to deploy the flashing blue lights to travel a distance of seven yards.

Then, finally, it was all happening, as the cry went up among the snappers that the Brownmobile was on the Mall. "Remember, don't shoot photographs," a helpfully free-spirited woman from Somerset chided them. "Shooting photographs is stealing pictures. Let pictures come to you. Let them manifest themselves ..."

She didn't get the shot as Brown manifested briskly past, but was not as disappointed as the Spanish lady who – when the PM manifested swiftly away 20 minutes later – seemed both confused and crestfallen at the contents of the vehicle. "No Angela Merkel? Why no Angela Merkel?"

Forgive us, madam, but we can only work with what we've got. What you and the others take away with you is the chance to say you were there when that man you couldn't name begged the Queen's pardon or something. And you'll agree that you really can't put a price on that sort of memory.

12 APRIL 2010

# These Republicans are like unhinged frat boys in *Animal House*, only angrier

GARY YOUNGE

In the classic teen movie *Animal House* there comes a moment when the ne'er-do-well students of the Delta fraternity finally realise their pranks have gone too far. Faced with expulsion from university, the most violent, antisocial drunkard of the group, Bluto Blutarsky (John Belushi), gives one last rousing, rambling speech to his crestfallen comrades. "Nothing is over until we decide it is," he yells. "Was it over when the Germans bombed Pearl Harbor? Hell, no!"

The other students look on confused. Bluto leads a charge but nobody follows. However, they soon fall in line after the fraternity's leader, the far more respectable, presentable, all-round-cad, Otter (Tim Matheson), backs Bluto's call to arms against the university authorities. "Bluto's right," he says. "Psychotic, but absolutely right.

We gotta take these bastards ... I think we have to go all out. I think that this situation absolutely requires a really futile and stupid gesture be done on somebody's part."

The Republican party in particular, and American conservatism in general, have taken to operating in a similar manner to the Delta fraternity – increasingly reckless, anarchic and strident. Faced with defeat they respond with desperation. Only where the Deltas were motivated by ribaldry, conservatives are driven by rage.

On the one hand there are the Blutos – characterised by their contempt for even the most basic facts. Their assertions are often not only verifiably false but patently ridiculous. The very people who claim that Obama is a Muslim were the ones who fumed about his relationship with Reverend Jeremiah Wright, his pastor in Chicago. Muslims don't have pastors. Last year the *Investor's Business Daily* claimed that if the renowned scientist Steven Hawking were British he would be dead: Hawking is British and alive.

These falsehoods are not limited to the fringes. A recent Harris poll reveals that a majority of Republicans believe Obama is a Muslim and a socialist who "wants to turn over the sovereignty of the United States to a one-world government". A *Daily Kos* poll in January showed that about two-thirds of Republicans either believe or are not sure that Obama is "a racist who hates white people", and more than half believe or are not sure that he was not born in the US and that he wants the terrorists to win.

So long as these people breathe the ever more fetid air of their own ecosystem – oxygen provided by Fox News – then these contradictions are of little concern or consequence to them. Cognitive dissonance is not the exception but the rule. But there is menace in this madness. A few weeks ago, shortly before the passing of the healthcare vote, conservative blogger Solomon

Forell tweeted: "We'll surely get over a bullet 2 Barack Obama's head!" He added: "The Next American with a Clear Shot should drop Obama like a bad habit. 4get Blacks or his claim to be Black. Turn on Barack Obama." Last week a man was detained for issuing death threats to Democratic senator Patty Murray. Speaking in Phoenix on a Tea Party tour, Joe the Plumber recently spelt out his plan for dealing with illegal immigration: "Put a fence in and start shooting."

So much for the Blutos. Far from reining them in, the Republican leadership increasingly reflects their excesses. Absent any legislative agenda or coherent ideological approach, they have spent the last two years crafting "a really futile and stupid gesture ... on somebody's part" that Otter would be proud of. Small government is a legitimate philosophical and political position. But in the hands of people who voted to bloat the deficit and unleash a huge state-grab of civil liberties, it is shorn of credibility. It isn't government they don't like it's Democrats in government.

So congressmen scream "liar" at the president and "baby killer" at their colleagues; senators repeat myths about death panels and legislators stoke up crowds from the balconies during the healthcare debate. On Friday at the Southern Republican leadership conference, Sarah Palin repeated her slogan: "Don't Retreat, Reload." This time she insisted it was "not a call for violence". The fact she would have to make that explicit tells us something about how dire things have become.

The potential for this kind of rhetoric to produce an unthinkable calamity should not be underestimated. Last year a Homeland Security report, *Rightwing Extremism: Current Economic and Political Climate Fuelling Resurgence in Radicalisation and Recruitment*, concluded: "The economic downturn and the election of the first African-American president present unique drivers for rightwing radicalisation and recruitment."

THE BEDSIDE GUARDIAN 2010

Such people are on the fringes. But those fringes are growing. In any case, it only takes one angry person with a gun to make the difference. If such a person were to emerge, they would not be acting alone. Thousands of others, from the blogosphere to Congress, have colluded in creating an alternative reality that would explain, if not justify, their actions. After all, if Obama truly were a foreign-born, white-hating, terrorist sympathiser who has usurped the presidency, drastic action would make sense.

Meanwhile, the brazen disregard for basic facts goes all the way to the top. The 2008 presidential contender John McCain recently insisted he never considered himself a "maverick", even though one of his books is subtitled *The Education of an American Maverick*, and he called himself "the original maverick" in campaign ads. It used to be assumed this was the tail wagging the dog. But by increments it is turning into an entirely new breed of dog. Establishment Republicans are not running away from Palin's wing of the party but towards it. McCain needed her endorsement to fight off a Tea Party challenge in Arizona.

This trend is not new. Ever since the Republican election rallies of 2008, where Obama's name provoked screams of "traitor" and "terrorist", this dialectic between leadership and base, margins and mainstream, populist reaction and legislative response, has been all too evident. Far from subsiding, the contradictions have sharpened.

Whereas in 2008 McCain grabbed the microphone from an audience member's hand and corrected her after she said she didn't trust Obama "because he's an Arab", the metaphorical mic has now been returned to her and she has been ushered to centre stage.

Having pitted fear against hope and lost, the Republican leadership has come up with no better alternative than to keep doubling down on fear. None of this puts food on Blutos' tables, but it does keep them angry. For those who peddle in rumour and angst, this is a lucrative market indeed. In a world where facts don't matter, their fears can never truly be assuaged.

Quite how reality will intrude into this parallel universe is as of yet unclear. But it will. Now that healthcare legislation has been passed, people will see that the state does not kill their grand-mothers and most Republican voters will see their healthcare costs fall. This week there will be an anti-tax rally – most of the protesters on it will actually see their taxes lowered by the Obama administration.

And how would the Republican party explain to most of its supporters that while their living standards stagnated or declined under George Bush they are set to improve under Obama? As Otter explained to one of the fraternity after trashing his brother's car: "You fucked up ... you trusted us!"'

13 APRIL 2010

# Glimmer in the darkness of Poland's second Katyn

TIMOTHY GARTON ASH

For the bereaved, this is a time for hearts opened in sympathy, not minds hastening with historical reflections. For Poland, however, and for Europe, there is a glimmer of hope in the dark-ness. This hope lies in the contrast between the two Katyns: the secret massacre of Polish officers by the Soviets in 1940, and last Saturday's plane crash that killed the Polish president and other leading figures on their way to mark the 70th anniversary of that crime. More accurately, it lies in the contrast between the historical circumstances revealed by the two events. These are like night and day.

The execution of thousands of Polish officers, at a time when the Soviet Union had joined Nazi Germany in the Hitler-Stalin pact, was a totemic crime of mid-20th-century European barbarism. There was no Polish state to mark their passing, because it had been erased from the map by the Nazis and Soviets.

The crime of 1940 was totemic, too, in the way it was concealed by giant lies. At first, widows and children knew nothing at all of the fate of husbands and fathers. Then in 1943, when bodies were unearthed in the Katyn forest by occupying Germans, the Soviets claimed they had been killed by the Nazis after Germany attacked in 1941. The Soviet Union persisted in this lie almost to its own dying day – and, shamefully, countries such as Britain were for decades complicit in the lie. I will never forget attending the ceremony to unveil a memorial in a west London cemetery in 1976. The obelisk bore the stark inscription "Katyn 1940" – and the date said it all. The British government sent no representative and forbade serving officers to appear in uniform. Russian guilt had not been proved "to Her Majesty's Government's satisfaction".

Compare this with the last few days. Although it has lost so many leading figures, the Republic of Poland has continued to function with constitutional dignity and efficiency. The Poles are mourning another national tragedy as only they know how, with flickering forests of flowers and candles, with the flags, the church services, the old hymns. In the past, when they struck up the patriotic hymn God, Who Protects Poland, they would sing "Return to us, O Lord, a free fatherland". Now they all sing, without hesitation, "Bless, O Lord, the free fatherland". For no one doubts that Poland is today a free fatherland.

Even more remarkable is the contrast in international reaction. This time round, the British party leaders fall over each other to join the US president and the chancellor of a democratic Germany in messages of condolence. The first Katyn catastrophe was concealed for decades by the night and fog of totalitarian lies; the second was immediately the lead item in news bulletins around the world. Most extraordinary has been the reaction of the former KGB officer Vladimir Putin, who has gone to exceptional lengths to demonstrate Russian sympathy, repeatedly visiting the crash site, announcing a national day of mourning, and ordering Andrzej Wajda's film *Katyn* (which spares you nothing of the cruelty of the KGB's forerunners) to be shown on primetime Russian TV.

In 1943, the head of the British Foreign Office wondered "how, if Russian guilt is established, can we expect Poles to live amicably side by side with Russians for generations to come? I fear there is no answer to that question." But history may even now be producing a most unexpected answer.

Let us, however, have no illusions: it is Poland, with the spirit of all those Poles who have died at Katyn – then and now – which has won itself that answer through its own exertions to secure its place as a free fatherland, anchored in Europe and a wider community of democracies. History helps those who help themselves.

14 April 2010

# Back to Salford, in search of the "classless society"

## SIMON HATTENSTONE

Marx and Engels, Salford's most celebrated pub philosophers, had a point when they said all history has been a history of class struggles. Mine certainly has been. When I was in nappies, Dad told me I was middle class. He was so proud of his recently discovered middle-classness. Dad might have left school at 14 and sold clothes door to door, but now we had a nice house and two cars we couldn't be more middle class. I was going to be a doctor or lawyer or accountant. No question about it – done deal.

As a little boy I revelled in my middle-classness – I was bright, worked hard, looked forward to grammar school. Then I got sick with encephalitis. By the time I emerged from two years of bed-bound illness I no longer felt middle class. I'd lost my friends, my aspirations, and my brain wasn't as good as it had been. Instead of a grammar school I attended a hospital school (a small room where I sewed furry animals), an "open-air" school (populated by children with Down's syndrome, asthma, kids on probation and me) and Kersal High (a sink-school comprehensive with the best teachers I ever had).

By the time I got to Kersal, I felt working class on a good day, and the solitary member of an elite underclass on a bad one. Middle class seemed so, well, middling. I'd been written off, so why should I be swaddled in middle-class norms. I wanted to be the angry working-class hero John Lennon sang about, or the romantic lion rising after slumber that Shelley wrote about. And yet at Kersal High I never felt so cursed by middle-classness. My peer group thought I talked posh and was rich, though as it happens Dad's business – by then a shop – was already going bust.

I did pass my exams, and ended up at Leeds University. Strangely, it was only when I "made it" to university that I began to feel less middle class. So many students had gone to grammar or even public school – I hadn't previously known any public school pupils. Now some students thought I talked common, were amazed that my school had no sixth form and only 6% had five or more decent O-levels. Eventually, through work, I mixed with people who had firsts from Oxford or Cambridge, and I felt more working class than I could have dreamed of.

Class has always confused me. And never more so than today. David Cameron says we're classless, Gordon Brown says pretty much all of us (except Cameron and co) are middle class, which kind of means we're classless. Can that be right? If so, where has the working class gone?

It's a gorgeous Sunday in Salford's Albert Park, which used to be known for muggings and sexual assaults. The grass is green and the daffodils nod contentedly in the sun. Two bull terriers are wrestling playfully, while two primped poodles walk by on leads. It's that kind of area – working class here, middle class a spit away where I was brought up. Or at least that's what we would have said before this election.

Local MP Graham Stringer is canvassing in Lower Broughton. He's a solid, principled man in his late 50s who admits he is uncomfortable going door to door. The relief is palpable when nobody answers and he can slot a leaflet through the letterbox. "Canvassing is like diving into a swimming pool. You don't want to do it, but once you get in it's nearly always pleasant." He has little to worry about, here. Almost everybody tells him they will vote Labour, even when they don't mean it. "Yes, I'll be voting

Labour," says one young man, "my girlfriend's in the bath." It sounds like an invite for some extracurricular canvassing, but the MP moves on.

"You can tell in their eyes. If they light up when you say Labour they mean it," Stringer says.

After an hour, I tell local resident Barbara Carter we're still looking for a Tory to convert. "There's one in the next street," she says. Then she apologises. "No, he's a Liberal Democrat."

Why are so many people voting Labour here? "Because we're workers. And they look after people. I live with a disabled bloke and you get looked after." What about Cameron? "Oh yes! He went to Eton, didn't he? Ordinary working person, aren't I? Could do with more money on the pension, though."

A couple of years ago Cameron tried to win over detractors who scoffed at his family's perceived privilege by revealing that his wife Samantha was rather "unconventional. She went to day school," he explained.

Later, Stringer sits on a park bench with the head of Salford council, John Merry. Both have been in politics for decades, and admit they are fascinated and baffled by class. "My background is working class," Stringer says. "I come from terrace houses in east Manchester. Then I earned my living as a scientist and MP, so it's difficult to class yourself as anything but middle class in an objective sense. But I still feel working class."

Merry says it's the other way for him – his father was a grammar-school boy but was forced to leave at 14 when Merry's grandfather died in an industrial accident. "So you could say he was middle class but then he went to work as a clerk in a very working-class environment in a brewery. Then he rose to be a personnel manager and councillor in Birmingham so I'm never quite sure if I'm middle class, upper working class or what really." What does he like to think of himself as? "Intellectual working class if I'm honest –

working-class background but many of the things I was brought into contact with were middle class, like theatre, music, cinema."

Stringer, in best Max Bygraves mode, wants to tell me a story. "You know Tony Wilson [the former presenter and music impresario]? When I first got to know him he didn't feel relaxed until he knew almost exactly which terrace street I came from. You know who are you talking to then, and after that you can have all these discussions about the music scene or architecture in Manchester. It sort of authenticates you." But he was a well-to-do boy, wasn't he? "Yes. He was from inner-city Salford but moved out to posh Pointon and Chester at quite an early age. But his reference points were still back into Salford."

Marx and Engels' local was the Crescent when they lived in Salford. Mine was the Star Inn, a scruffy, working-class pub with the most miserable landlord in the world – one-armed Wally. But we liked it. Today, it's just as scruffy but one of the country's few community pubs owned by the people who drink there. The workers have finally taken control of the pumps of production.

Margaret Fowler, a university lecturer with silver hair and an easy manner, is one of the shareholders. I ask if there are any Tories in the pub. She shakes her head. "How would anyone around here identify with them?" But don't people move fluidly between classes these days? "No, upper class is a closed shop. You have to be invited in or you're born into it." Fowler's father was a postman's son who became an accountant – she says her parents would have expected her to be where she is in life. She feels she has neither under-achieved nor over-achieved, so is comfortably middle class.

It's Sunday evening and I'm in a spartan working men's club in West Gorton, one of the most troubled areas in Manchester, which inspired TV's *Shameless*. It's a battered old place – snooker cues with no tips, thinning carpets, vintage people listening to covers of vintage hits by Marty Wilde and Frankie Lymon and the Teenagers. There is also a warmth, a camaraderie here – plus free live music.

Bob Johnstone is 75, and used to work on the buses. He says in his 29 years in Gorton he has never seen a politician round here at election time – Labour takes them for granted, the others don't bother. There is mass unemployment here in an area where the factories have long since closed. Brown might get a slightly easier ride if he turned up, but not Cameron, he says. "They'd take the mickey out of him. Out of the way he talks for a start. A lot of kids wag school here, but they're streetwise. You can't take them for fools. Cameron's not a man of the people, is he?" What does that mean? "Getting your hands dirty now and again. Anybody can fall off a bike, even I've done that."

Johnstone asks me to guess how much he was earning on the buses. A hundred pounds a week? "You're way out. Fifty-five pound a week. I retired in 1981 on that."

What class does Johnstone identify with? He thinks carefully. "Middle class," he finally says. Why? "Well, I'm not down on my uppers. If I was on my uppers I'd call myself working class, and I always worked for a living." It's not just for the politicians that the term working class has become pejorative.

It's 10pm in Cloud 23 at Manchester's Hilton hotel. This is where the prosperous younger people come to look down on the rest of Manchester. The view is magnificent and the prices are steep – £8.30 for a large glass of wine or cocktail, as opposed to £2.40 for a small bottle of wine in West Gorton.

Just as I've not found a Conservative all day, now I can't find a Labour voter. Forty-year-old Rob, a planning manager, left school with one O-level, started out on £25 a week and now earns £40,000 a year. He will vote Tory. He worries that we've become a benefits society. His girlfriend Julie says there's a reason for that. "There's

5 MAY 2010
Alastair Campbell at Granada studios in Manchester following a speech
by Gordon Brown in the fifth week of the campaign. MARTIN ARGLES

8 MAY 2010
Party leaders Nick Clegg, David Cameron and Gordon Brown at the
VE Day commemoration in Whitehall, London. DAN CHUNG

21 MAY 2010

Gordon Brown speaks to Nick Clegg on the telephone in the minutes before leaving No 10. See Ian Jack article, page 218. MARTIN ARGLES

21 MAY 2010

Gordon Brown, his family, staff and colleagues photographed for the final time in the prime minister's office. MARTIN ARGLES

not a lot out there for people at the moment. The job market is very tight – there's nothing like the YTS scheme that helped me."

The next morning I'm at the People's History Museum in Manchester. It used to be known as the National Museum of Labour History, but it was felt that implied allegiance to the political party. It considered "working class" and "working people" before settling on the simpler people's museum.

Whatever it doesn't say in its title, this is as class-conscious a cultural centre as there could be. Upstairs is a reminder of how far the working classes have come over the past two centuries. Last year, two swords were discovered in a family home. They belonged to the Manchester and Salford Yeomanry Cavalry, who so violently charged the people demanding a vote at what became known as the Peterloo massacre in 1819 – 15 people were killed and it led to the foundation of the *Manchester Guardian.*

The museum's director, Nick Mansfield, tells me he has also had his share of class crises. His mother was a working-class Tory and for so many years he couldn't understand why. "I railed against it when I was young, but as you got older you realised there were logical reasons. We lived in Cambridge and she was a bedder at the university – which meant she changed the beds of the students." Mansfield explains that bedders got to take home leftovers from the college kitchen and they got tips from the wealthy students: "They'd have loved Cameron and his chums."

I think my father was also a working-class Tory when he started out. He ended up a middle-class Labour voter. Perhaps he was as confused about class as I am. Who knows where they really belong? I don't think Dad did. Nor me. So many of us bop back and forth on the working-, middle-class continuum as we go about our daily business. The one thing everybody I met agreed on was that they were not upper class. And despite Cameron's conviction that we are now classless, this is where he might have problems.

17 April 2010

# Election briefing: the yellow surge could soak us all

## MALCOLM TUCKER

OK, look, I'm knackered. I'm as cranky as Janette Krankie was when she found out there was a new Jimmy Krankie auditioning and stayed up all night doing crank. I've been up for 36 hours trying to get my head round the debate numbers. I've read the whole of Twitter. I've watched both Dimblebuds, *QT*, all the local news. Rewound the worm polls, and checked the backgrounds of the focus group members. And still hungry for the red meat of reaction at 6.30am, I put the paper lad in a half-nelson and made him give me three key words on each party leader's performance. The good news is he was very encouraging. We may also need to sort out a quiet visit to Harley Street re a compacted shoulder joint.

As you know, I always said Clegg would be a formidable opponent. Any suggestion he would be a mere Weetabix with a Dictaphone sellotaped to him was to put you at your ease. I always said the debates were going to be game changers. They were exciting, they were engaging, and we should see if there is any possible way in the world for us to get the fuck out of the rest of them.

Obviously we can't lead on this. But can we have a back-channel chat and see if we can't get the Tories to withdraw, claiming that public debates over policy are a distraction from the real business of debating policy publicly?

*Clegg:* I know there's a view that Clegg winning is OK for us. And I was fine with Peter running Spin Alley. You need control.

You can't just have a bunch of cabinet ministers bouncing around the room like bollocks in a tumble drier. And journalists like Peter. People feel they know where they are with a sociopath. But the thing about promoting the Yellow Surge is that although a tidal wave of piss obviously sounds very attractive, everyone can get soaked. It's all a great laugh when the Tories are seeing their cocks cut off into their pints of cider in the West Country. Not so funny when we get kicked in the bollocks in the Ribble.

*Hot Buttons:* I think in the world where the man with the golden tie is doing well we may need to reposition ourselves on some hot button issues. On gays and Europe there has been a residual fear that if we point out too much that the Tories are homophobes and xenophobes we will deliver unto ourselves the liberals and the homos and the people who have three kinds of olive oil, but these may actually be outweighed in this great country of ours by the queer-bashers and closet racists – so our moral stand could leave us marginally worse off. That's not the kind of moral stand I like. Let's all stamp on a paedo. That's my kind of brave crusade.

I've looked at the numbers and the maths are difficult to calculate even using Mosaic, but if we look at proxy questions like "Are you relaxed about the introduction of new varieties of breakfast cereal?" (87% of homophobes aren't) or "Would you agree with the statement that in general the Cox's Orange Pippin is superior to the avocado pear?" (79% of racists hold this view) compared with the numbers who agree 3-D films are primarily an innovation to drive up cinema revenue (83% liberal), then it does seem that this nation is actually basically decent, so far as we can tell. But only marginally.

One thing we know for certain is that the people of this country do not enjoy humour or fair play. These are our defining national characteristics. Polling suggests the public are more comfortable with the humourless and want to escape economic pain for themselves while others pay the price. They just very much like to be told they enjoy humour and fair play. Remember this next time around. No jokes. It's going to be tough. But not for you.

Finally. Just a note regarding the repeated claim that this is going to be at some point The Dirtiest Election Campaign In History. Please, can people stop saying this shit to me unless they mean it, because you know how excited it gets me.

*Regards, Malcolm*

*(As dictated to Jesse Armstrong)*

17 APRIL 2010

# Why I moved into an old people's home

## DIANA ATHILL

Very few events in my life have been decided by me. How I was educated, where I have lived, why I am not married, how I have earned my living: all these crucial things happened to me rather than were made to happen by me. Of course an individual's nature determines to some extent what happens, there will be an interplay of causes, probably too complex to disentangle, in which intention usually plays a part but moments at which a person just says, "I shall now do X" and does it are rare – or so it has been in my life, anyway. Perhaps my decision to move into a home for old people is not quite the only one, but it is certainly the biggest.

This is not to say that outside events contributed nothing to it, because two of them did set the scene. The first was a visit to a friend, Rose Hacker, after I had learned that she had made such a move. This shook me, because Rose, though well over 90, was a lively and independent woman. Rose in an old people's home? It seemed unthinkable. I decided I must summon up the nerve to visit her: "summon up the nerve" because the image in my mind of such homes was a grim one.

This one, behind a high wall in Highgate, north London, was set in a large, well-kept garden surrounded by trees and appeared to be uninhabited. I realise now most of the residents were in the library, where tea is served to those who don't prefer to have it in their rooms, and that the reason there were no nurses to be seen was that there aren't any nurses: it is not a nursing home, although carers are available to those who need them. I found Rose's room and knocked on the door. Silence. So I opened it, and there was Rose, who must by then have been rising a hundred, having a nap in a splendid extending armchair.

She woke at once, unabashed, and no sooner had she greeted me warmly than she said: "My dear, you must come and live here. It is the most wonderful place." I had no intention of living in any such place, however wonderful, but I was so pleased to find her happy that I urged her to tell me more. It was run by a venerable charity with the aim of giving its residents as normal, independent and pleasant a life as possible, while at the same time providing whatever care they needed until they died. Was it expensive, I asked. Four hundred and forty pounds a week (it has now gone up to £550), and a bit more if a lot of care was needed. When I said there must be a long waiting list, Rose answered blithely: "You needn't worry about that, we're dying all the time."

I thought then only that I was relieved to find Rose so well-suited, but I suppose I must have tucked away the thought: "If one day ..." And that thought was still to be there when I needed it.

The other piece of scene-setting was less agreeable. My oldest friendship, dating from the moment when we first sat down beside each other for breakfast as nervous "freshers" at Oxford's Lady Margaret Hall, was Nan Taylor, three months younger than me. Nan weathered less well than I did. A breast cancer was caught early enough for her to consider herself cured, but drastic radiation did her a good deal of harm, and she persisted in smoking heavily in spite of the horrible cough which she called "my boring old bronchitis". As she approached her 80s she became tottery, broke her hip as a result of a bad fall, and was soon reduced to immobility and incontinence. She was able to employ agency nurses to come in morning and evening, because the one thing she was determined to do was die in her own bed, but it was hard work for her friends.

There were five of us to share the burden, but for two years a burden it was. At every visit there was a nerve-racking wait: was she dragging herself precariously towards the door, or had she fallen, in which case she couldn't get up? More and more often it was the latter, whereupon one prayed that her neighbours were in, and would support one through the anxious moment of finding the crumpled heap on the floor and sorting it out. If they weren't in one had to call the police who, I must say, would rise to the occasion with surprising kindness. And once Nan was re-established in her chair and tea had been made and poured, it became with every visit less easy to penetrate her increasing deafness, and her indifference to any subject apart from querulous complaints about her carers. She had been for many years a dear, generous and entertaining friend, so we all went on being fond of her, and wanting to help, but I'm pretty sure I was not the only one whose sorrow at her death was mingled with relief. And in my case vanity (I suppose) filled me with dismay at the thought of ever inflicting such an experience on my friends.

In the winter of 2008 I went down with flu, and was soon reduced to such a state of inertia that I no longer reached for the glass of water beside my bed which I knew I ought to be drinking, nor could I summon up the energy to telephone anyone. Eventually a dear friend, Xandra Bingley, happened to telephone me, after which she fed and cared for me with the most generous willingness and good humour until I was better. There was no question of Xandra making heavy weather of it, and I felt nothing but the purest gratitude and relief, but later I remembered that post-Nan dismay. Nan's decline had been gradual, so I had not realised until now that an old person can be reduced to helplessness – can reach the stage of having to be looked after – almost overnight. If I'd had children I suppose I would have accepted, albeit reluctantly, that it could be done by them, but by one's friends? Very occasionally, and if one were able to reciprocate, perhaps; but if it was likely to become more frequent, if it was possible that one might soon become as dependent on their help as Nan had been? No! And how, having reached my 90s, could I fool myself into thinking that I was not moving into that territory? It was then that I decided to call Rose's home and ask them to send me their brochure.

As a result I visited their office and ended by saying that I would like to be considered as a resident if a room came free in about a year's time. I was able to feel that I had made what was probably a sensible decision but was not tied down to it. So for the next 12 months, on the rare occasions when I did think about it, I was able to feel that moving into an old people's home was a comfortably distant event.

By that time I knew a good deal about the home – the Mary Feilding Guild. I learned that the quality of the care was wonderful, and that their rooms were tiny. Visiting Rose, I had not been particularly struck by her room's smallness, I suppose because I had not yet envisaged living in such a room myself, but now I had talked to someone who had just moved in and who was still vividly aware of what she had given up in order to be there, and it was alarming.

You were not, of course, a prisoner in your room. You lunched in the dining room, and at tea-time had the choice between a tray in your room or having it in the library. There was also a computer room and various utility rooms, including kitchens with ovens for those who wanted to cook. And the garden was large and very pleasant. It would, I saw, be like going back to live in college. Except that when you went to college you had no accumulation of possessions to be sacrificed.

It was that which made it such a violent shock when the letter came saying that a room was now available. It was one of their best rooms, with big windows looking out over the garden and a balcony large enough for several flower pots and a chair. But it would hold a single bed, a desk, two chairs plus a desk chair – and that was that. The built-in storage space for clothes would hold – perhaps – a quarter of those I possessed; there was only one wall about 12 feet long for pictures. And what would I do about my books?

I came home, sat down in my little sitting room, looked round at the magpie's nest of beloved things accumulated in a long lifetime, and felt: "But this is me." The extent to which a personality depends on the space it occupies and the objects it possesses appeared to me at that moment overwhelming. How could I perform an act of what amounted to self-destruction? The answer was: I can't! I can't and I won't, I'd rather die.

At that stage it would have taken only one word of encouragement from one person, and I would have called the Guild and told them I had changed my mind. I did not get that word. The two people I relied on most for support, my nephew Philip Athill and

Xandra, had agreed that in deciding to move to a home I was doing a sensible thing, and I knew both of them felt relief at that decision, as I would have done in their position. Both, when they saw that now I might panic out of it, were perceptibly disturbed at the possibility, again as I would have been. They were not being selfish or unkind. They were simply aware that over their full and busy lives hung the possibility that affection might plunge them into a very onerous responsibility. Of course they didn't want this to happen. It was their reaction that made me suppress the panic.

This horrible feeling came in surges, like fits of nausea – just as excruciating and irresistible, so that while it was going on I was entirely possessed by it and, like fits of nausea, it passed. It was a relief, gradually to realise this: that what one had to do was hold tight and wait it out, whereupon reason would re-establish its hold: a sensible decision did not become less sensible when it finally led to the action decided on. I must accept that fact, calm down and get on with it.

This became less painful when I discovered to my surprise that getting rid of possessions by giving them to friends or members of my family who would, I was sure, enjoy them turned out to be easy – even a positive pleasure; but unfortunately my books were too many to be disposed of in that way. Some could be given, but most had to be dealt with in bulk. I finally managed it. Philip spent the best part of a day holding up, one by one, every book in that daunting mass and saying, "In or Out?" then boxing it as appropriate. But even with a lot of help, just before the final move I experienced a physical collapse serious enough to lead to a night in hospital, which I'm now sure was the result of stress.

That peculiar little physical collapse seemed to rid me of an accumulation of misery at one go. Almost at once on arrival at the home I knew that it was going to suit me. And sure enough, it does. A life free of worries in a snug little nest (my room really is charming), good friends among my neighbours, freedom to do everything I'm still capable of doing, and knowing one will be beautifully looked after if necessary: what could be better?

19 APRIL 2010

# Volcanic ash is the new swine flu hysteria

SIMON JENKINS

A ship, a ship, my kingdom for a ship. Refugees now herded in airports on the west coast of America are harking back to Conrad. Thousands of us, entombed in the hotels round LA airport, live by rumour. A fleet of racing canoes is said to have left New Zealand waters, re-enacting the ancient Polynesian migration to Easter Island. Bring them on, we cry. Any vessel will do to escape.

Across the world, air travellers to Europe are in limbo. Mysterious websites tell of riots on Spanish ferries, $1,000 taxi rides from Scandinavia and a million desperate Britons wandering the continent. We hear they are fighting to get on trains and buses, huddled, exhausted things with sacks like those fleeing an advancing army. The Vikings of Iceland, who gave us herring wars and dodgy credit, have capped it all by cutting the Atlantic. Come back Columbus, come back the Cunarders. Death to Iceland.

What did we do before planes? We hear of pandemonium in New York as travellers queue for precious boat tickets. Is the Panama Canal open? Or might we get up to Alaska and cross to the Trans-Siberian railroad to St Petersburg. The rumour is Portugal is open, suddenly free of ash. Everyone screams for seats to Lisbon. Consortia form in corners to charter executive jets. Might some cowboy take a propeller plane to Greenland and fly down through the ash to London? Every crisis is an opportunity.

The health-and-safety Armageddon I long expected has arrived. It was bad enough to have an idiot with a shoe bomb stirring equally idiotic regulators to enforce billions of pounds of cost and inconvenience on air travellers in the cause of "it might happen again". Now we have a volcano and a bit of dust. It is another swine flu.

The truth is that putting large, heavy bits of metal into the air is just too much for the psyche of modern regulators. They panic. The slightest risk cannot be taken or someone might blame the regulators, whose job is not to assess risk but avert it. Even an airline company, with everything to lose, is not allowed to assess its own risk. Many more will die on roads and elsewhere because of the anarchy the air controllers have unleashed on Europe, but that is not their business. They don't care.

I will find it hard to trust airlines again, not because they are too risky but because what they do panics authority too easily. Air travel has become hellish. For the moment, we must pray for another Dunkirk. The skies over the Atlantic must fill with planes, big and small, swooping out of the jet-stream to pluck the poor bloody infantry of globalisation off the beaches of the new world, and get them home to fight another day. Please come soon.

20 APRIL 2010

# Sir Peter Tapsell: still the dish of the day at 80

SIMON HOGGART

To Lincolnshire, to visit Sir Peter Tapsell in his home. It is his 15th parliamentary election, and if he wins next month – something he won't take for granted, though everyone else does – he will become Father of the House.

This is largely an honorary title, but it does mean that he will be in charge of proceedings for the election of the Speaker on the first day of the new parliament. With several Tories hoping to get rid of John Bercow, this could be quite a tricky job, and he has already been briefed about the problems he might face – if he is elected, as he invariably says.

He believes it is vital for the new parliament to get off to a good start, and begin to recover from the horrors of the recent past. And the main reason he is running again at the age of 80 is because he doesn't want to be lumped in with the flippers and duck house people who have been obliged to quit.

It's something of a pilgrimage for me. Like all sketchwriters, I love it when Sir Peter speaks, his words seemingly carved into instant stone as he utters them. I once compared him to George Best and to Alfred Brendel (though to resurrect the old joke, Best couldn't play the piano, and Alfred Brendel is a lousy footballer). My encomium appears prominently in his election address. There was of course a considerable degree of irony in what I wrote, which Sir Peter well knows, though he hopes that the voters of Louth and Horncastle won't spot it. It would be easier if there were a typeface called ironic bold.

I was invited for lunch, at his wonderful house. My visit was at an hour's notice, so I assume they eat like this every day. Lady Tapsell, who is from Normandy, served us a velvety watercress soup, accompanied by chilled Sancerre. Sir Peter, a well-known Eurosceptic, said he had some anxiety about Ukip, as there is much anti-Brussels feeling in the area. However, the Ukip candidate, Pat Nurse, seems more concerned with health. "I support lifestyle choice and an end to the denormalisation [sic] of adults who do not take on board health propaganda," whatever that means. As a rallying cry against fisheries policy and the CAP it seems lacking.

Lady Tapsell brought us delicious local roast beef, plus fried potatoes and a glass of Châteauneuf-du-Pape. Sir Peter described his typical day, which consists of driving round the villages and market towns in an ancient Land Rover. He speaks for 10 minutes then asks for questions. People are too polite these days, he thinks. There is not enough heckling, though in Alford four or five very big men stood nearby in a threatening way and swore at him. "We don't want any of your fucking nonsense," one of them said. "Bring back national service," said another. "Yes," Sir Peter replied, "and you would be a fine candidate for it."

Lady Tapsell produced a platter of French cheeses with fresh fruit. "I am told that the Liberal candidate is conducting a campaign based entirely on the email," Sir Peter said. He once remarked that he didn't have "an internet" and doesn't wish to consult "Mr Google" every time he wants to know Tory policy.

Lady Tapsell brought us the first of two desserts, caramelised strawberries, with dessert wine.

Sir Peter suspects that the strains in the eurozone will, ultimately, lead the Germans to renegotiate their relationship with the rest of Europe, and that will be our chance to do the same. Lady Tapsell produced home-made café glace, coffee ice cream. I could hardly get behind the wheel to drive away.

23 April 2010

# *Guardian* journalists meet to discuss election leader line

## MATT SEATON

This morning Comment is free posted an open thread inviting you, *Guardian* readers and users, to share your views with us about who or what the *Guardian* should support in the election editorial that will be published sometime before 6 May. The purpose of this "have your say" was to open up, as far as we could, an important bit of *Guardian* tradition: the editor's meeting at which all *Guardian* journalists can air their views of what the leader line should be, before the leader writers retire to some hallowed inner sanctum to compose whatever oracular statement the *Guardian* finally makes on the subject.

Your response was spectacular. Between 7.30am and the start of the meeting at 1.15pm, in excess of 1,200 comments were posted. At the time of writing, the total stands at more than 1,500. Even a cursory skim through the thread will tell you two things. While this is no scientific sample (and no opinion poll), an overwhelming majority of commenters urged the *Guardian* to back the Liberal Democrats. The chief reason why most of those who posted wish to see that is – necessarily summarising and simplifying hundreds of fascinating contributions – because you want to see real political change, vitally including electoral reform. And to most of you, Nick Clegg's Liberal Democrats look like that change or the best bet for it.

That was the message we Ciffers took into the meeting – in the *Guardian*'s Scott Room, whose walls were lined with sheets displaying a selection of your comments from the thread. With at least 200 people in the room, one issue at least was immediately clear: the air conditioning wasn't up to the job. As is also traditional at such gatherings, the *Guardian*'s instinct for democracy and egalitarianism wars with an obscure combination of deference to the senior editors and columnists and an "I'll-sit-at-the-back-of-the-class" rebelliousness. This tension gets resolved in a delicate hierarchical compromise, with inner circle chairs occupied by the big beasts, with some secondary ranks behind, and then a standing crowd of silent spectators and occasionally noisy dissenters.

The editor, Alan Rusbridger, kicked off proceedings by reminding us why we were there – to honour the unique institution in Fleet Street of a news media organisation, independent and not beholden to proprietor or shareholders, holding such a consultative, "sounding-board" meeting with staff about such a central question of editorial policy. He then laid out seven areas of policy and principle to guide discussion: the economy, constitutional reform, foreign policy, public services, social justice, the environment and civil liberties. From here, I'm observing Chatham House rules and not attributing remarks, but will try to summarise and give you a flavour of the debate.

On the economy, the discussion focused on Labour's record: on the one hand, its management of the recession has been creditable and things could have been so much worse; on the other hand, the responsibility for the regulatory failures during the previous decade's boom is largely Labour's too. The bottom line, though, is that Labour is still the most redistributive party – for all its failures and timidity on that score. As one said: "Labour always remembers the poorest," whereas, historically, the Liberal Democrats are a party of the centre that looks out for the middle strata of society and tackling poverty is not in their DNA, as it is for Labour.

Jumping to foreign policy, a consensus soon emerged that the *Guardian*'s editorial positions are most closely aligned, of all the three parties, with the Liberal Democrats' prospectus. On Europe, especially, Cameron's Conservatives are a cause for concern, in contrast to a more realist Liberal Democrat attitude than in past times. Clegg's scepticism on replacing Trident suited many, too; and on Britain's role in the world, a less fetishistic attitude towards the "special relationship" with the US, and human rights, the Lib Dems tick *Guardian* boxes that Labour leaves blank. Brown's attack on Clegg in the leaders' debate for being "anti-American" seemed clumsy and ill-judged, it was said; after all, it was only the Liberal Democrats, of the main parties, who had shared the *Guardian*'s opposition to the Iraq war.

Moving to public services, the debate was wide open. There is doubt about Labour's centralised mode of delivery and its target-driven record. Have people had enough of the big state, and are both the Tories and Lib Dems more in tune with the public mood by promising more devolved services and local control? As one said: "Labour has real achievements, but there are big questions to answer." On the other hand, the older hands at the *Guardian* – and among the electorate – still have the memory of past recessions under Conservative governments when cuts in public spending were harsh and not "humane". A voice from the standing contingent also observed crisply that, whatever Clegg and Cable might say about public spending, there is plenty of evidence of Liberal Democrats in local government being anything but liberal in their approach to services and cuts.

Constitutional reform energised discussion. A senior web editor observed that not just in today's open thread, but throughout our election coverage, there has been an incredibly high level of engagement from users and the dominant theme has been the desire for change and reform – for a new politics. Where the *Guardian* has long been on political reform (in some areas, for more than a century), there also, by and large, are the Liberal Democrats. And on civil liberties, which the *Guardian* has championed, most recently through liberty central, the Lib Dems score a home run, it was agreed.

On the environment, the verdict is that Labour has come late to the party, but has finally started to get things done – slowly building a new green economy, with jobs and growth in the renewable energy industry, for instance. There was a feeling, too, that however strongly Cameron had run on the environmental message in the early days of his leadership, he has not ultimately succeeded in selling that message to substantial portions of his party base and hierarchy. Again, the Liberal Democrats have long been on the right ground on the environment – although, as a senior editor observed, their opposition to nuclear power is hard to square with Britain's commitment to cutting carbon emissions.

The editor moved the debate on to the decisive questions of how to translate the *Guardian*'s values and principles into a succinct editorial message – as he put it, separating the matters of principle from the pragmatic issue of how to reconcile them with the first-past-the-post system we have.

Opening, one said there was "a consensus in favour of some form of 'Lib-Lab-ery'"; as another then chimed, "If there were a box [on the ballot paper] you could tick, it would be for a hung parliament – but you can't vote for that." So immediately, we were into the mechanics of how to get the reform we all want. But how to address the question of "progressive alliances" and tactical voting in the most unpredictable, poised and unstable general election in decades?

There was a strong feeling from several quarters that the *Guardian* should not necessarily plump for one party over another, but instead, in tune with what feels like the public mood, "vote with our values" – say that we want change and reform, and leave it to voters to decide the rest. And this is where your Cif representatives in the room spoke up to convey a sense of what you had been telling us, reading from the thread: strong support for the Liberal Democrats, not necessarily to see them in government and Nick Clegg as prime minister, but with a powerful current of desire for a new politics – the resurgent great theme of the last year.

Some election veterans and harder-headed realists wanted to see a firmer message in favour of Labour, on the grounds that there is a real risk that a collapse in Labour's vote, even with a big turnout for the Liberal Democrats, would be most likely to deliver a minority Conservative government or even a majority for Cameron.

What is certain, though, is that creating at least some kind of window for the world to this internal *Guardian* exercise brought an even greater sense of energy and engagement to an already unexpectedly exciting election. Thank you for sharing your views with us. The *Guardian*'s election leader will be written and published in the newspaper and on Comment is free later next week.

23 APRIL 2010

## Readers live blog the second televised leader debate

COMMENT IS FREE OPEN THREAD

Is anyone else a bit nervous? Or am I just a wimp? CLAIREMcW 8.01PM

Like the set. Is this a graphic representation of "broken Britain"? ROYMAYALL 8.01PM

Good to see Clegg playing his ace straight off – we should not have gone. To. Iraq. Maybe he read that Martin Kettle blog. OZKT29B 8.04PM

Both Brown and Cameron targeting their opening speeches at those who might vote Lib Dem. Clegg having the confidence to ignore them and wrap himself in the flag – British values etc. Pretty good move. CHASM 8.07PM

I wonder how many people are now Googling about paedophilia just because Nick told them to. NICKDAS 8.11PM

Every time Gordon "smiles" a tiny part of me dies. HERMIONEGINGOLD 8.14PM

That bath-time joke was horrific. RUPERTMYERS 8.14PM

Dave is doing a lot better this week. It's not changing my mind, but he's much better today. CLAIRE McW 8.19PM

Cameron went to Afghanistan and was "blown away". Whoops. SCAMANDER 8.21PM

Ridiculous question designed so that each one tells more fricking anecdotes. What we should be hearing is how the only way of dealing with climate change is radical aggressive policies. ADAMRUTHERFORD 8.28PM

This is really interesting, actually. Brown is doing much better, Clegg is assured and assertive, Cameron looks ineffectual and almost sidelined. CHASM 8.31PM

I'm listening to this on radio and finding it hard to differentiate between Cameron and Clegg's voices. MSCHIN 8.39PM

Is it a risk in British politics for Clegg to say he's not a man of faith? Would be in US presidential debate. GEORGINA HENRY 8.40PM

@georgina I reckon he dealt with that in a perfectly British way, basically saying, it's not an issue. ADAMRUTHERFORD 8.42PM

Am I being silly, or is Cameron actually coming out better than Clegg? NWERDINE 8.45PM

@nwerdine You are being silly, yes. Cameron is definitely running third. CHASM 8.47PM

Brown and Cameron have improved marginally, so Clegg looks less brill. Marginally. GRUBHATER 9.03PM

Clegg is SO on form. He is very well briefed. He is fresh and makes a great deal of sense, But Brown is ON FIRE! Cameron just gave a commitment on the hoof. He is panicking. STEPHENSOBO 9.03PM

Cameron's winning this debate. RUPERTMYERS 9.14PM

@RupertMyers How? Cameron sounds like a broken record. TRUE-BLUETAH 9.16PM

Oh, god, immigration again! Will somebody here marry me so that I don't have to endure feeling like an outsider any more? BALAJIRAVICHANDRAN 9.17PM

@truebluetah I'll tell you. He is speaking with the right tone. Clegg's charmingly naive approach is wearing thin, and Gordon just can't come back from that bathtub line for me. RUPERTMYERS 9.19PM

Gordon the clear winner. By a knockout rather than just points. APOINT 9.30PM

Clegg 93rd min winner ! Bravo! MAITAIMIK 9.33PM

YouGov/Sun polls says Cameron wins the debate – Sky gives Cameron 36%. WTF? I definitely need to ditch this Freeview lark because it's distorting reality. UBERMORLOCK 9.47PM

*The above is an edited selection of comments posted at guardian.co.uk/ commentisfree*

27 APRIL 2010

# Blair Peach: after 31 years, Met says "sorry" for role of riot police in killing

PAUL LEWIS

A former police inspector tonight denied involvement in the notorious killing of the anti-racist protester Blair Peach, after a report released earlier in the day suggested he may have been the officer who struck the "fatal blow".

Alan Murray, who is now a university lecturer but was a 29-year-old Metropolitan police inspector in 1979, said he was the victim of a bungled investigation into Peach's death. "I did not kill Blair Peach. Of that I am certain," he said.

Murray was speaking after the release of more than 3,000 previously secret documents that shed new light on the death of Peach, a 33-year-old teacher from New Zealand whose skull was crushed by a single blow to the head during a protest against the National Front in Southall, west London, on the evening of 23 April 1979.

The documents appeared to confirm the long-held suspicion that Peach was likely to have been killed by an officer from the Met's riot squad, the special patrol group (SPG).

The key document was produced by Commander John Cass, who ran the Met's internal complaints bureau and led the inquiry into Peach's death. He concluded that Peach was "almost certainly" killed by one of six SPG officers, some of whom then lied to cover up the actions of their colleague.

No officers were ever charged over Peach's death, although the event marked one of the darkest moments in Scotland Yard's history. Sir Paul Stephenson, the Metropolitan police commissioner, recognised as much when he said the report made "uncomfortable reading". He unequivocally accepted the finding that a Met officer was likely to have been responsible for the death and, in an unusual move, expressed his regret.

"I have to say, really, that I am sorry that in over 31 years since Blair Peach's death we have been unable to provide his family and friends with the definitive answer regarding the terrible circumstances in which he met his death," he said.

Asked if he was apologising for the death of Peach, he replied: "I am sorry that officers behaved that way, according to Mr Cass."

Murray, who retired from the Met soon after the death and now lectures in corporate social responsibility at Sheffield University, was not named in the documents that were made public. But he accepted that from evidence given at Peach's inquest and other material, he was easily identifiable. The former inspector is among dozens of police officers questioned over the death more than 30 years ago who can now be identified.

They include Tony Lake, who attended the Southall demonstration as an SPG sergeant, and later rose through the highest ranks of the constabulary, becoming the chief constable of Lincolnshire police.

Lake, who once chaired the national DNA database and was awarded an OBE when he retired two years ago, declined to comment last night on Peach's death but said that a 1981 newspaper report linking him to the officers identified in the Cass report was "fundamentally wrong".

The Met agreed to release the documents last year in the aftermath of the death of Ian Tomlinson, a 47-year-old newspaper seller who died after being attacked by police at the G20 protests in London. The officer filmed striking Tomlinson was a member of the territorial support group, which replaced the disbanded SPG in 1987. The Crown Prosecution Service is still considering whether to charge the officer with manslaughter.

Yesterday's publication marked the culmination of a 31-year campaign by friends and family of Peach for full disclosure of the Met's inquiry into the death. The Cass report was suppressed in 1980 by the late Dr John Burton, the coroner who oversaw the inquest into Peach's death.

The inquest controversially returned a verdict of "death by misadventure", but recently disclosed documents suggest Burton was biased in favour of the police. He wrote to ministers before the end of the inquest, dismissing the belief that Peach was killed by an officer as political "fabrication".

After the inquest, Burton penned an "unpublished story" about the Peach death which railed against what the coroner saw as a leftwing campaign to destabilise the legal establishment. Senior civil servants managed to persuade him not to publish his account. One official wrote: "An article like this would be a heaven-sent opportunity to those who wish to get maximum publicity out of this incident to argue that the coroner was biased and for this reason the inquest was unsound."

Peach's long-term partner, Celia Stubbs, said yesterday she felt totally vindicated by the Cass report. She described its release as "the beginning of the end" of her campaign for answers.

She repeated her long-held belief that Peach would not have wanted to be known as a political martyr, but accepted that the search for answers over his death had for many become a political cause in itself, galvanising concern over what were considered the brutal actions of corrupt and unaccountable police.

When Peach's body was finally buried – 51 days after his death – thousands of activists marched across London. Around 8,000 mainly Sikhs from Southall had already paid their respects at his open coffin, which lay in a nearby theatre the previous night.

The suspicions of most of those mourners – that a police officer killed Peach – were all but confirmed in yesterday's report.

Stubbs said: "It is fantastic after 31 years. I have only read 200 pages of the report but I feel that we have really been vindicated because we have always said that Blair had been killed by a policeman. It says in the report that it was an officer that struck Blair. I never really expected a prosecution. I don't regret that, I am just pleased that we have the report so we can see what happened on the day."

The Cass report was written at the end of the summer of 1979, following months of inquiries.

In laying out his terms of reference he said: "My brief is to investigate the circumstances surrounding the death, so I do not propose to enlarge much further on the events of that day except to emphasise that it was an extremely violent, volatile and ugly situation where there was serious disturbance by what can be classed as a 'rebellious crowd'.

"The legal definition 'unlawful assembly' is justified and the event should be viewed with that kind of atmosphere prevailing. Without condoning the death I refer to Archbold [Criminal Pleading, Evidence and Practice] 38th edition para 2528: 'In case of riot or rebellious assembly the officers endeavouring to disperse the riot are justified in killing them at common law if the riot cannot otherwise be suppressed.'"

If Cass was seeking to exonerate his men, it was an endeavour he found difficult in the face of more than 3,000 pages of witness testimony, forensic evidence and tense interviews with officers. After reviewing hundreds of pages of evidence, he reached his conclusion: that it could "reasonably be concluded that a police officer struck the fatal blow". Despite this, he said there was insufficient evidence to bring charges of unlawful killing.

Cass had narrowed his investigation down to six SPG officers in carrier U11, the first vehicle to arrive in Beachcroft Avenue, the suburban street where Peach was found stumbling around, barely able to talk. Moments earlier, 14 witnesses had seen "a police officer hit the deceased on the head" but, according to Cass, there were discrepancies in their evidence and most could not identify an officer from repeated identity parades.

Although he did not recommend charges over the death, Cass did name three officers he proposed should be prosecuted for perverting the course of justice, believing they had lied to his investigators to cover up the actions of their colleague.

Analysing their statements, he found some had been engaged in a "deliberate attempt to conceal the presence of the carrier at the scene at that time".

In a key passage, he wrote: "It is now clear that [carrier] U11 was at the scene and almost certainly the officer who struck the blow had come from that carrier. It will be appreciated that the explanation given by the crew of the carrier would be of paramount importance to the investigation." He went on to express concern over the "attitude and untruthfulness" of some of the officers in the van, and found their responses "seriously lacking".

His recommendation that three officers be prosecuted for lying to their seniors was apparently overruled by the then director of public prosecutions, Sir Thomas Hetherington, who within weeks of receiving the Cass report announced there was insufficient evidence to bring any charge against any officer. After the Met reviewed the conduct of the officers, it was felt that none should be disciplined.

Of the six SPG officers, Cass said there was an "indication" that one officer in particular – the first to emerge from the carrier – struck the "fatal blow", but emphasised that there was "no evidence of a conclusive nature". The name of that officer was redacted from today's published version of the report, but last night Murray acknowledged that it was a reference to him. He accepted he was the first out of the van and said he was aware at the time that Cass had made him a "prime suspect" in the inquiry. But he criticised the investigation, and accused Cass of turning to him in the absence of more concrete evidence.

"In a report like that, that man [Cass] can write anything he likes," he said. "So he is pursuing me and trying to fit me up for a murder that I didn't commit, and then he tells people that I am stressed."

Cass, 85, who retired 20 years ago, said last night he was unwilling to comment on the allegations being made by Murray. But the Met stood by Cass, saying his findings were the result of an extensive and robust inquiry. Commander Mark Simmons, the officer who now runs the Met's complaints department and oversaw the release of his predecessor's report, said "a significant amount of resources" had been put into the investigation. "I've got no reason to disagree with Commander Cass's conclusions," he added.

Cass's findings were also welcomed yesterday by Deborah Coles, a co-director of Inquest, an organisation that was set up in 1981 partly in response to Peach's death and provides advice on contentious deaths. However, she raised questions about the institutions that hold police to account. "The whole police investigation into what happened on 23 April 1979 was clearly designed as an exercise in managing the fallout from the events of that iconic day in Southall, to exonerate police violence in the face of legitimate public protest," she said. "The echoes of that exercise sound across the decades to the events of the G20 protest and the death of Ian Tomlinson in 2009."

29 APRIL 2010

# Digested election: Bigot-gate

JOHN CRACE

GILLIAN DUFFY: What are you going to do with all those illegal immigrants?

GORDON BROWN: I deported them all last weekend.

MRS DUFFY: No you haven't. Mr Cameron's black man in Plymouth says there are still millions of them.

BROWN: You're just a bigoted old woman.

SKY TV: We heard that!

BROWN: I said: "You're a big-hearted woman." *(To Duffy, whispering)* Oi, you, come indoors, you mad old bat.

MRS DUFFY: That's not very nice.

BROWN: I said, "I'll feed your cat." How much cash do you want to shut up? You could certainly do with a hearing aid.

MRS DUFFY: Ooh, Mr Brown, you're breaking my arm …

BROWN: And if you look carefully, you'll notice I'm also not smiling.

MRS DUFFY: Thank God for that.

BROWN: So it's a deal. A couple of grand, we get rid of all the foreigners in your street and you say you'll still vote Labour.

JEREMY VINE: So, prime minister. Do you think your intemperate remarks might have cost you the election?

BROWN: Go fuck yourself, you prick.

VINE: I'm sorry?

BROWN: I said: "With a bit of luck it will pass in a tick."

DAVID CAMERON: I'm walking on sunshine …

NICK CLEGG: I'm walking on water.

1 May 2010

# The liberal moment has come

## GUARDIAN LEADER

Citizens have votes. Newspapers do not. However, if the *Guardian* had a vote in the 2010 general election it would be cast enthusiastically for the Liberal Democrats. It would be cast in the knowledge that not all the consequences are predictable, and that some in particular should be avoided. The vote would be cast with some important reservations and frustrations. Yet it would be cast for one great reason of principle above all.

After the campaign that the Liberal Democrats have waged over this past month, for which considerable personal credit goes to Nick Clegg, the election presents the British people with a huge opportunity: the reform of the electoral system itself. Though Labour has enjoyed a deathbed conversion to aspects of the cause of reform, it is the Liberal Democrats who have most consistently argued that cause in the round and who, after the exhaustion of the old politics, reflect and lead an overwhelming national mood for real change.

Proportional representation – while not a panacea – would at last give this country what it has lacked for so long: a parliament that is a true mirror of this pluralist nation, not an increasingly unrepresentative two-party distortion of it. The *Guardian* has supported proportional representation for more than a century. In all that time there has never been a better opportunity than now to put this subject firmly among the nation's priorities. Only the Liberal Democrats grasp this fully, and only they can be trusted to keep up the pressure to deliver, though others in all parties, large and small, do and should support the cause. That has been true in past elections too, of course. But this time is different. The conjuncture in 2010 of a Labour party that has lost so much public confidence and a Conservative party that has not yet won it has enabled Mr Clegg to take his party close to the threshold of real influence for the first time in nearly 90 years.

This time – with the important caveat set out below – the more people who vote Liberal Democrat on 6 May, the greater the chance that this will be Britain's last general election under a first-past-the-post electoral system which is wholly unsuited to the political needs of a grown-up 21st-century democracy.

TACTICAL OPTION

The pragmatic caveat concerns the danger that, under the existing electoral system, switching to the Liberal Democrats in Labour-Conservative marginal constituencies might let in an anti-reform Tory party. So, voters who share this principled enthusiasm for securing the largest possible number of Liberal Democrat MPs next Thursday must, in many constituencies, weigh the tactical option of supporting Labour to prevent a Conservative win.

Hopefully, if this really is the last election under the old system, such dilemmas between head and heart will apply less in future. For now, however, the cause of reform is overwhelmingly more likely to be achieved by a Lib Dem partnership of principle with Labour than by a Lib Dem marriage of convenience with a Tory party which is explicitly hostile to the cause and which currently plans to redraw the political map for its own advantage. The momentum for change would be fatally undermined should the Conservatives win an overall majority. The Liberal Democrats and Labour should, of course, have explored much earlier and more explicitly how they might co-operate to reform the electoral system. During the campaign, and especially since the final leaders' debate, the appetite for co-operation has clearly increased and is increasing still. Mr Clegg's *Guardian* interview today underscores the potential for more productive engagement with Labour and is matched by fresh, untribal thinking from his potential partners.

This election is about serious choices between three main parties which all have something to offer. David Cameron has done what none of his immediate predecessors has understood or tried to do: he has confronted the Conservative party with the fact that it was out of step with the country. He has forced the party to become more diverse and to engage with centre-ground opinion. He has explicitly aligned himself with the liberal Conservative tradition which the Thatcherites so despised during their long domination of the party. He has promoted modern thinking on civil liberty, the environment and aspects of social policy.

Mr Cameron offers a new and welcome Toryism, quite different from what Michael Howard offered five years ago. His difficulty is not that he is the "same old Tory". He isn't. The problem is that his revolution has not translated adequately into detailed policies, and remains highly contradictory. He embraces liberal Britain yet protests that Britain is broken because of liberal values. He is eloquent about the overmighty state but proposes to rip up the Human Rights Act which is the surest weapon against it. He talks about a Britain that will play a constructive role in Europe while aligning the Tories in the European parliament with some of the continent's wackier xenophobes. Behind the party leader's own engagement with green issues there stands a significant section of his party that still regards global warming as a liberal conspiracy.

The Tories have zigzagged through the financial crisis to an alarming degree, austerity here, spending pledges there. At times they have argued, against all reason, that Britain's economic malaise is down to overblown government, as opposed to the ravages of the market. Though the Conservatives are not uniquely evasive on the deficit, a large inheritance-tax cut for the very wealthy is the reverse of a serious "united and equal" approach to taxation. Small wonder that the Cameronisation of the Conservative party sometimes seems more palace coup than cultural revolution. A Cameron government might not be as destructive to Britain as the worst Tory regimes of the past. But it is not the right course for Britain.

If this election were a straight fight between Labour and the Conservatives – which it absolutely is not – the country would be safer in the hands of Labour than of the Tories. Faced in 2008 with a financial crisis unprecedented in modern times, whose destructive potential can hardly be exaggerated, the Labour government made some absolutely vital calls at a time which exposed the Conservatives as neoliberals, not novices. Whether Labour has truly learned the right lessons itself is doubtful. Labour is, after all, the party that nurtured the deregulatory systems which contributed to the implosion of the financial sector, on which the entire economy was too reliant. How, and even whether, British capitalism can be directed towards a better balance between industry and finance is a question which remains work in progress for Labour, as for us all. At the highest levels of the party, timidity and audacity remain in conflict. Nevertheless, Labour, and notably Alistair Darling, a palpably honest chancellor who has had to play the most difficult hand of any holder of his office in modern times, deserves respect for proving equal to the hour. Only the most churlish would deny the prime minister some credit for his role in the handling of the crisis.

## LABOUR'S FAILINGS
But this election is more than a verdict on the response to a single trauma, immense though it was. It is also a verdict on the

lengthening years of Labour government and the three years of Gordon Brown's premiership. More than that, any election is also a judgment about the future as well as a verdict on the past. A year ago, the *Guardian* argued that Labour should persuade its leader to step down. Shortly afterwards, in spite of polling an abject 15.7% in the European elections, and with four cabinet ministers departing, Labour chose to hug Mr Brown close. It was the wrong decision then, and it is clear, not least after his humiliation in Rochdale this week, that it is the wrong decision now. The *Guardian* said a year ago that Mr Brown had failed to articulate a vision, a plan, or an argument for the future. We said that he had become incapable of leading the necessary revolution against the political system that the expenses scandal had triggered. Labour thought differently. It failed to act. It thereby lost the opportunity to renew itself, and is now facing the consequences.

Invited to embrace five more years of a Labour government, and of Gordon Brown as prime minister, it is hard to feel enthusiasm. Labour's kneejerk critics can sometimes sound like the People's Front of Judea asking what the Romans have ever done for us. The salvation of the health service, major renovation of schools, the minimum wage, civil partnerships and the extension of protection for minority groups are heroic, not small achievements.

Yet, even among those who wish Labour well, the reservations constantly press in. Massive, necessary and in some cases transformational investment in public services insufficiently matched by calm and principled reform, sometimes needlessly entangled with the private sector. Recognition of gathering generational storms on pensions, public debt, housing and – until very recently – climate change not addressed by clear strategies and openness with the public about the consequences. The inadequately planned pursuit of two wars. A supposedly strong and morally focused foreign policy which remains trapped in the great-power, nuclear-weapon mentality, blindly uncritical of the United States, mealy-mouthed about Europe and tarnished by the shame of Iraq – still not apologised for. Allegations of British embroilment in torture answered with little more than a world-weary sigh. Large talk about constitutional change matched by an addiction to centralisation. Easy talk about liberty and "British values" while Britain repeatedly ratchets up the criminal justice system, repeatedly encroaches on civil liberties, undermines legal aid and spends like there is no tomorrow on police and prisons. Apparent outrage against the old politics subverted by delay, caution and timid compromise.

There are reservations, too, though of a different order and on different subjects, about the Liberal Democrats. The Liberal Democrats are a very large party now, with support across the spectrum. But they remain in some respects a party of the middle and lower middle classes. Labour's record on poverty remains unmatched, and its link to the poor remains umbilical. Vince Cable, so admirable and exemplary on the banks, nevertheless remains a deficit hawk, committed to tax cuts which could imply an even deeper slashing of public services. Though the party has good policies on equality, it has not prioritised the promotion and selection of women and ethnic minority candidates.

## MATCHED PRIORITIES

Surveying the wider agenda and the experience of the past decade, however, there is little doubt that in many areas of policy and tone, the Liberal Democrats have for some time most closely matched our own priorities and instincts. On political and constitutional change, they articulate and represent the change which is now so widely wanted. On civil liberty and criminal justice, they have remained true to liberal values and human rights in ways that the other parties, Labour more than the Tories in some respects, have not. They are less tied to reactionary and sectional class interests than either of the other parties.

The Liberal Democrats were green before the other parties and remain so. Their commitment to education is bred in the bone. So is their comfort with a European project which, for all its flaws, remains central to this country's destiny. They are willing to contemplate a British defence policy without Trident renewal. They were right about Iraq, the biggest foreign policy judgment call of the past half-century, when Labour and the Tories were both catastrophically and stupidly wrong. They have resisted the rush to the overmighty centralised state when others have not. At key moments, when tough issues of press freedom have been at stake, they have been the first to rally in support. Above all, they believe in and stand for full, not semi-skimmed, electoral reform. And they have had a revelatory campaign. Trapped in the arid, name-calling, two-party politics of the House of Commons, Nick Clegg has seldom had the chance to shine. Released into the daylight of equal debate, he has given the other two parties the fright of their lives.

A newspaper that is proudly rooted in the liberal as well as the labour tradition – and whose advocacy of constitutional reform stretches back to the debates of 1831-32 – cannot ignore such a record. If not now, when? The answer is clear and proud. Now.

7 MAY 2010

# Death and destruction in Athens

STEPHEN MOSS

It began as a fiesta, a mass march in the sun against the deflation-
ary programme the Greek people are being told can alone save
their country. At 10 on Wednesday morning, Klathmonos Square
in Athens was filling with protesters. A union official was making
an interminable speech (Greeks never use one word when 300 will
do), and music was blaring out of vans – those Chilean-style revolutionary songs without which no demo is complete: "The people,
united, will never be defeated." Not today, anyway.

People had said there would be no violence – or at least if there
was, it would be "ritual" violence: a broken window here, a
wrecked ATM there. One Greek journalist had told me the protests
so far had been subdued – "equivalent to what would normally
happen here if the electricity board sacked a few people". He said
the public were resigned to the economic hardships to come –
salaries of state employees cut by 25%, pensions to fall by 15%,
unemployment likely to rise to 18% – and that they recognised the
only alternative was national bankruptcy; not just junk bonds but
a junk country.

A few hours later, three bank workers, one a woman who was
four months pregnant, lay dead in a burned-out bank on Stadiou
Avenue, the victims of anarchist firebombs. Ritual violence this
was not, and by Wednesday evening Athens feels drained and
lifeless. "This will make people stop and think," teacher Anna
Tsiokou tells me, as we stand beside the police cordon on the
edge of the area where the firebombing had occurred. "The

demonstrations will have to stop for the moment. We have legitimate grievances, but the anarchists are using the crisis for their own ends."

The writer Apostolos Doxiadis, whom I had met the previous day, rings me as I sit in a cafe close to Stadiou, and offers to come down from his office 20 minutes away and help me make sense of what has happened. Doxiadis has an interest in terrorism because last year his office was firebombed, after he and two fellow writers had taken a public stand against political violence and disruption of artistic events by sympathisers of the riots of December 2008 (when the police shooting of a schoolboy led to weeks of unrest).

"What's so surprising is that there haven't been more deaths before," Doxiadis says. "Those of us who have been outspoken against violence from the beginning are not, I'm sorry to say, surprised, because there's been extreme violence of many forms. But this tragedy will start to make people think seriously, and find other ways to register their dissent. We are in a complex situation, and we have reached a tipping point today."

Just before midnight on Wednesday, as Athens finally starts to rest after a fearful and violent day, I have a coffee with an anarchist in Omonia Square, the traditional heart of violent protest in the city. He tells me he was close to the attack on the bank. His emotions are confused. He is sorry for the deaths, but will not accept the anarchists are to blame.

"The government are presenting this as murder," he says, "but it was a tragic accident. Anarchism is about material damage; it is not about taking life." Perversely, he blames the bank for allowing workers to be there on a day when it should have realised banks would be targeted.

"I am shocked, devastated," he says. "It will make me rethink whether I will ever throw a petrol bomb again." Yet, a few minutes later, he tells me that he will do just that if faced with a line of policemen who threaten him and his "comrades".

"When one of us is killed in a non-combat situation, it doesn't even get reported. I said people were going to die in Greece. This isn't the G20 protest outside RBS; this is about people's lives. Everyone here will be affected in some shape or form."

He believes Greece is at a potentially revolutionary moment – a point of view held by virtually no one except anarchists, communists and the fringe left – and, while he sympathises with the three innocent bank workers, mostly he is disappointed that the cause has been set back, the revolutionary momentum lost. The deaths have given even the anarchists pause for thought, and the evening's battles in Omonia and the neighbouring district of Exarchia have been less extensive than might otherwise have been the case.

The general strike, the mass demonstration and the deaths occur on my third day in Greece, a country now in such crisis that it is being painted as an international pariah. "This is the biggest crisis for Greece since the dictatorship [the 'rule of the colonels' from 1967-74]," says novelist Petros Tatsopoulos, at his flat in the northern suburbs of Athens, two days before the killings. "But this is not only our fault. There has been a chain reaction from the [subprime mortgage] crisis starting in the US two years ago, and Greece was the weakest link in the chain in Europe. Traders have been gambling on the bankruptcy of Greece, and that is a very dirty game."

Tatsopoulos accepts Greece is now the "black goat" of Europe – it takes me a while to grasp the slight difference between the English and Greek expressions – but again stresses it is not solely the fault of his country. The collapse in relations between Greece and Germany – the latter was tardy in agreeing the loans needed to prop up Greece – becomes evident. "The Germans think we are the black goat, and that there would be no problems in the euro-zone if Greece wasn't a member," he says. "But the Greeks think the Germans are the last people to talk, because they didn't pay reparations to us after the occupation in the second world war."

The number of tourists from Germany is predicted to drop by two-thirds this summer, a further disaster for an economy danger-ously dependent on tourism and the service sector. Tatsopoulos foresees the severe public sector cuts and tax rises imposed by the EU and International Monetary Fund – the quid pro quo for their £95bn bailout package – provoking a social crisis; particularly as the country is being led by an ostensibly socialist government. "The Greek people can't stand any more," he says. "Greece is a very expensive country; prices are very high, but salaries are already low, and they won't be able to take more cuts in wages. There will be a revolt in the streets."

The taxi driver who takes me from Tatsopoulos's flat to Syntagma Square, home of the Greek parliament, tells me in broken English how fearful the public are. In part, he blames jour-nalists. "They have made the people scared. The people don't know what they should do to get out of this." He also says journalists should have warned of the gathering crisis. "I think they are taking money from the government and the banks," he says. Greeks, several people tell me, are great conspiracy theorists.

There have been smaller daily demonstrations in Syntagma Square in the run-up to Wednesday's mass demo. Now it is the turn of the town hall workers, and John Maravelakis, who is sell-ing copies of *Workers Solidarity*, explains why he has come. "If the working class succeed in their conflict with the government and stop this offensive, things are going to be better for Greece. Otherwise, we are going to live in hell. Working conditions will be destroyed, we will earn less, and there will be no jobs for younger people."

Maravelakis describes his paper as representing the anti-capitalist left, and has no time for George Papandreou's government. "We have a socialist government like Stalin was a socialist in Russia. They did not vote for Papandreou last October to implement monetarist policies. That is why people are angry."

That anger is palpable everywhere. That afternoon, I am sitting outside a cafe close to Syntagma, when a waiter offers to put up an awning. "No, I like the sun," I say, "the good Greek sun." "That's all we have left," he says. I laugh. "Don't laugh," he says. "We don't have the motivation right now to go to work. We hear bad news every day, and that affects us in a bad way. We are responsible for this, because we are electing the same people every time to be the government. They took the money, most of them; they are corrupt. And now they ask us to make sacrifices. We didn't steal the money. My salary here is €700 a month. I can't afford to pay more taxes or lose my Christmas and Easter bonuses." Greeks call those bonuses the "13th and 14th salaries", and the fact they are being removed is cited repeatedly.

Why has Greece reached this desperate state, I ask Alexis Papahelas, executive editor of the national newspaper *Kathimerini* and Greece's best-known journalist, when I meet him at his paper's offices overlooking the Aegean. "Politicians failed to exercise any kind of leadership," he says. "They let populism take over. And the public have been in denial. Somebody said to me recently it was all media hype, just like swine flu – that nothing would happen in the end. Well, we are going through the realisation process right now, and this week's announcements were the final shock. People now recognise it's for real, it's going to change our lives, and there's no going back. But somebody has to sell them some hope. We need a positive narrative about how Greece can get out of this."

What will the political impact be? "It's very hard to predict," Papahelas says. "People are looking for a messiah. They'd like some successful businessman, a Berlusconi figure, to come forward, and that is a scary thought. Papandreou has one more chance to re-establish his government, but I think the period of pain will be too long."

Like many pundits in Greece, Papahelas points to the dead weight of the public sector as the single biggest factor dragging Greece down, making the government deficit impossible to deal with, and killing enterprise. "It's been the dream of every kid coming out of high school or university to be appointed some-where in the state apparatus – to get a permanent job on good money and not necessarily work hard. That's over. It delivered jobs for a while, but now the state is bankrupt."

Tax evasion is also endemic: the black economy accounts for almost 30% of the total economy. Inefficiency is rife: everyone points to the education system, where the pupil-teacher ratio is the lowest in Europe (about seven to one), yet standards in state schools are relatively poor.

Neoliberal economists, such as former finance minister Stefanos Manos, believe Greece needs a Margaret Thatcher, will-ing to take on vested interests, sweep away the occupational closed shops, and sack hundreds of thousands of state employees. Others, while admiring his ideological purity, think the cure would prob-ably kill the patient.

The novelist and cultural commentator Takis Theodoropoulos, whom I meet at the foot of the Acropolis shortly after it has been occupied by protesting trade unionists, likens Greece's current condition to emerging from a nightclub at dawn. A cultural conservative with a shock of grey hair, he believes that the past five years have been a social, as well as an economic, disaster, marked by an obsession with materialism, the rejection of trad-itional Greek values, and a belief that people could spend as much as they liked without ever having to pay.

"We transformed Greece into a nightclub," he says, "but how long can you live in a nightclub? It's not only a matter that at five in the morning, you have to pay the bill. There's also the fact that psychologically you get out and you are ruined. You are a wreck. This is a society which is tired and depressed, profoundly depressed. That is not just a privilege of Greek society – the whole of European society is more or less depressed – but I don't know how we are going to get out of here."

Theodoropoulos, who has mined Greek history in his novels and essays, says that in many ways Greece's travails mirror the collapse of Athenian society that Plato described in *The Republic*. Perhaps the mention of Plato cheers him up, because he suggests the current crisis might offer a form of catharsis. "In Greek, the word 'crisis' has two meanings," he explains. "One is the same as in English, a situation which is uncertain and not under control. But it also means the intellectual energy you need in order to realise what's happening to you. In Greek you can say, 'This man is in a crisis,' but you can also say, 'This man has crisis.' That is our only hope."

Theodoropoulos may be able to see the cathartic benefits of social purification, but the workers I meet each day protesting in Syntagma Square think more viscerally. When the teachers hold their own demo on Tuesday afternoon, I ask Elena Tsiadi whether she really believes the protests will achieve anything. "I don't know if we are going to achieve anything," she says. "Realistically speaking, I don't think we will. But when you are led to the corner, you have to react. We want someone to pay for what we will suffer. In Iceland, they went bankrupt and already six ministers are on trial. Here, we have a series of governments which have committed crimes, and no one is paying. They are asking us to pay the bill. Greeks are a particular kind of people who say, 'We are willing to work, willing to suffer, willing to make sacrifices,' as long as we have leaders who pay first. Somebody has got to set an example."

The following day, I am back in Syntagma with the huge crowd – estimated by the police at 30,000, by the protesters at almost double that – marking the day of the general strike. For an hour or so, the crowd confronts the police ringing parliament. Even before the masked anarchists in their black uniforms arrive, there are violent scenes, with bottles, sticks and metal railings being thrown by small groups of protesters on the ramparts at each side of the building. This, though, is containable, and has a theatrical element, the crowd venting their feelings like an audience as the mini-battles play themselves out.

But once the anarchists enter the square, with the police in pursuit firing tear gas, the atmosphere changes instantly. The gas chokes you and makes your eyes stream. Anarchists wielding heavy mallets, with which they break off pieces of concrete to use as weapons, are arguing furiously with middle-aged women in the fleeing crowd. The latter accuse them of having wrecked the march, though the extent of the disaster is not yet clear.

I try to take refuge alongside other journalists in the parliament building, which commands a view of the entire square – by now a battlefield. But the policeman on the gate tells me I lack the necessary permit. "No money, no honey," he says with a laugh. I pass a man in an immaculate suit who is clutching a handkerchief to his mouth, and ask him whether he works in the parliament building. "No, I am an honest Greek," he responds in a flash. He tells me he is a lawyer. "I wanted to be in the square with the people, but the stench is too much."

While the battle rages and before news of the deaths has emerged, I have to go to do a prearranged interview with Antonis Liakos, professor of modern history at the University of Athens. This must be the strangest interview I've ever conducted, because it takes place in a cafe only a couple of hundred metres away from Syntagma, in a pedestrianised street where people are still sitting outside, despite the whiff of tear gas from the square.

Liakos is critical of the austerity measures, and says the approach needs to be more "nuanced". A government with more bargaining power would, he suggests, be able to pick and choose which of the measures to apply. Like several of those I talk to, he argues that you can't have European monetary union without political union, because the states will never be in synch economically. Many leading figures in Greece now back political union, and it is possible to foresee inexorable pressure towards a superstate that would leave the UK, always lukewarm on matters European, entirely out in the cold. The Greek crisis is the first chapter of a Europe-wide story that could go anywhere.

Liakos believes there is a danger that, as in the 1930s, economic crisis may encourage the rise of anti-democratic groups across Europe. "We don't know how things are going to change in the rest of Europe," he says. "If Spain is in the same situation as Greece, then the whole euro stability pact will come under threat. The worst scenario is that European monetary union is going to sink. Imagine you are living in 1932: you can't anticipate the second world war and the catastrophe that was derived from the economic crisis. Perhaps we, too, can't see what is before our eyes."

After the meeting, I return to the square. The battle is over, an eerie calm has descended, and the pall of gas is dispersing. The police are still lined up in front of the Tomb of the Unknown Soldier, just beneath the parliament, but the only people left are two young men sitting on the kerb holding red flags. One, a student who has smothered his face in special white paint that mitigates the effects of the gas, tells me his friend has two degrees but can't get a job, and he doesn't want to be in the same position when he graduates.

I ask whether, at the height of the battle, the Tomb came under assault. "No," says the student, "we respect the monument. It is not the enemy, the cops are not the enemy – it's the people inside the parliament who are the enemy, but they don't come out."

At that point, another young man who has been listening to our conversation approaches. He disagrees with the student. "Just look at this," he says, pointing to the line of policemen in front of the Tomb. "People gave their lives in the war so that this monument to freedom could be built. Now the police stop the people from getting to it. The monument is shit. Today we have lost our freedom."

We don't know it yet, but on the broad avenue that leads down to the square, three people have lost much more – their lives. This peculiar calm in Syntagma, with Japanese tourists taking pictures of the debris, policemen slowly removing their gas masks and lighting cigarettes, and a young man walking past holding a broken violin, precedes a storm that will shortly break, exploding the myth that violence can be ritualised, theatrical, innocent.

The staff of the ornate Grand Bretagne hotel, which adorns one side of the square, are already scrubbing the anarchists' graffiti from its marble facade, but the lives lost today cannot be restored. Greece's monumental debit column now has its starkest entry.

7 May 2010

# The tug of war for No 10

## PATRICK WINTOUR

Gordon Brown and David Cameron were locked in a constitutional standoff early today, as the Tory leader claimed Labour had lost the right to govern – but the prime minister, confident that the Tories had not secured an overall majority, said he would look to see if he could form an alliance with the Liberal Democrats.

With more than half the seats declared, Cameron asserted that his party was on course to gain more seats than at any time in 80 years. He said it was clear that the country wants change that requires new leadership.

Amid vastly different regional swings, the results also showed strong Labour resilience outside the south, and the Lib Dems had badly underperformed against euphoric expectations of only a week ago. It looked as if they might end up with only 62 seats, down one.

Nick Clegg, the Lib Dem leader, was said to be depressed by the result, and wary of forming "a coalition of the defeated" that might be seen as ignoring the public mood. Brown flew to London from his Scottish constituency to offer the Lib Dems the chance to form a stable government, culminating in a referendum on electoral reform for the Commons.

Clegg will wait to see the final result and meet his new group of MPs tomorrow. Some in his party will claim he can form a stable coalition for two years to deliver recovery and political reform, but others will be nervous of appearing to shun the electorate's will.

Shadow ministers warned that the bond markets would not tolerate the lack of stable government. The shadow chancellor, George Osborne, told Labour to "get real" about trying to cling to power.

But Cameron took a more measured tone, saying: "I believe it's already clear that the Labour government has lost its mandate to govern our country. The Conservative party is on target to win more seats at this election than we have done at any election in perhaps as long as 80 years. What's clear from these results is that the country, our country, wants change. That change is going to require new leadership and we will stand ready to do all we can to help bring that leadership."

The Tory leader, reflecting the coming battle for power with Brown, promised to put the national interest first in the "hours ahead, or perhaps longer than the hours ahead". Speaking after he had been returned in Kirkcaldy with an increased majority, Brown openly held out the prospect of trying to secure a coalition with the Lib Dems built round electoral reform. He said: "The outcome of this country's vote is not yet known, but my duty to the country coming out of this election is to play my part in Britain having a strong, stable and principled government able to lead Britain into sustained economic recovery and able to implement our commitments to far-reaching reform upon which there is a growing consensus in our country."

Brown's aides said they would try to form a progressive alliance if the Tories did not score as high as 320 seats. Private talks between intermediaries started almost as soon as the polls closed, but with such conflicting results few were willing to predict the outcome.

The former home secretary Jacqui Smith was the most high-profile victim of the expenses scandal, losing her ultra-marginal Redditch seat by 6,000 votes to the Tories. Other Labour casualties included Vera Baird, Mike O'Brien and Bill Rammell, but Ed Balls held his seat. Defeated Liberal Democrats included Lembit Opik and Evan Harris.

Lord Mandelson described the result as a cliffhanger while an openly bewildered Ed Miliband, the energy secretary, said the people had spoken, but "we don't know quite what they have said".

7 MAY 2010

# Parliament is hung, drawn and quartered

MARINA HYDE

Set your sights on adventure, voters. Britain is heading for a parliament not so much hung as drawn and quartered, while Lembit Opik has lost his seat, leaving the vital All Party Asteroid Defence Committee without its leader, and the human race in deadly peril. Cleggmania? Beginning to assume all the historic import of an argument in a car park, though paradoxically its figurehead could yet hold Britain's future in his hand.

"What I will do is put the national interest first," insisted a distinctly nervous-looking David Cameron in Witney. But earlier had come news apparently fashioned to restore hope to a grateful nation: in the event of a hung parliament, Mr Gordon Brown would himself try to form a coalition government. So the PM's glass was very much half full. Of mescaline. There was "a growing consensus for political reform", he euphemised in Kirkcaldy, suggesting that come lunchtime he really could be on the TV sofas explaining that he's always been a collegiate sort of politician, which even by his own standards would surely be the most screamingly hilarious whopper of recent years.

Whether the necessary preparations for the introduction of martial law were already under way was unclear but the serially smooth rode the uncertainty. Owing to his supernatural powers of regeneration, Peter Mandelson used the energies released by projected seat losses to form a psychic cage around his personage, from within which he was able to toy with the likes of Theresa May. "You're losing your legitimacy to govern," Theresa scoffed at him. "But you don't seem to be acquiring it," his lordship smiled pityingly.

It was "a decisive rejection of Gordon Brown", explained the Tories. It was "nothing like an endorsement of David Cameron", countered Labour. Questions about what Nick Clegg would do were "way above my pay grade", said Lembit, which was certainly accurate as he no longer has a pay grade, while the Queen was presumably dreading the post-Diana retread of a week to come, complete with fatuous YOUR COUNTRY NEEDS YOU, MA'AM headlines.

Fittingly for a nation in the twilight of its first world days, the Electoral Commission swiftly announced an investigation into the inability of many to cast their vote, while in Sheffield, some shut out of polling stations marched on Nick Clegg's house. The #nickcleggsfault Twitter hashtag had finally moved from the virtual to the physical world.

As for the visuals ... there's really nothing like a month of gruelling campaigning and the wildly unforgiving glare of high definition television to showcase the political class at its most cadaverously horrifying. The likes of Eric Pickles and Ann Widdecombe looked like the provisional wing of the Addams Family.

On the BBC, Andrew Neil was at the London Eye hosting some sort of Imbeciles' Ball, or certainly a gathering of media liggers who wouldn't be the most enormous loss to British public life were the luxury boat on which they were gathered to be torpedoed. Throughout the night, we heard from a selection of people whose opinions were so fist-gnawingly moronic or teeth-grindingly irrelevant that caring about them would be grounds for being stripped of the vote in perpetuity.

"Yay David Cameron!" glossed Joan Collins, channelling Noam Chomsky. "What did you think of the exit poll?" Neil asked Bruce Forsyth. "I ... I thought it was high," gibbered Bruce eventually, before trying to get fellow guests to bellow his catchphrase at him.

In the middle ages, some sorcerers practised tyromancy, which was basically divination by cheese – foretelling the future according to the omens found in cheese. The formation of holes, the pattern of the mould – all these seem somehow the very definition of predictive science when compared with the practice, several centuries of alleged progress later, of asking the tenuously coherent host of *Strictly Come Dancing* to extrapolate an election exit poll.

Still, though that may have been the first occasion to deploy the phrase "a new low" on the night, it looks likely to be very far from the last in the coming days. We can only await Britain's next lurch into self-parodic chaos with the baffled laughter it deserves.

8 MAY 2010

# Voted Clegg, got Cameron

LETTERS TO THE EDITOR

Voted Clegg, Got Cameron. Not happy.
*Pete Dorey, Cardiff*

Not enough staff on the polling stations? And not enough voting slips? Can't vote? These are efficiency savings. Get used to it.
*Geoff Fimister, Newcastle upon Tyne*

Is there any better comment on the general election results than Roger McGough's The Leader? I wanna be the leader / I wanna be the leader / Can I be the leader / Can I? I can? / Promise? Promise? / Yippee I'm the leader / I'm the leader / OK what shall we do?
*Dr Hilary Lloyd Yewlett, Cardiff*

Brown lost because, despite his manifest leadership strengths, he's irredeemably tainted by the mistakes of the last 10 years. Clegg lost by lacking the courage to get off the fence, and Cameron failed to win by lacking the courage and leadership to reform even his own party. Could this be the first election to result in the replacement of all three party leaders?
*David Lewin, Oxford*

I have little doubt Brown, Clegg and Cameron could sit round a table and easily sort out the election result. Of course that's Mrs Brown, Mrs Clegg and Mrs Cameron.
*Pete Bibby, Sheffield*

What a wonderful opportunity for our newly elected representatives to hang up their party hats and prove their ability to work
together for the good of our fragile country. Do we think they
are up to the task – or will their party games drag us further into
the mire?
*David Evans, Stonehouse, Gloucestershire*

Judging by his success with the Ulster Unionists and the European
rightwingers, David Cameron doesn't really have a great track
record on doing deals with other parties does he?
*Pat Oddy, Yarm, Cleveland*

I should like to check a couple of things in the British
Constitution. Where can I buy a copy?
*Julian Oddy, Weymouth, Dorset*

11 MAY 2010

# Gordon Brown: a gifted man, ground down by the success of a rival

MICHAEL WHITE

Few of Gordon Brown's friends and admirers would have predicted
during his dominant decade as chancellor that his life's journey
from the Presbyterian manse in Kirkcaldy to No 10 would end in
such a painful exit. Many of his enemies in Labour's ranks and
beyond predicted it long ago. Both camps will regret it.

Both also knew a man who had been a gifted student politician who ran rings around the stuffy Edinburgh University establishment, rose almost effortlessly through Labour's ranks to be shadow chancellor, but saw the ultimate prize snatched from him by a younger rival, less substantial but more confident: his friend and nemesis, Tony Blair. "You've ruined my life," became a taunt he would hurl at Blair. It gnawed at him.

The paradox of Brown's career is that of a man blessed with intellectual gifts, drive and ambition who was simultaneously cursed with a debilitating self-doubt that easily turned to mistrust and suspicion of all but the most devoted allies. For every MP who spoke of his personal acts of kindness and his high-minded strivings to curb child poverty – not just in Britain – another would recall brusque, high-handed rudeness.

Blair, with whom Brown was yoked in a dysfunctional political marriage throughout the New Labour project, would count himself as a friend, one who feared rather than hoped that his unavoidable successor would not rise to the challenge of leadership and reinvent himself, liberated after finally taking over in June 2007.

For a few months it looked as if it might prove so. Brown handled a series of crises, floods, Islamist bombs and a cattle cull, with quiet competence. He set out plans to decentralise Britain and make good the more evident weaknesses of Blairism, not least its disregard for civil liberties and taste for celebrity.

But two developments soon derailed the new prime minister's hopes.

In August 2007 the first cracks appeared in the international banking system, cracks that would lead to the run on the Northern Rock bank – the first in Britain for 150 years – and its eventual nationalisation by New Labour.

Almost in parallel Brown allowed speculation to build towards a snap general election in October of that year. In theory it would smash yet another Conservative challenger as well as secure Brown his own mandate for five years. But the Tories pulled a rabbit out of the hat – a thoroughly regressive promise to slash the unpopular inheritance tax – and bounced back in the polls.

Brown blinked and cancelled the election, foolishly denying that he had been influenced by the polls. The subsequent jibe about "Bottler Brown" crystallised voters' doubts about his character and capacity to lead.

Had not Blairites and officials muttered for years about his inability to take the rapid-fire decisions needed at No 10, but not No 11? Had they not complained about his temper, his bullying treatment of colleagues, Blair among them?

This fateful judgment meant Brown would prove unable to regain lost ground via the substantial and serious success of his premiership: the decision to recapitalise British banks after the collapse of Lehman Brothers in 2008.

As the western banking system tottered it was Brown, his underrated chancellor, Alistair Darling, and their officials who moved first on 8 October to pump billions into banks to prevent a wider collapse. Other beleaguered governments followed the British lead and the system survived.

The following spring Brown chaired a crucial meeting of the G20 industrialised states to coordinate a global economic stimulus to fend off another Great Depression, to boost IMF lending, thwart protectionism and uphold the world trading system.

Again Brown's role was praised. But his enemies were already making a concerted effort to persuade voters that, whatever good calls Downing Street had made in the crisis – much better than the Tory opposition, economic analysts agreed – the former chancellor had taken crucial decisions that either caused or compounded Britain's unique vulnerability in the crisis. The result? A huge rise in the public borrowing deficit.

Much of that deterioration was attributable directly to the reckless profligacy of the banks in repackaging and selling on questionable debt in ways which – theoretically – spread the risk, but when the bubble burst proved to have contaminated all but the most prudent.

Gordon Brown's role in this cast a long shadow over a chancellorship that Blair had routinely praised as the greatest of modern times. During what became known as the "Great Moderation" – low interest rates, low inflation, a record decade of economic growth – Brown himself routinely boasted that he had put an end to "Tory boom and bust".

Now the sharpest recession since the 1930s had proved that to be a hollow claim. Worse than that, Brown's critics were able to claim that in hiving over responsibility for regulating the banking system from the Bank of England to the Financial Services Authority, his first, bold initiative as chancellor in 1997 had fatally weakened it. The FSA was fretting about solvency when liquidity was the problem.

But the wounding charge in 2010 has become Brown's creation of a structural hole in the budget, more serious than the cyclical hit that the recession made in tax receipts, at least 4% of GDP. "Brown used bankers' taxes to pay nurses and it was unsustainable," as one shadow minister warned. The failure to build up reserves during the boom years will make recovery that much harder.

How it all happened is intertwined with Brown's own character and experience. Early on, the assistant lecturer turned TV producer had shown signs of ducking challenges where the outcome could not be guaranteed, unwilling to take on the frontrunner for Labour's nomination in the Hamilton byelection, one George Robertson, as early as 1978.

Robin Cook, five years his senior, was an early Scots rival. But Blair, the callow young lawyer elected with him in Margaret

Thatcher's landslide year of 1983, was always a protégé. It was Brown who was promoted to be shadow trade secretary by Neil Kinnock in 1989, then to be shadow chancellor when John Smith took over in 1992. Blair trailed.

As such Brown made himself unpopular by taking a tougher stance on public spending pledges to restore Labour's credibility, a reason for Blair's subsequent success, he persuaded himself. He was luckier over sterling's brief membership of the European monetary system (EMS), forerunner of the euro. Smith and Brown backed it, but when sterling was rudely ejected in September 1992 John Major took all the blame.

The crisis allowed sterling to regain its competitiveness, opening the road to the boom decade. Brown learned a lesson. Later, when prime minister Blair became eager to take Britain into the new eurozone, his chancellor agreed in principle but announced "five tests" – dreamed up by his consigliere, Ed Balls, in a taxi – that would postpone it indefinitely. The Blair camp saw the euro dispute as yet another of tactics, not of principle, though it has proved to be one of New Labour's best calls.

When Blair faced down Brown over which of them would run for the Labour leadership after Smith's death in 1994, he promised Brown unique sway over economic domestic policy. It allowed him to build a power base that would hamper Blair's (sometimes ill-considered) pro-market plans for reform.

Often there was merit in the case being made by both men and goodwill between them too. They spent billions to reverse, albeit only modestly, the Tory legacy of child poverty and inequality. They rebuilt schools and doubled the NHS budget – slashing waiting times – to better effect than the *Daily Mail* would concede. They introduced the national minimum wage.

What so often poisoned their dealings and repeatedly mangled New Labour's effectiveness in its early, popular years was the personal dimension. Blair rightly felt his chancellor was blocking him. Brown felt with equal justice that Blair had promised to step aside as early as 2003. Witnesses confirm both views.

So it continued, with barely coded sniping at Labour conferences. In 2004 Blair said he would not seek a fourth term: it did not heal the wound. In September 2006 Blair, weakened by the Iraq debacle, was forced to tell party activists it would be his last conference as leader.

Brown said he was eager for a contest (a mistake Blair felt he had made in not beating Brown openly in 1994) but did his best to organise a "coronation". Potential rivals were undermined and more than 300 Labour MPs lined up to nominate him. Within six months some were regretting it. Despite his dogged election campaign this month, one which turned looming disaster into a manageable defeat, more and more have abandoned him in recent days.

It will not have been easy for Brown to make last night's decision; he believes he is the man to steer Britain out of recession. But he will have been persuaded to put party first.

The tragedy is that Brown's many admirable qualities and instincts – his social conscience and moral compass – could have been more constructively and generously deployed in shaping Blair's salesman's skills.

An introvert who, some say, could never live up to his father's high expectations, his gloomy side must have been enhanced by his traumatic experience of near-blindness in his teens. Blair's sunny disposition must have rankled; the loss of his first child, Jennifer Jane, was a further cruel blow.

Brown made his private comfort a low priority compared with his career, his love life as neglected as his chaotic flats.

Sarah Brown brought domestic happiness and a young family to his life relatively late, he is 59. It should provide a much-needed balm in his hour of defeat.

11 MAY 2010

# Only one coalition is legitimate: Lab-Lib

## POLLY TOYNBEE

This is the moment of truth, when finally and irreversibly the Liberal Democrats have to define themselves, something they have for so long avoided. Whose side are they really on? The establishment has leaned heavily on the Lib Dems to suggest that they have no such choice but must put into power the party with most seats. The bombast of a rightwing press is doing its damnedest to dragoon them into putting Cameron into Downing Street, by threatening the wrath of the people. The question now is whether Lib Dem leaders have the intellectual, political and moral fibre to resist bogus claims that "legitimacy" obliges them to favour the Conservatives.

The Lib Dem leadership must not be spooked by an inauthentic view of legitimacy. Nick Clegg knows full well from his European experience – where coalition-building of every kind is the everyday norm – that legitimacy falls on whatever grouping can command enough votes in a parliament to form a government. That is often not the party that happens on its own to have more seats than any other, while still failing to represent the majority sentiment in a country. After all these years of advocating pluralism, the Lib Dems will surely not be trapped by old first-past-the-post thinking that "strong and stable government" must be the least plural.

True legitimacy resides in a coalition of principle between the parties that stood for election on the most closely shared values. Their voters are the ones that confer legitimacy. Most who voted

Lib Dem would feel the deal illegitimate if they found their vote diverted into the Cameron camp. Lib-Con may work locally, but never nationally. The Lib Dem manifesto has almost nothing in common with Conservatism, nor with what Nick Clegg rightly called the "nutters" among the Tories' EU partners. Cameron's marriage bonus, the inheritance tax gift to the richest, Trident, shrinking Sure Start, and an austerity budget cutting £6bn from the fragile recovery within 50 days – these are not the principles Lib Dem voters chose. But tax reform to help the lower paid, closing tax loopholes for the rich, and electoral reform are core radical Lib Dem policies that they cannot legitimately abandon.

According to Ben Page of Ipsos Mori, the greater part of Lib Dem voters lean towards Labour, with only 22% leaning toward the Conservatives. That makes an alliance with Labour the more legitimate, as well as the expedient, choice. Turning to Cameron would mean quick death at the next election. Once the deal was done, the Lib Dems would soon be mangled, trampled and jettisoned. The Tories would trap the Lib Dems, who would fear being held responsible for bringing the government down. Nick Clegg would find himself with about as much influence as Tony Blair had in Washington once he had signed up in blood to the Iraq war, poodles both.

With Gordon Brown gone and a new Labour leader installed, the fear of "illegitimacy" will be doubled. No doubt the Tory press will hammer on about another "unelected" prime minister – but prime ministers are not elected, they are not presidents. Legitimacy springs from the clear case that Britain is not a Conservative country. It has become an essentially social democratic one since the Tories last won in 1992.

Any doubt about that was laid to rest in last week's election. If Conservatism cannot win a majority under dream circumstances with every fair wind blowing in its favour, it has become a minority rump belief in British life. Labour was on its knees with a singularly disliked leader. Cameron was better by far than the Tories' last four leaders, astute in trying to adapt his party to changed times. The crash and its aftermath have unseated governments everywhere, and Labour was partly blamed. The Conservatives outspent the other parties by millions, sending Lord Ashcroft's gilded missiles into the marginals. After 13 years, it really did feel like time for a change. So for Cameron to win a meagre 36% of the vote was a phenomenal failure. Not a failure of Cameron's personally, nor of his campaign. The Conservatives were beaten because this is no longer a Conservative country.

Here at last is the historic chance to heal the pointless rift between two near-identical progressive parties, divided only by history, tradition and a rotten voting system. Clegg would badly misread the mood of this country if he opted for the Conservatives now – despite their "final" AV offer late yesterday.

The Labour offer laid before the Lib Dems is, instead, a coalition of equals, forming a government under a new leader, together with the SDLP, Plaid Cymru, SNP and others. The conventional British view is that a multi-party coalition would be unstable, but that's how most of Europe is governed. It would be in none of their like-minded interests to bring down this coalition government. There are few Labour policies that would not be negotiable under a fresh leader, able to think anew about everything. Who would be there to die in a ditch for ID cards or 28-day detention?

Elections change everything – that's what they are for. A radical blend of reform to the tax system, a splitting of the banks between casino and retail, positive towards Europe, protective towards services for the vulnerable, creating financial stability in the joint council with all parties that the Lib Dems propose – why not? Above all, real electoral reform. The days of triangulating would be over, and each party would improve the other.

Suddenly everything looks possible. Not easy, but a legitimate coalition of the voters' expressed wishes.

11 MAY 2010

# Election live blog

ANDREW SPARROW

8.13AM: Who's going to govern the country? We're into day five of the post-election power vacuum and, as Patrick Wintour reports in the *Guardian* today, the Lib Dems are saying today is "crunch time". It looks as though we might get a decision before the day is over. But I said almost exactly the same 24 hours ago, at the start of yesterday's live blog, and events didn't turn out quite the way most of us were expecting.

Nick Clegg faces a very difficult decision. If he forms a pact with the Tories, there will be howls of protest from his progressive allies on the left. If he goes into coalition with Labour, he will be accused of propping up the party that lost the general election.

There isn't an easy solution and Clegg's leadership skills are about to be tested to the hilt. Will he be decisive? Can he hold his party together? Can he explain what he is doing to the public? And can he use this moment to reshape politics, showing himself to be a master of events, rather than someone who has been constrained by them? We'll find out soon.

8.39AM: George Osborne, the shadow chancellor, has just been on the *Today* programme. He dismissed suggestions that the Tories could form a minority government.

9.31AM: David Cameron and Nick Clegg both made statements as they left their respective homes this morning. Cameron said it was "decision time" for the Lib Dems and urged them to make the right one. Clegg said: "The discussions between the political parties have now reached a critical and final phase. I'm as impatient as anybody else to get on with this, to resolve matters one way or another."

Quote of the day so far has come from former home secretary David Blunkett, who was on BBC Radio 4's *Today* programme. He warned that a "coalition of the defeated" between Labour and the Lib Dems would "lose very badly" at the next general election. He added: "Can you trust the Liberal Democrats? They are behaving like every harlot in history."

10.16AM: The key event this morning will be the meeting between the Labour negotiating team and the Lib Dem negotiating team which has just started in the House of Commons. A Labour-Lib Dem coalition would be dependent on the support of other smaller parties. But Labour is not planning to strike a formal coalition agreement with them. Labour and the Lib Dems would not have a majority, but they would be confident that parties such as the SNP would not vote against the Queen's speech. Labour seems to be planning to negotiate with parties like the SNP on a case-by-case basis.

10.47AM: Senior Tories have been trying very hard to be polite about the Liberal Democrats. When William Hague briefed journalists in the House of Commons last night, he adopted the tone of someone who was mildly disappointed by the behaviour of his negotiating partners but determined not to let one episode spoil a promising relationship. George Osborne took much the same tack in the broadcast interviews he gave this morning.

**10.52AM:** My colleague Julia Kollewe is writing a market turmoil live blog. She says the government's auction of gilts went very well this morning. There was speculation that the markets might take fright at the prospect of a Labour-Lib Dem minority government. But it does not seem to stop people wanting to lend money to the government.

**11.20AM:** Nick Clegg has just left his south-west London home. "I'm certainly hopeful of getting a resolution as quickly as possible," was all he would say.

**11.37AM:** Gary Gibbon on his Channel 4 blog has been speaking to MPs who were at the Lib Dem meeting last night. He thinks a Tory-Lib Dem deal is now looking more probable.

**11.51AM:** Caroline Lucas, the new Green party MP, would not enter a formal coalition with Labour and the Lib Dems (or the Tories and the Lib Dems). She will vote in the Commons on a case-by-case basis.

**12.09PM:** Lord Kinnock told the BBC's *Daily Politics* show that a Labour-Lib Dem deal would last, but that there needs to be a decision soon: "It's certainly possible, and a deal would be durable over a limited period of time, 24 to 36 months, say, with a clear declaration that an election were held in that time."

**12.19PM:** I've been fielding some interesting questions from readers and colleagues. Here's an attempt to provide some answers.

*How long will this last?* David Cameron has said he wants a decision very soon. Waiting five days for a government may seem like a long time. But by international standards it is not long at all

*Would Labour MPs vote in favour of a referendum on PR?* Most would, but not all. Some Labour MPs are strongly committed to first-past-the-post.

*Do Labour and the Lib Dems need to get the smaller parties to join a coalition?* No. Gordon Brown is prime minister and he is entitled to remain prime minister until defeated in the House of Commons on the Queen's speech or a motion of confidence. A Labour-Lib Dem government would have to cooperate with the smaller parties on a case-by-case basis, but it would not need a formal agreement.

*Is a national government, involving Labour and the Tories, unthinkable?* Yes. At one stage Frank Field floated the idea, but there is no support for it at Westminster.

12.23PM: Douglas Alexander, Labour's general election coordinator, has ruled out a coalition with the SNP. "I can't envisage circumstances in which we enter coalition with the SNP," he said.

12.53PM: My colleague Polly Toynbee has been taking soundings from some Lib Dems and she writes on Comment is free that they are getting the impression that some on the Labour side are not serious about striking a deal.

1.01PM: This could be significant. Conservative Way Forward, a Thatcherite ginger group within the Conservative party, has issued a statement saying it has "considerable concern" about the state of the coalition talks with Lib Dems. It wants David Cameron to form a minority Conservative government.

1.27PM: The Unite union (Labour's largest single financial backer) has issued a letter backing a Labour-Lib Dem deal. The letter, from the joint general secretaries Tony Woodley and Derek Simpson, has been sent to the 100-odd MPs who belong to the Unite parliamentary group.

**1.31PM:** Sir Malcolm Rifkind's language is getting more colourful by the hour. This morning he was expressing his anger at the Lib Dems. Now he is saying that Gordon Brown's attempt to cling on to power "comes straight out of the Robert Mugabe school of politics".

**1.36PM:** The Tory negotiating team is talking to the Lib Dems this afternoon. William Hague has just announced this on Twitter: "Will be returning to the Cabinet Office shortly to resume negotiations with the Liberal Democrats."

**1.48PM:** David Cameron and Nick Clegg met for an hour this morning, Lib Dem sources have revealed.

**1.54PM:** Ed Miliband, a member of the Labour negotiating team, told the BBC that there was a "good atmosphere" in his talks with the Lib Dem team this morning. He said there were "many points of agreement", but certain points had to be "worked through".

**2.00PM:** The Lib Dem negotiating team has gone into the Cabinet Office for their talks with the Tories. They did not say anything on the way in. The Conservatives are coming now.

**2.52PM:** Andy Burnham has said that Labour should "respect the results of the general election". He has clearly indicated that he is opposed to a Labour-Lib Dem deal. Burnham said that David Blunkett – who set out his views in a *Guardian* article today – has spoken with "real authority" on this matter. Burnham is a member of the cabinet. If a Labour-Lib Dem coalition does happen, will he resign? Or is he only speaking out because he has concluded that the Labour-Lib Dem talks are heading for the buffers?

**3.06PM:** On the BBC just now the Tory blogger Iain Dale said that he thought Nick Clegg and Vince Cable were both firmly in favour of deal with Cameron, but that they were being opposed by Lord Ashdown and Sir Menzies Campbell.

**3.19PM:** Sam Coates from the *Times* has put this on Twitter: "Against Lab-Lib coalition at Cabinet yesterday – Burnham Straw Byrne Khan Ainsworth."

**3.48PM:** A deal between the Tories and the Lib Dems is now looking likely. The Lib Dem negotiating team is now talking again to the Tories. Last night the Conservatives did not have any plans to talk to the Lib Dems again. William Hill have stopped taking bets on who the Lib Dems will form a pact with after a flood of money came in from punters betting on a Tory-Lib Dem deal.

**4.00PM:** Laura Kuenssberg has just said on BBC News that she has seen bags being loaded into cars at the back of Downing Street. "Large hold-alls", she said. She is implying that the Browns are getting ready to leave.

**4.19PM:** Sky News has is running a news strap saying: "*Evening Standard* newspaper reports Gordon Brown has quit as prime minister." I've just called Downing Street. Brown is still prime minister. He has not resigned – yet.

**4.50PM:** Lord Mandelson has just left Downing Street. He was wearing his impassive, non-responsive face as he got into his car. He did not respond to questions.

**4.56PM:** Isn't 24-hour news mad? Earlier I mentioned Laura Kuenssberg's observation that hold-alls were being loaded into a car at the back of Downing Street. She suggested that it might be a sign the Browns were leaving. A few minutes late the BBC reported that they did not belong to the Browns. Then someone suggested they might belong to the Darlings. Now Jon Sopel has said that they weren't the Darlings' either. It turns out they contained police kit.

5.00PM: This is good. We've got a picture of the notes on which Nick Clegg set out his negotiating demands. You can read Graeme Robertson and Allegra Stratton's story about it, and read the note itself, alongside the *Guardian*'s crib as to what it means.

5.15PM: George Pascoe-Watson, the former *Sun* political editor, thinks the Lib Dems will get six cabinet posts in a Tory-Lib Dem coalition, and that Nick Clegg will become deputy prime minister.

5.47PM: Events have moved very quickly in the last two hours. Westminster is now on standby for a change of government soon, perhaps tonight. Nothing has been announced formally, and journalists have been making what has now become a collective assessment on the basis of unattributable briefings and nods and winks. But *Gordon Brown is expected to resign as prime minister at some point soon.*

6.21PM: Labour's national executive committee met this afternoon. Members agreed to meet "in the days and weeks ahead" to determine the timetable and the procedures for electing a new leader.

6.35PM: According to Nick Robinson, Gordon Brown and his colleagues are putting a brave face on things in No 10. Robinson has just said that he's been told they've been telling jokes. Brown is with his closest allies: Ed Balls, Lord Mandelson, Sue Nye, and

Douglas Alexander. Tony Blair has spoken to Brown by phone. New Labour started with Brown, Blair and Mandelson. As the government comes to an end, they're still yoked together.

7.10PM: Outside Downing Street they've set up the podium. Brown will be coming out soon to resign.

7.19PM: Brown is speaking. He says he is going to go to the Queen and resign. He will advise the Queen to invite the leader of the opposition to become prime minister. He wishes the new PM well.

7.22PM: Holding hands with Sarah, he goes back into Downing Street and comes out again with his children, John and Fraser. As a family, they walk hand in hand down to the car, which is not parked immediately outside the front door. Some of my colleagues find the pictures a bit sugary, but I found it sweet and touching.

7.49PM: Gordon Brown has finished his audience with the Queen. He is now heading to Labour HQ.

7.53PM: Brown has arrived at the Labour HQ on Victoria Street. Ed Miliband looked morose, Yvette Cooper gave Brown a warm hug, Douglas Alexander looked glum. Brown shook hands with and greeted a crowd of party workers. Then he went inside.

8.06PM: David Cameron is in the car on his way to the Palace now. But he seems to have to got stuck in traffic. He'll have to take it up with Boris.

8.29PM: David Cameron is prime minister, Sky tells us. In the old days these things used to appear in the *London Gazette*. Nowadays it's a newsflash on Sky.

**8.41PM**: David Cameron is leaving Buckingham Palace. Lord Mandelson has told the BBC that the Lib Dems were never serious about a pact with Labour.

**8.45PM**: Cameron is arriving in Downing Street, with his wife, Samantha. He says the Queen has asked him to form a government and he has accepted. He says he and Nick Clegg are forming a joint government. They are both leaders who want to put aside party interest and work in the national interest. I thought Cameron's speech was a bit lacklustre. It was very short of memorable phrases. But I suppose Cameron has had other things to worry about.

**9.12PM**: Simon Hughes has just told Sky that the coalition agreement covers a full four years.

**9.40PM**: Amid the excitement of the appointment of a new prime minister, a rather bitter war of words has broken out between Labour and the Liberal Democrats. They are both blaming each other for their failure to create a "progressive" coalition.

**10.23PM**: Cameron is addressing Tory MPs in the Commons. Clegg is addressing a joint meeting of Lib Dem MPs and the Lib Dem federal executive. Cameron has already been appointed prime minister and the new government is starting to tick into action. As far as we can tell, Tory and Lib Dem MPs seem delighted. But we still don't know the details of the agreement and backbench MPs are only now finding out. Effectively, they signed up to the deal before they had read the small print.

**11.06PM**: Downing Street has confirmed that Nick Clegg has been appointed deputy prime minister.

12.38AM: Nick Clegg is giving a press conference now. He starts with a tribute to Gordon Brown. And he says he wants to produce not just a new government, but a new kind of government.

12.51AM: David Cameron has just arrived home. At his west London home, not the new one.

1.00AM: That's it. Britain has got its first coalition government for more than 60 years. And Nick Clegg will be sitting in cabinet alongside Liam Fox and William Hague. Will it work? Who knows? But it is a bold project, and it will be certainly be interesting. We'll get our first good look at it tomorrow (rather, later today) when the Cameron cabinet is expected to meet for the first time. And we've also got a new (interim) Labour leader. And the Labour leadership contest will soon begin in earnest. Time for bed. Thanks for the comments.

*The above is an edited selection of posts from the live blog*

12 MAY 2010

# A political crapstorm, but no new world

MARINA HYDE

Having begun this election standing outside Buckingham Palace waiting for Gordon Brown to clock in and out of Her Majesty's car park, there was a certain symmetry to ending it in similar fashion, with the added bonus of being able to watch David Cameron's driver execute the same epic constitutional manoeuvre half an hour or so later.

It would be nice to tell you that it was a whole new world out there after the political crapstorm that has been electrifying our planet, but things felt decidedly similar. "Gordon Brown?" queried one man from Florida when asked for his thoughts on being present at the end of an era. "Who is Gordon Brown?" It doesn't especially matter now. "Sorry," he chortled, "but I have no idea who your prime minister is." Please don't apologise: we haven't had the first clue ourselves for days.

Yet Nick Clegg had now accepted Cameron's Invitation to Join the Collapse of the Next Conservative Government – which meant there was a strong whisky with Gordon's name all over it at the palace.

He arrived just as *EastEnders* started (terrible form, but what can you do?) though didn't linger. Mr Brown's last natter with Her Majesty would play out behind closed doors, of course – then again, what hasn't these past few days? It was just a better class of door. Happily, we have yet to reach that landmark in human civilisation where the Queen tweets, "PM just offered me his resignation & I totes accepted!!! :-)". But it's presumably just the one election away.

Next through the gates was Mr Cameron, who interrupted *Cowboy Builders* on Five, though by this point Her Maj was presumably resigned to the night's telly being a write-off. A much bigger crowd had gathered for the new PM, most of whom seemed to be Londoners. His car drew both cheers and boos. "Surely he should have come on the bike," someone observed tartly.

"I miss Gordon already," giggled someone else. Yet by mid-afternoon, it had become abundantly clear that any deal between Labour and the Lib Dems was off – fairly predictable, given the increasingly vocal opposition within Labour. Rumours swirled that the talks between the two parties had been Ballsed up by that master negotiator Mr Ed, whose hard man act the Lib Dems are said to have found somewhat distasteful. The only real sadness is that Balls wasn't around at those moments in history which called for a touch as famously gossamer as his – the Cuban missile crisis would have had a livelier outcome, for instance, while the Louisiana Purchase would have fallen through within 10 minutes of Ed's greeting Napoleon with the words: "Listen, you'll give us the ports and be grateful, you revolting little frog."

To say that by the end of this saga the media had begun to eat itself wouldn't begin to cover the cannibalistic orgy that has been raging in Westminster. News channel helicopters drowned out their own ground-level broadcasts, ably assisted by megaphone-wielding members of the public who chanted things like "Sack Kay Burley!" Ever more outlandishly repellent pundits were exhumed. Kenneth Baker ... oof, mine eyes! For political junkies it had the flavour of Pokémon – gotta catch 'em all.

For less insane members of the public, this week has presumably acted as a sort of politics aversion therapy, ensuring that every time someone even says the words "strong and stable government", intense feelings of nausea and images of Alastair Campbell will flood their brain.

The geographically tiny village of Westminster has resembled nothing so much as a meth-assisted version of Camberwick Green, with the Sauron-like capabilities of news channels allowing viewers to follow dramatis personae round this weirdo toytown. There were the Lib Dems leaving their headquarters; there they were walking to the Cabinet Office; there they were a few minutes later arriving. And, oh look – there's Windy Miller talking to Kay Burley on College Green.

Unbelievably – although not really within the context of the past few days – a giant rainbow appeared over the palace just as Cameron's car swept in. In the coming days, do expect unicorns to follow.

12 MAY 2010

# The Wags strike back

## JESS CARTNER-MORLEY

Every cultural tribe has its day on the front pages, its moment in the full unforgiving glare of being where-it's-at. The hippies had Woodstock in 1969; the acid house generation had the summer raves of 1988 – and the Wags had Baden-Baden in 2006, when the wives and girlfriends of the England football team stole the attention of the entire British media from right under their spouses' noses.

It ended badly, both for the footballers and for their better-looking halves. The term Wag, previously an innocent acronym of "wives and girlfriends", became a totem of a shallow, consumerist and celebrity-obsessed culture. Four years on, as he names his provisional World Cup squad, Fabio Capello has made great show of sidelining the Wags, the implication being that Alex, Coleen, Carly et al wrecked their boys' focus and fitness in 2006, presumably by clattering into their hotel rooms giggling and tipsy on their Louboutins and then disturbing the athletes' beauty sleep by wanting to hold late-night marital conferences about what best to wear to brunch with the girls the next day – an analysis which strikes me as both far-fetched and misogynistic, but never mind. This time, the Wags are apparently to be accommodated in a sort of holding pen out of harm's way, possibly in

Mauritius, and only allowed to visit the players for one day after each game.

But against all the odds, the Wags are back in the fashion game. Those who assumed Coleen Rooney, Abbey Clancy and other footballers' partners would be happy to while away the rest of their lives spending their mornings at the gym and the afternoons at the beauty salon, treading water in the back pages of the trashier gossip weeklies while real life moved on without them, have been proved wrong. In the four years since the last World Cup, they have regrouped, adjusted to the new cultural terrain, dialled down their aesthetic to suit a sobered world and are back where they belong – setting trends.

Like it or not, the Wags matter. They are far and away the best style bellwether we have, because they occupy the strategically important territory between cutting-edge fashion and the mainstream. Yes, their look is derivative, but that's the whole point. Lady Gaga's stage wardrobe and the more outré output of Paris fashion week do influence what you wear, but they have to go through a whole sequence of filtering processes along the way. What makes the Wags important for fashion-watchers is that they have an appetite for new trends, but that this is always tempered by a strong sense of vanity. Unlike, say, Agyness Deyn, they will never even consider wearing a dress that does not enhance their cleavage, or shoes that are anything but leg-lengthening. Unlike the fashion avant-garde, their status is dependent as much in looking attractive as in looking on-trend, and this makes them a truer reflection of real women's concerns.

The Wag look of 2010 is a far cry from the teeny hotpants and enormous handbags of the old days. For a start, the new Wag is often to be found in trousers. This is an extraordinary turnaround, since trousers – with the exception of super-tight designer jeans and velour tracksuit bottoms for the gym – were conspicuously absent from the Wag wardrobe a few years ago. This spring, within a time period of a few weeks, a Wag icon, an ex-Wag and a current Queen Wag – Victoria Beckham, Cheryl Cole and Abbey Clancy – were all photographed not just in trousers but in a peg-leg trouser shape, loose at the hip and tight at the ankle.

On the fashion desk we're calling the look for summer 2010, which the Wags have nailed, Daytime plus. Daytime plus is a pair of harem-ish or skinny trousers, with very fashion-forward shoes: either chunky platform heels, or ankle boots, or a cut-out hybrid of the two. On the top, this is paired with a tailored jacket, a new arrival in the Wag wardrobe, which projects a sober, I'm-on-the-school-run-just-like-you message. Under the jacket will be a loose, very fine-weave Alexander Wang-ish vest top. This is important because (a) the filminess of the vest layer is essential for showing a bit of breast curvature, an aesthetic to which the Wags are wedded, and (b) those filmy vest layers are surprisingly expensive, but are a status symbol which only those who spend time flicking through the rails in Cricket or Matches will clock. For slightly more dressed-up occasions, the Wag look once revolved around Herve Leger dresses which were not so much body-conscious as anatomically accurate, and supersized blow-dries. For summer 2010, the Wags who are nailing it – see Stacey Giggs at the Manchester United Player of the Year awards – have updated the look with looser, cooler dresses and hair given edge with great accessories.

The Wags may not be allowed out on the tiles in Cape Town this summer, but if you think that'll keep them out of the limelight, you're dreaming. I'm backing the girls to win.

13 MAY 2010

# Digested election: Cameron and Clegg speak to the country

JOHN CRACE

DAVID CAMERON: Nick is an extremely attractive man.

NICK CLEGG: May I add that Dave is well fit.

CAMERON: Nick and I share many values ...

CLEGG: A public school education, *noblesse oblige* ...

CAMERON: And we are both committed to making this coalition work.

CLEGG: Because we both know that most people in our parties hate it.

CAMERON: We know we have differences, but we are united.

CLEGG: In an insatiable lust for power. And each other.

CAMERON: So in the spirit of compromise ...

CLEGG: Dave has agreed to a referendum on the alternative vote.

CAMERON: Because it doesn't make any real difference to us.

CLEGG: And to tax breaks for low earners.

CAMERON: I had my fingers crossed there.

CLEGG: We are now going inside No 10 for the first time.

CAMERON: To roll up our sleeves.

CLEGG: And compare our biceps.

13 MAY 2010

# After a whirlwind
# romance, the big day

## SIMON HOGGART

"This is what the new politics looks like," said Nick Clegg as he stood in the sun-drenched garden of 10 Downing Street. It looked like a civil ceremony. A press conference like that might be illegal in 45 American states.

There were trees in the bright green colours of early summer, a trimmed lawn, the happy couple in their smartest clothes. All it needed was a marquee, a band, and a table for the presents.

All the guests marvelled at how happy they looked. And they have so much in common. The groom is from Eton and Oxford. The groom is from Westminster and Cambridge.

They handed round copies of the prenup, or "coalition agreements reached document" as they call it.

Earlier they had posed on the steps of No 10. They might have been conjoined twins. You felt that if they ever fall out, they'll need to go to Great Ormond Street to be surgically separated. The man who told us that we had to vote Conservative or risk the horrors of a hung parliament was bubbling over with the joys of a hung parliament.

It was going to usher in the new politics, in which the national interest was more important than party interest. It was a historic, seismic shift! And so quick. By contrast, St Paul spent years changing his mind.

Apparently it had nothing to do with the electoral arithmetic. It was all to do with inspiration. "We did both have a choice," said the prime minister. "We looked at minority government, and we thought: this is so uninspiring!"

He was asked how he felt the morning after the night before, hooked up to someone he barely knew and had barely spoken to. As with so many whirlwind romances, the thrill was still electric.

"I woke up thinking: 'This is so much better than the alternative.' I had a great sense of inspiration and excitement."

Now they would be two teams trying to form one strong team. "Perhaps we'll share a car, to save petrol!" It's one of those truisms that are actually true – two can live as cheaply as one.

It turns out that Clegg will take prime minister's questions when Cameron is away. It will give him something to occupy himself during those long, lonely times when Dave is in Tokyo, or Brussels.

"I'm looking forward to a lot of foreign travel," Dave said. Nick gave him a big happy smile.

They'll be sharing accommodation, of course.

"There's a corridor connecting No 10 with where I am, but I don't yet know where I am," the deputy prime minister said. That was existential angst. He'll be told, soon enough.

It got more metaphysical. "This will succeed through its success," said Cameron. Chew on that one.

Inevitably there was a bad fairy, who pointed out: "When you were asked what was your favourite joke, you said, 'Nick Clegg.'"

"Did you?" asked Clegg.

"I'm afraid I did," the prime minister replied.

"Well, I'm off," said Clegg, but with a merry smile. All the happiest partners remember when they couldn't stand each other! It's utterly romantic, like *The Taming of the Shrew*.

All too soon it was over. "Bye, and thanks so much for the lovely gifts, especially the fondue sets and hostess trollies!"

(No, of course not.)

13 MAY 2010

# A new politics? With a top table that looks like that?

### KATHARINE VINER

So we got Theresa May! She wasn't good enough to feature in the foreground of the Conservative campaign; she wasn't good enough to be involved with the manifesto; she wasn't good enough to be part of the negotiating team. But apparently she's good enough to be home secretary. Three cheers for that!

From a total of 29 attending cabinet, there will be just four women. (One of them, Sayeeda Warsi, is unpaid, unelected and a "minister without portfolio". She is also the only non-white member of the cabinet.) It's quite a contrast with Nick Clegg's comments on Tuesday: "I hope this is the start of a new kind of politics I have always believed in. Diverse, plural, where different points of view find a way to work together."

This cabinet, diverse? With less than 14% women? Spain manages 53%, Germany 37%. Plural? With not a single minority ethnic MP? A new kind of politics? When two thirds of the top table went to private school – three each to Eton and Westminster – compared with 7% of the population?

If this is the new government's definition of diversity, perhaps someone can explain to the charmed double act of David Cameron and Nick Clegg what the rest of the country looks like. It's not their fault that these 43-year-old white ex-public schoolboys have piles of cash and nuclear families. But they need to realise that they, and their cabinet, are anything but reflective of the country.

If they care at all about representation – and I'd have thought that Cameron must, since in 2008 he promised in the *Observer* that he would give a third of the jobs in his first government to women – then the new cabinet is an embarrassment to both of them.

How did this happen? Until now the Tories have been impressive; it is largely down to them that the presence of women in parliament increased at this election, from 19.5% to 22%. They also dramatically improved the number of their ethnic minority MPs. The Lib Dems, by contrast, have an appalling record: a 100% all-white parliamentary party with just seven female MPs – and even fewer female candidates than at the last two elections. All the women in the cabinet are Tories; if you're going to have a Lib Dem "who he?" with David Laws, why not a "who she?" with Lynne Featherstone?

The new appointments cap an election that has surely marked a nadir for women in modern public life. The lack of women in the campaign was much discussed – with no discernible response from any party. There were no women promoting manifestos, making speeches, representing their parties in the media. There were few women on TV at all, as Nick Robinson and Adam Boulton tried to out-macho each other with testosterone-fuelled aggression. Pundits were white men to a man – the sight of Lib Dem Olly Grender on *Newsnight* was almost shocking: women exist!

The Labour party, which has by far the best record on the representation of women, nevertheless hid them away: Harriet Harman, now its second female "acting" leader, was barely seen; nor Yvette Cooper – pressed by Jeremy Paxman about the content of her "pillow talk" with husband Ed Balls and now asked repeatedly if her hubby is standing for leader; nor Margaret Hodge, who made the best speech of election night on defeating the BNP in Barking.

Those delectable wives did get noticed, of course. Sarah Brown, Samantha Cameron and Miriam Gonzalez Durantez got a brilliant press – because they are quiet, good-looking, well-dressed and, best of all, know their place: as wives and mothers, in support of their powerful men. Herding their beautiful families, looking lush, standing pregnant on the threshold of No 10 like the Virgin Mary in Renaissance blue. The wives were the Madonnas, the good women; the women MPs the bad. All were silenced.

Does representation matter? Is it any better to have May as home secretary when she's voted against gay rights and women's access to abortion? It surely counts for something. May, who once wore a T-shirt bearing the slogan "This is what a feminist looks like", has campaigned against sexual violence and worked hard on getting more Tory women MPs. She is far more likely to ask questions about how a policy will impact on women than her male colleagues. Whether or not you like her answer is another matter, but she knows to ask.

For an institution to be democratic it has to be "of the people" – democracies simply don't work unless they represent those they govern. The millionaire who slashes away at public services can have no true understanding of the effect of the loss of those services on the single mother with nowhere else to go.

And so a stranded quartet carries the torch for women in a scandalously undiverse cabinet, almost a century after women got the vote. We have a parliament that is not representative of the people, and a cabinet not even representative of parliament. A cabal of rich, white, middle-aged, soft-handed men is to rule over this mixed-up, multiracial, aging, 51%-female, gloriously diverse country of ours. A new politics? I don't think so.

15 MAY 2010

# Gordon Brown: the picture that says it all

IAN JACK

For several months in the late 1870s the painter William Frederick Yeames worked on a canvas in his studio in St John's Wood. For some of that time his nephew, James Lambe Yeames, stood before him. The boy was aged five or six and dressed, according to the evidence of the picture, in a light-blue costume that suggested an earlier age. The English civil war was a fashionable subject at the time and Yeames, a successful though poorly reviewed artist, painted in the then popular style that invited viewers to consider the story, or even the moral question, which the details in the picture revealed.

His nephew takes up only a small proportion of the canvas but all eyes are on him: he's the centre of a narrative that Yeames invites us to imagine. Parliamentary forces have invaded a Royalist house, but the Royalist owner has fled. The householder's son stands innocent and erect to face his Roundhead inquisitors. "And when did you last see your father?" is the question, but how will the boy reply? Will he tell the truth, as all good boys should, and condemn his dear father to capture and imprisonment or worse? Or will he be clever enough to dissemble – to lie in a good cause? His family looks on fearfully. A little girl, presumably his sister, is in tears.

We like to think that we have different sensibilities to our Victorian ancestors: what suckers they were for sentimentality and melodrama, how childishly fascinated by pictorial detail, how easily they could be made to weep! But this photograph by Martin Argles, one of the set he took on Tuesday to record Gordon Brown's last hours in Downing Street [published in this volume's selection of photographs], suggests that we're much the same. At first glance all that it has in common with Yeames's painting are Brown's two sons standing on a desk. Nobody is hiding in an oak tree out of shot; nobody faces a beheading. The question "And when did you last see your father?" has been turned into a statement: "At last you will see your father!" Brown has spent so much time not at home.

Still, at least one person in the picture seems to be crying and others have cried at the sight of it. Alastair Campbell confessed on his blog that its publication in the *Guardian* had "set off the waterworks", and not just because he's in the picture and had witnessed the scene. Campbell remembered blubbing when his own son, then aged eight, asked "Are we going to win?" on the night of the 1997 election – or perhaps the tears came when he read the line again in his published diaries.

"There is indeed something so special about kids and their insights into big moments of drama," Campbell wrote on his blog, though the truer impact that children make may not be their insights (as Argles took his pictures he overheard one of Brown's sons say, "Daddy, you know everything") but their guileless presence. Politicians have been kissing random babies for a very long time, but only relatively recently have they been advertised as themselves keepers of children. Prime ministers are younger now, couples have children later and notions of private life have changed. But there's also something else – the political need, common to all the big parties, to speak of the electorate as "families", often "hard-working", instead of as citizens or social classes antagonised or bound together by mutual interest. The family above all else: Yeames's little boy must have had the same thought, just as Brown had it in his last speech as prime minister when he stood outside No 10 and said that as he left "the second most important job I could ever hold, I cherish even more the first – as a husband and father". Soon after, he and his wife and children walked down the street to their car; a good leave-taking, lumps in many throats.

Argles took his picture only a few minutes before – when prime ministers go, they go quickly. The time according to Sky on the wall-mounted screen is 19.17 and Brown was in the street at 19.20.

Where are we? In what's known as the "war room" on the ground floor of No 12 Downing Street and therefore no older, as a room, than circa 1960, when architect Raymond Erith rebuilt the house from scratch. Later Erith's pupil, Quinlan Terry, remodelled the interiors of No 10 for Margaret Thatcher. The style is neo-Palladian: a broken pediment above the door, wood panels from floor to ceiling, and all looking rather new. The candelabra may be from John Lewis, as may the pencil-pleated silk curtains (butterscotch?) hanging from their brass rails. Rooms in expensive Indian hotels sometimes have this look, with its unpersuasive nod to the 18th century, but we can be sure that Gordon Brown has never patronised the room's appearance with snobbish remarks, or even noticed it. As any visitor to his North Queensferry home will attest, he can never be accused of an interest in comfort or fashion; the one picture on the wall when I went there was a black and white photograph of Jim Baxter, who played left-half for Raith

Rovers, Rangers and Scotland, while the living room floor was a sea of plastic toys.

Now Brown is leaving his war room for the last time. In another, more private room, Argles has photographed him on the phone to Nick Clegg – "Nick, Nick, I can't hold on any longer" – and now in the bigger room he's just finishing a brief speech of farewell to his staff and colleagues. His children run over and are hoisted to the desk. Brown ends his speech, the audience applauds. Argles takes his picture, and in a fraction of a second manages two extraordinary achievements. First, a record of how Labour's 13 years in power ended that also includes (you might argue) three great architects of its early success – Mandelson, Campbell and the TV screen. Second, a picture of Brown that for once shows spontaneous happiness: the man who people who know him say they know him to be. A painter could have struggled for years to get it all in, only to have his painting disbelieved.

Time for the slideshow and the pointer: who and what can be seen. Note the nice blue box on the desk in the foreground. It's probably where an assistant kept Brown's cufflinks – there's been no time for a leaving present. Then, between the two computer screens, a bottle of hand-soap. The swine flu scare? Next, the people, who from left are: Sarah Brown with six-year-old John; Justin Forsyth, director of strategic communications (against the curtains); Gordon Brown with three-year-old Fraser, who has cystic fibrosis (though that's a poor definition of an obviously buoyant personality); Ed Miliband (half seen) and Ed Balls, potential successors; Joe Irvin, political secretary; the Lords Adonis and Mandelson; Campbell; Gavin Kelly, deputy chief of staff (there was no actual chief of staff); Stewart Wood, European adviser; Kirsty McNeill, speechwriter; Leanne Johnson, diary secretary.

The only person who looks uneasy is Sarah Brown. She and John are those most aware of the camera. Both have struck poses, as you do. She looks sadder than her husband, who in cuddling Fraser has found something to do. The bracelet she wears is plastic and made by one of the children, probably John. Other parts of the house have their paintings stuck to the walls. Sarah is 46 and Gordon 59. They met properly on a plane taking them to a Scottish Labour party conference in 1994 and had their relationship disclosed via a photograph taken in a restaurant for the *News of the World*. Charlie Whelan, then Brown's spokesman, set it up and had the shots retaken when he decided that his boss needed to look more romantic. All this seems long ago.

As for the others, at how many of them has Brown aimed a mobile? Perhaps none, or perhaps the victims have forgiven him. Almost certainly not at Mandelson – it would be like trying to hit a cat at 200 yards with a brick – though his grievance against him over siding with Blair runs very deep. Now, like the rest of this small audience, Mandelson looks genuinely sorry and admiring. Anyone familiar with workplace farewells will recognise the emotions, the lumpy throat and the prickly eyes, which come with the realisation that not only is a significant part of the leaver's life ending but a good part of yours is as well. "You've been wonderful friends as well as colleagues ... I wish you all the best" and so on. Mandelson's face is composed to reflect similar thoughts back to Brown, and it would be unfair to doubt his sincerity. So many "ups and downs" in the past are turned in the present from mountains to molehills – say what you like about Gordon, but ... To quote the managerial euphemisms of Campbell in his blog: "As my diaries reveal, I have had a lot of ups and downs with GB and his team. But I really do believe he behaved with incredible courage and dignity in the last days of his premiership, and that whilst he may not have had all the roundedness of the TB political skillset, in particular his comms skills, he certainly had resilience and a deep belief in the power of politics to do good."

All leave-takings tend to promote the same atmosphere. With a prime minister, to quote Walter Bagehot on the weddings of princes, they may be no more than a brilliant edition of a universal fact. On the other hand, Brown on this day has behaved particularly well. According to people there, he has cracked favourite jokes to keep spirits up and sat with people with his arm around them and remembered how much this or that piece of work had helped him. And, as one of them said, it was a family house, with the Brown children favourites of doorkeepers, advisers and civil servants. Family eviction, then, on top of brave political failure, Henry V's pre-Agincourt tour of the tents, and final resignation: no wonder there were tears.

Brown's career is often described as "a tragedy" – I've done so myself – with the fatal flaw stemming from a doubled-edged character divided between the New Testament and Machiavelli, between public rectitude and private scheming. It may be so, but a much more visible flaw (at least in a modern politician) was the burden of his self-consciousness and the feeling, reinforced by dozens of media consultants and millions more critics on their sofas, that he never looked or sounded right. His nemesis in that regard hangs on the wall above the fireplace, already shimmering with news of his going.

Argles's picture shows, among many other things, a man relieved of a job that he should never have wanted. Already, it's beginning to look unfair of us; Thursday night's BBC show *Have I Got News For You* was soon made unfunny by kicking a man – a suddenly better man – when he was down.

Socially and geographically and for reasons beyond party politics, he will probably be missed. When will we next see a prime minister from northern Britain or one who attended a state school? Unless William Hague mounts a coup, not for a very long time. When the Browns left Downing Street on Tuesday, a certain kind of Britain went, too. The Royalists have evicted the Roundheads: the thought, maybe even a tear, is difficult to resist.

22 MAY 2010

# Hoggart's week: the untimely death of novelist JG Farrell

## SIMON HOGGART

Wonderful that JG Farrell won the "lost" Booker prize for his novel *Troubles* this week. I read it in 1978, eight years after it was published, but thought it was marvellous and I voted for it last month. It's sad, very funny, elegiac, beautifully written, and has unexpected delights on every page. The central metaphor, the crumbling, cat-infested Majestic hotel standing for the British empire, is so lightly worn that it might not represent anything except itself.

The other day at the Irish embassy Farrell was feted as a great Irish writer, although while his parents were at least part-Irish, he firmly thought of himself as British. However, he did live in County Cork at what turned out to be the end of his life. His great friend David Simpson went to visit him there for a week in May 1979, and Farrell announced that he was going to learn to fish; Simpson could teach him. Simpson said he had never fished in his life, so they learned together, standing at a point where a local later told them: "You'd as likely catch a fish in your kitchen sink as there."

Three months later he was dead, aged 44. As a young man he'd had polio, which left him weak. He was trying to cast from a ledge

8ft above the sea, and his necessarily clumsy action made him lose his footing. A woman who was there saw him drowning and tried unsuccessfully to help. So we were deprived of more superb books that can never now be written.

The other day I was writing about the great cliches of Sunday evening television mystery drama: you know, the way that rich or upper-class people are always rude to the police ("Must you, inspector? The lord lieutenant will be here any minute"). The detective is hidebound by his superior officer, who is obsessed with procedure. None ever says: "Tear up the rule book. We need to nail this bastard!"

Any young woman who works with horses is no better than she ought to be. The crucial clue is often available on Google, even if it dates from before the internet was invented: "Bingo! It turns out that he worked as an Elvis impersonator in Doncaster in the 1960s. I think we have our man!"

The great American film critic Roger Ebert gets his readers to send their own favourite movie cliches. If any character imitates another character rudely, that person – usually his boss – will walk in and stand at the back. When a car screeches up to a building, there is always a parking space in front.

Some are simple misdirection. The villain is never the choleric character who's always exploding with rage. Nor the chap trained in kung fu. Or the evasive, secretive one. This would be handy for real police work. "He was seen waving a shotgun and threatening to kill the victim, inspector."

"Hmm, rules him out then."

If you have any thoughts on these lines, I would be delighted to hear them.

I helped at the annual charity quiz on Monday, the one where the well-to-do folk of Notting Hill help out the poor who live in the streets just to the north of them. David and Samantha Cameron used to come; for some reason, they couldn't make it this year. The toughest question by far was "Spell the Icelandic volcano, Eyjafjallajökull – including all dots." Tough for me, that is – I had to learn to pronounce it. It's *Aya* – to rhyme with layer – *Fi-alla Yerkul*. You can do it with practice.

I think one table got it right.

We are burying Alan Watkins on Monday. All professions mourn their own, although journalists are among the few who can inflict their friends on the rest of the world. But Alan was undoubtedly a great man.

As a lad, starting out on the *Guardian*, I thought his light, elegant prose was almost magical; he knew very well that personality in politics is far more important than mere policy, so he wrote illuminatingly about people's foibles, often to their annoyance, always to the delight of colleagues and rivals. Just sitting at the next table in a restaurant when I was 23, I felt I had arrived at the top of the trade. If you had told me that we would spend companionable evenings drinking with other hacks in El Vino's East (the one near Blackfriars bridge) I would have been thrilled beyond measure.

He was friendly with some politicians, but it was because he liked them; he was utterly unmoved by office and power. He was also very kindly. There was one celebrated bore from whom, at party conferences, people would try to flee while he was in the loo. Alan forbade this because it would be cruel and unfair. It didn't stop the bore being vicious about him in print, but that is in the nature of bores, desperate for attention they can't otherwise earn. Alan shrugged it off. He did a good shrug, often before sipping more champagne.

Mick Paine writes from Gainsborough to complain that he'd been in WH Smith, Lincoln, to buy a couple of magazines. Since Christmas, there has been a young lady stationed by the exit who accosts customers as they leave. Once he was collared and asked: "Would you mind telling me who your power supplier is?"

He told her he would indeed mind, and later reflected that he would no more go to a bookshop for electricity than to the electricity company for a newspaper. He wrote to Smith's head office and got a vague reply saying it was only a trial. I see it as yet another invasion of privacy – we are allowed no time now not being assaulted by advertising and promotions.

And Mick has got his revenge: he has subs to the magazines now, so he doesn't even need to go into Smith's.

# Summer

# Obituary: Louise Bourgeois

## ADRIAN SEARLE

Louise Bourgeois, the French-born, American-based artist best known for her sculptures of vast metal spiders, died yesterday in a New York hospital at the age of 98. Bourgeois, who only found widespread acclaim late in life, had suffered a heart attack at the weekend, a spokeswoman said.

With her death, American and European art has lost not only a tremendous and hugely influential artist, but a direct link between the art of the 21st century and Belle Époque Paris, with cubism, symbolism, surrealism and abstract expressionism, and all that followed.

Born in Paris, on Christmas Day 1911, she recounted that the attending doctor had told her mother, "Madam, you are quite ruining my day." Her personality and her art were to match, and there are few artists who have claimed so outspokenly that their work has been founded in childhood and adolescence.

Her parents ran a prosperous family business devoted to the repair and resale of medieval and 17th- and 18th-century tapestries and textiles, living above the showroom in Paris.

As a child, Bourgeois had a talent for mathematics. In adolescence, she began helping in the workshop of the business, repairing the destroyed lower portions of old tapestries, sewing fig-leaves on to the genitalia of the naked figures on works destined for prudish American collectors. At about this time her philandering father introduced his lover, an Englishwoman called Sadie, into the household as the children's tutor. From her, Bourgeois learned English, as well as jealousy and hatred.

All of this became part of the Bourgeois legend and the engine of her art. As an émigré French artist who moved to New York in 1938, her career developed slowly. Critical and commercial success only came when she was in her 60s. Although it was not until 1982 that New York's Museum of Modern Art gave her a retrospective – the first it had ever mounted of a woman artist – she was by then already well-known, if regarded as uncategorisable, marginal, even eccentric. The exhibition transformed her into the grande dame of American art.

In the same year, the photographer Robert Mapplethorpe took a number of famous portraits of Bourgeois. She wore a black coat of monkey fur and carried something under her arm as a sort of prop: a big, obscene black latex sculpture, resembling a gigantic penis and balls. She insisted it was not a phallus at all. It was, she said, her little girl. In Mapplethorpe's images, Bourgeois smiles mischievously for the camera. The image is immensely seductive.

Bourgeois made sculptures in all kinds of media; she made wonderful prints and drawings, created claustrophobic installations and fabricated little sewn dolls and giant metal spiders with equal care. She even recorded herself singing childhood songs, broadcast in an empty Venetian tower.

There were many-breasted creatures, beautifully carved marble hands, things that were sexual and strange and filled with secrets and barely suppressed violence. Refusing to describe herself as a feminist, she was one anyway. She has lessons for all artists alive now – in persistence, commitment and individuality, and in the difference between art made as an adjunct to a career, and art borne out of inner necessity.

Bourgeois made great work and bad work, and didn't care to choose. She even published her insomniac bedside drawings.

"My memories are moth-eaten," she wrote recently, in a crabby hand, next to a beautiful, abstract drawing. We have lost a great artist, but the art goes on.

9 JUNE 2010

Barbara Kingsolver, winner of the 2010 Orange prize for fiction for her novel *The Lacuna*. FELIX CLAY

**11** JUNE **2010**

The opening ceremony of the World Cup 2010 at Soccer City,
Johannesburg. TOM JENKINS

11 JUNE 2010

A South African supporter at the opening game of the World Cup 2010 at Soccer City, Johannesburg, versus Mexico. TOM JENKINS

23 JUNE 2010

Cattle hang after slaughter at John Penny and Sons in Leeds.

CHRISTOPHER THOMOND

5 June 2010

# Gaza flotilla diary: "A man is shot. I am seeing it happen"

## HENNING MANKELL

25 MAY, NICE It is five o'clock in the morning and I'm standing in the street waiting for the taxi that will take me to the airport in Nice. It's the first time in ages E and I have had some time off together. Initially we thought we'd be able to stretch it to two weeks. It turned out to be five days. Ship to Gaza finally seems to be ready to set off and I'm to travel to Cyprus to join it, as arranged.

As instructed, I've limited my luggage to a rucksack weighing no more than 10 kilos. Ship to Gaza has a clearly defined goal: to break Israel's illegal blockade. After the war a year ago, life has become more and more unbearable for the Palestinians who live in Gaza. There is a huge shortage of the bare necessities for living any sort of decent life.

But the aim of the voyage is of course more explicit. Deeds, not words, I think. It's easy to say you support or defend or oppose this, that and the other. But only action can provide proof of your words.

The Palestinians who have been forced by the Israelis to live in this misery need to know that they are not alone, not forgotten. The world has to be reminded of their existence. And we can do that by loading some ships with what they need most of all: medicines, desalination plants for drinking water, cement.

The taxi arrives, we agree a price – extortionate! – and drive to the airport through empty, early morning streets. It comes to me now that I made my first note, there in the taxi. I don't remember the exact words, but I'm suddenly disconcerted by a sense of not quite having managed to register that this is a project so hated by the Israelis that they might try to stop the convoy by violent means.

By the time I get to the airport, the thought has gone. On this point, too, the project is very clearly defined. We are to use non-violent tactics; there are no weapons, no intention of physical confrontation. If we're stopped, it ought to happen in a way that doesn't put our lives at risk.

26 MAY, NICOSIA It's warmer than in Nice. Those who are to board the ships somewhere off the coast of Cyprus are gathering at Hotel Centrum in Nicosia. It's like being in an old Graham Greene novel. A collection of odd people assembling in some godforsaken place to set off on a journey together. We're going to break an illegal blockade. The words are repeated in a variety of languages. But suddenly there's a great sense of uncertainty.

The ships are late, various problems have arisen, the coordinates still haven't been set for the actual rendezvous. The only thing that's certain is that it will be out at sea. Cyprus doesn't want our six ships putting in here. Presumably Israel has applied pressure.

Now and then I also note tensions between the various groups that make up the leadership of this unwieldy project. The breakfast room has been pressed into service as a secretive meeting room. We are called in to write details of our next of kin, in case of the worst. Everyone writes away busily. Then we are told to wait. Watch and wait. Those are the words that will be used most often, like a mantra, in the coming days. Wait. Watch and wait.

27 MAY, NICOSIA Wait. Watch and wait. Oppressive heat.

28 MAY, NICOSIA I suddenly start to wonder whether I may have to leave the island without getting onto a ship. There seems to be

a shortage of places. There are apparently waiting lists for this project of solidarity. But K, the friendly Swedish MP, and S, the Swedish female doctor, who are travelling with me help keep my spirits up. Travel by ship always involves some kind of bother, I think. We carry on with our task. Of waiting. Watching and waiting.

29 MAY, NICOSIA Suddenly everything happens very quickly. We are now, but of course still only maybe, to travel sometime today on a different, faster ship to the point out at sea where the co-ordinates meet, and there we will join the convoy of five other vessels that will then head as a single flotilla for the Gaza Strip.

We carry on waiting. But at about 5pm the port authorities finally give us permission to board a ship called the *Challenge*, which will take us at a speed of 15 knots to the rendezvous point, where we will transfer to the cargo ship *Sophia*. There are already lots of people aboard the *Challenge*.

They seem a bit disappointed to see the three of us turn up. They had been hoping for some Irish campaigners who have, however, suddenly given up the idea and gone home. We climb aboard, say hello, quickly learn the rules. It's very cramped, plastic bags full of shoes everywhere, but the mood is good, calm. All the question marks seem to have been ironed out now. Soon after the two diesel engines rumble into life. We're finally underway.

23.00 I've found a chair on the rear deck. The wind is not blowing hard, but enough to make a lot of the passengers seasick. I have wrapped myself up in blankets, and watch the moon cast an illuminated trail across the sea. I think to myself that solidarity actions can take many forms. The rumbling means there is not a lot of conversation. Just now, the journey feels very peaceful. But deceptively so.

30 May, at sea, south-east of Cyprus, 01.00 I can see the glimmer of lights in various directions. The captain, whose name I never manage to learn, has slowed his speed. The lights flickering in the distance are the navigation lights of two of the other ships in the convoy. We are going to lie here until daylight, when people can be transferred to other vessels. But I still can't find anywhere to sleep. I stay in my wet chair and doze.

Solidarity is born in dampness and waiting; but we are helping others to get roofs over their heads.

08.00 The sea is calmer. We are approaching the largest vessel in the flotilla. It's a passenger ferry, the "queen" of the ships in the convoy. There are hundreds of people on board. There has been much discussion of the likelihood of the Israelis focusing their efforts on this particular ship.

What efforts? We've naturally been chewing that over ever since the start of the project. Nothing can be known with any certainty. Will the Israeli navy sink the ships? Or repel them by some other means? Is there any chance the Israelis will let us through, and repair their tarnished reputation? Nobody knows. But it seems most likely that we'll be challenged at the border with Israeli territorial waters by threatening voices from loudspeakers on naval vessels. If we fail to stop, they will probably knock out our propellers or rudders, then tow us somewhere for repair.

13.00 The three of us transfer to the *Sophia* by rope ladder. She is a limping old cargo ship, with plenty of rust and an affectionate crew. I calculate that we are about 25 people in all. The cargo includes cement, reinforcement bars and prefabricated wooden houses. I am given a cabin to share with the MP, whom I view after the long days in Nicosia more and more as a very old friend. We find it has no electric light. We'll have to catch up on our reading some other time.

16.00 The convoy has assembled. We head for Gaza.

18.00 We gather in the improvised dining area between the cargo hatches and the ship's superstructure. The grey-haired Greek who is responsible for security and organisation on board, apart from the nautical aspects, speaks softly and immediately inspires confidence. Words like "wait" and "watch" no longer exist. Now we are getting close. The only question is: what are we getting close to?

Nobody knows what the Israelis will come up with. We only know that their statements have been menacing, announcing that the convoy will be repelled with all the means at their disposal. But what does that mean? Torpedoes? Hawsers? Soldiers let down from helicopters? We can't know. But violence will not be met with violence from our side.

Only elementary self-defence. We can, on the other hand, make things harder for our attackers. Barbed wire is to be strung all round the ship's rail. In addition, we are all to get used to wearing life jackets, lookouts are to be posted and we will be told where to assemble if foreign soldiers come aboard. Our last bastion will be the bridge.

Then we eat. The cook is from Egypt, and suffers with a bad leg. But he cooks great food.

31 May, midnight I share the watch on the port side from midnight to 3am. The moon is still big, though occasionally obscured by cloud. The sea is calm. The navigation lights gleam. The three hours pass quickly. I notice I am tired when someone else takes over. It's still a long way to anything like a territorial boundary the Israelis could legitimately defend. I should try to snatch a few hours' sleep.

I drink tea, chat to a Greek crewman whose English is very poor but who insists he wants to know what my books are about. It's almost four before I get to lie down.

04.30 I've just dropped off when I am woken again. Out on deck I see that the big passenger ferry is floodlit. Suddenly there is the sound of gunfire. So now I know that Israel has chosen the route of brutal confrontation. In international waters.

It takes exactly an hour for the speeding black rubber dinghies with the masked soldiers to reach us and start to board. We gather, up on the bridge. The soldiers are impatient and want us down on deck. Someone who is going too slowly immediately gets a stun device fired into his arm. He falls. Another man who is not moving fast enough is shot with a rubber bullet. I think: I am seeing this happen right beside me. It is an absolute reality. People who have done nothing being driven like animals, being punished for their slowness.

We are put in a group down on the deck. Where we will then stay for 11 hours, until the ship docks in Israel. Every so often we are filmed. When I jot down a few notes, a soldier comes over at once and asks what I am writing. That's the only time I lose my temper, and tell him it's none of his business. I can only see his eyes; I don't know what he is thinking. But he turns and goes.

Eleven hours, unable to move, packed together in the heat. If we want to go for a pee, we have to ask permission. The food they give us is biscuits, rusks and apples. We're not allowed to make coffee, even though we could do it where we are sitting. We take a collective decision: not to ask if we can cook food.

Then they would film us. It would be presented as showing how generously the soldiers had treated us. We stick to the biscuits and rusks. It is degradation beyond compare. (Meanwhile, the soldiers who are off-duty have dragged mattresses out of the cabins and are sleeping at the back of the deck.)

So in those 11 hours, I have time to take stock. We have been attacked while in international waters. That means the Israelis have behaved like pirates, no better than those who operate off the coast of Somalia. The moment they start to steer this ship towards Israel, we have also been kidnapped. The whole action is illegal. We try to talk among ourselves, work out what might happen, and not least how the Israelis could opt for a course of action that means painting themselves into a corner.

The soldiers watch us. Some pretend not to understand English. But they all do. There are a couple of girls among the soldiers. They look the most embarrassed. Maybe they are the sort who will escape to Goa and fall into drug addiction when their military service is over? It happens all the time.

**18.00** Quayside somewhere in Israel. I don't know where. We are taken ashore and forced to run the gauntlet of rows of soldiers while military TV films us. It suddenly hits me that this is something I shall never forgive them. At that moment they are nothing more to my mind than pigs and bastards.

We are split up, no one is allowed to talk to anyone else. Suddenly a man from the Israeli ministry for foreign affairs appears at my side. I realise he is there to make sure I am not treated too harshly. I am, after all, known as a writer in Israel. I've been translated into Hebrew. He asks if I need anything.

My freedom and everybody else's, I say. He doesn't answer. I ask him to go. He takes one step back. But he stays.

I admit to nothing, of course, and am told I am to be deported. The man who says this also says he rates my books highly. That makes me consider ensuring nothing I write is ever translated into Hebrew again.

Agitation and chaos reign in this "asylum-seekers' reception centre". Every so often, someone is knocked to the ground, tied up and handcuffed. I think several times that no one will believe me when I tell them about this. But there are many eyes to see it. Many people will be obliged to admit that I am telling the truth. There are a lot of us who can bear witness.

A single example will do. Right beside me, a man suddenly refuses to have his fingerprints taken. He accepts being photographed. But fingerprints? He doesn't consider he has done anything wrong. He resists. And is beaten to the ground. They drag him off. I don't know where. What word can I use? Loathsome? Inhuman? There are plenty to choose from.

23.00 We, the MP, the doctor and I, are taken to a prison for those refused right of entry. There we are split up. We are thrown a few sandwiches that taste like old dishcloths. It's a long night. I use my trainers as a pillow.

1 June, afternoon Without any warning, the MP and I are taken to a Lufthansa plane. We are to be deported. We refuse to go until we know what is happening to S. Once we have assured ourselves that she, too, is on her way, we leave our cell.

On board the plane, the air hostess gives me a pair of socks. Because mine were stolen by one of the commandos who attacked the boat I was on.

The myth of the brave and utterly infallible Israeli soldier is shattered. Now we can add: they are common thieves. For I was not the only one to be robbed of my money, credit card, clothes, MP3 player, laptop; the same happened to many others on the same ship as me, which was attacked early one morning by masked Israeli soldiers, who were thus in fact nothing other than lying pirates.

By late evening we are back in Sweden. I talk to some journalists. Then I sit for a while in the darkness outside the house where I live. E doesn't say much.

2 June, afternoon I listen to the blackbird. A song for those who died.

Now it is still all left to do. So as not to lose sight of the goal, which is to lift the brutal blockade of Gaza. That will happen.

Beyond that goal, others are waiting. Demolishing a system of apartheid takes time. But not an eternity.

*Translated by Sarah Death*

7 JUNE 2010

# Cumbria mourns its dead

HELEN PIDD

When the residents of west Cumbria were told it was finally safe to leave their houses last Wednesday afternoon, they came out squinting into the sunlight to share news of unimaginable horror. It was the loveliest weather for the most awful of days.

Yesterday, about 1,500 people gathered at two services to remember the 12 people killed by Derrick Bird four days earlier. This time, the weather reflected the mood. All was grey.

By the beach at Seascale, a short walk from where Bird murdered his final three victims – Jane Robinson, Michael Pike and Jamie Clark – a service was held for locals to pay their respects to the dead, while about 1,000 later gathered for a vigil of "recollection and remembrance" in Whitehaven, just round the corner from the taxi rank where Bird shot fellow driver Darren Rewcastle.

Earlier, Bird's two sons had released a statement saying that they were "devastated" by the death of their father, who they said was "the nicest man you could ever meet".

Among those sheltering under umbrellas at Seascale were Sheena Pike, widow of Michael, and other relatives of the dead.

Jordan Williams, a nine-year-old who witnessed Mr Pike's murder, was also present.

"The real community is not a faceless community," said the Reverend John Woolcock, vicar of Seascale, who led a minute's silence for the victims. "We know each other. Tragedy does not take all of our love – it increases it."

Throughout the service, Woolcock referred only to the "12 dead" – there was no mention of the final death, of Bird himself, in a Lake District wood.

"I suspect that nearly every one of you knew at least one person who was killed," said the Reverend Richard Teal in an address that praised "the resilience and strength of west Cumbrians". Worshippers recited Psalm 121, which promises: "The Lord will defend you from all evil; it is he who will guard your life."

Teal acknowledged that many people would ask where God was when Bird went on the rampage. "I know many of you will question why this happened – for those going through suffering and bereavement, no theoretical answer will do," he conceded.

Accompanied by a music group, the crowd sang Be Still for the Presence of the Lord, The Lord's My Shepherd, and Amazing Grace. During the last hymn, sobs could be heard above the music.

"Please don't ask us how we feel," said Joan Bell, looking out from under her hood with watery eyes. She was at the front of the crowd with her friend Anne Cox during the service, defiantly umbrella-less. The 70-year-olds were friends of Robinson, murdered as she delivered catalogues. The pair had seen Robinson's twin, Barrie, in Seascale's St Cuthbert's church yesterday.

Cox said: "Jane was a bird lover, and during the service a sparrow flew into the church. I said to Barrie: 'Take that as a sign she's still with you.'"

There was no anger at the emergency services, condemned by the press for failing to stop Bird sooner. By the end of the service, collection buckets for the Cumbria Air Ambulance were full of coins and soggy notes. Bell said she had returned from a boat trip on the Danube last Tuesday. "People kept asking me where I came from. I said: 'Seascale – you won't have heard of it.'" She paused for a moment. "They will now."

8 JUNE 2010

# Somalia's invisible war, the new frontline against al-Qaida

GHAITH ABDUL-AHAD

On a side street off Mogadishu's Wadnaha Road frontline a young officer is explaining the unwritten rules of the city's intractable civil war as his men exchange fire with an unseen enemy.

The fighters shooting at him are from the Hizb al-Islam, he explains. He knows this because they fight longer than al-Shabab, the other main Islamist group besieging Somalia's tiny government-held enclave, but also because they told him. "We have friends there. They tell us before they leave their base that they are going to attack. When they want to fire mortars they tell us so we can take cover."

If the conflict that has turned Mogadishu into a virtual no-go zone for 19 years occasionally resembles a grim farce, there is nothing farcical about the scene around us.

Nearby lies an array of flip-flops in different shapes and sizes and always in singles: blues, reds, purples, tiny plastic ones with flower designs and large leather ones attesting to previous skirmishes, advances and retreats. A jungle of trees and shrubs has taken over the deserted street so that the soldiers have to push the branches with their elbows and guns to make a path. Houses and shops are shattered, empty and riddled with bullet holes.

Somalia is the world's invisible conflict, and perhaps its least comprehensible. Since January last year, when Ethiopia pulled out of the country, the Islamist government of Sharif Ahmed has been locked in an attritional struggle with al-Shabab, a more radical offshoot of the Islamic Courts movement, the alliance of tribal sharia courts which once controlled most of southern Somalia. The government is also under attack from Hizb al-Islam, many of whom fought alongside Ahmed against Ethiopia.

Al-Shabab and Hizb al-Islam control most of Mogadishu and south and central Somalia, having squeezed the internationally backed government into a sliver of land defended by an African Union force. But it is hard to keep up with the shifting frontlines of this conflict: when I was in Mogadishu last May the government controlled all of Wadnaha and Factory roads, the main arteries that cross the city.

Soon after I left, the commanders and their troops in that area joined the opposition, and the government lost three miles of territory including the camps at the ministry of defence and the stadium.

When the warlord Yousuf Neda Adi switched sides again – this time rejoining the government with his troops – the government line stretched back and gained another few hundred metres. But Adi now believes the government may have been behind a recent assassination attempt against him.

But there is more at stake here than a few square miles of terri-tory. Al-Shabab have established themselves as the Somali franchise of al-Qaida, aspiring to be named as al-Qaida in Somalia – just as with jihadi groups in Yemen and Morocco. They are imposing a regime of extreme sharia law on the areas they control that makes the Taliban seem moderate. Western security experts, Somalis living abroad and local fighters say the country is fast becoming the favoured destination for wannabe jihadis.

The addition of the whine of US drones to Mogadishu's symphony of tank, mortar and machine gun fire is evidence of the deep anxiety the conflict is causing in Washington and other western capitals. As one minister told me over a breakfast of goat liver, bananas, papayas, chapattis and sweet milk tea: "For the first time in many years the international community is interested in Somalia, not because of our suffering but because of al-Qaida. The British and the Americans are interested in helping us because they see the anarchy in Mogadishu is hitting them back home."

BEHEADING VIDEO
Abdey Qadir is a tall figure with small, sunken eyes and a thick beard that grows only under his chin, giving him the appearance of a fierce goat. He is an intelligence officer in the Amniyat or security division of al-Shabab.

We meet in a room on the government side of the frontline. He pulls a Chinese mobile phone from his pocket, fiddles for a bit, then holds it in his giant hands and shows me a grainy bluish film.

A man dressed in a white shirt and dark trousers is lying on his stomach on the ground. He is blindfolded with a black cloth, his arms tied behind his back. Another man is standing astride him, one foot pinning his shoulder to the ground. The victim's feet shake but he is silent and his mouth is closed. There are trees around and the person who is filming shouts, "*Allahu akbar. Allahu akbar.*" The "executioner" pulls the man's short hair up, the head lifts, he stretches his right arm under his neck and starts cutting from left to right. In short fast moves, the knife moves up and down, in and out. The body shakes and a pool of blood flows calmly and gathers under the head. The executioner pulls the knife to the right and then goes back to the start and cuts deeper this time to separate the head.

The film stops and there is a thick cold silence in the room.

"We killed him because he was a spy," Abdey says calmly. "We captured him trying to cross from the government lines."

Qadir explains that the practice of beheading and removing limbs, for which al-Shabab have become notorious, has been an important element in establishing the group's grip on large areas of the country.

"One of the reasons for our strong name is not only the war, it's the strong fierce rule that is based on cutting heads as punishments for the crimes," he says. "We have gained respect. We implement a strong rule that no one can deviate from which has also made us very popular with Arab and other mujahideen. We have courts all the time that implement sharia, but when we are in the middle of war and the fighter captures the traitors and the apostate soldiers of the government then we implement the sharia immediately and cut the head."

Qadir tells me proudly that he doesn't himself carry a gun. "My duties are to bring news, watch the people who move weapons to the government side from the weapons markets and find the enemies of al-Shabab in our area ... To kill people you don't need a gun ... Not always."

I ask him why he fought a government that imposed sharia on Somalia and is led by one of their former allies in the Islamic Courts movement. "According to our beliefs Somalia was never an Islamic country – it has to be liberated from the apostasy. After that we move to Kenya, Ethiopia, Djibouti ... The resistance never stops at specific borders."

Al-Shabab's origins date to the mid-1990s when a group of militant jihadis split from the Itehad al-Islami, the main Islamist organisation at the time, in Somalia and later joined a loose alliance known as the Islamic Courts.

The more militant elements in the alliance gave Ethiopia, ever nervous about the Islamist presence on its doorstep, the pretext to invade.

Ethiopia's occupation was backed by the US but after a war of insurgency led by the Courts alliance, the Ethiopians withdrew, handing security to the African Union.

In a clan-based society such as Somalia where it's not uncommon to hear someone say of a close cousin: "We meet in the 10th grandfather" – or approximately 300 years ago – the militias are tribal; the forging and breaking of alliances happens according to tribal interests. Even the parliament is a tribal entity based on a sub-sub-clan representation.

## FOOT SOLDIERS

Al-Shabab's success – like other Islamist organisations – can partly be attributed to their "modern structure", based more on merit rather than tribal loyalties. Beliefs, rituals and loyalty to the commander of the faithful replace the traditional loyalties.

Their foot soldiers are young men, radicalised by years of war, many from the marginalised tribes of the farming south that have been dominated for the past two decades by the strong pastoralist tribes. Their tribal elders can no longer offer any resemblance of respect.

"Most of the new recruits joining us now are the zealous young, their hearts are filled with passion and zeal, who can't wait to face the enemy. They are 14, 15, 16," said Qadir.

"They empower the young," a writer in Mogadishu who lives in al-Shabab-controlled Bakara market told me. "They go to the young, give them power, the power to face that rotten structure of the tribe, power in the shape of a gun. Power as self-esteem and belief ... This is why they succeed. Now I am worried about my own young brother."

With power, discipline and structure, al-Shabab managed to provide "security" to the local population, making it possible for people to safely leave their houses, go shopping, do business and, unlike government soldiers who are known to be little better than looters and criminals, their fighters enjoy a good reputation.

They also levy taxes from businesses and farmers and even local herders.

"We tax the people, the companies, the farmers and the herders. But we don't use the word tax. Instead we use the term aid. We also control some ports and airports that give us revenues. The big money transfer companies, we go to them once a month – they pay between ten thousand dollars and twenty during the war, at the time of peace few thousands only," says Qadir.

Al-Shabab is in nominal alliance with Hizb al-Islam but they often clash with each other over control of "liberated" areas and a war of assassination is going on between the two parties. Recently they have started to outbid each other on radicalism. When Hizb banned radios in Mogadishu from broadcasting music, al-Shabab issued a statement a week later banning schools from ringing bells. After al-Shabab started getting support from al-Qaida in Yemen and other jihadi groups, Hizb called on Osama bin Laden to come to Mogadishu.

FOREIGN BACKING

Just as the government receives military and financial support from Ethiopia, Djibouti, the EU and US, al-Shabab also look abroad for money, weapons and fighters.

"The government takes support from the west so we take support from our brothers the muhajiroon – immigrants," says Qadir. "Some are part of the fighting brigade, some don't leave their hiding places. They work in manufacturing explosives and strategy and those are not seen.

"They are Asians, Yemenis and Arabs with American passports, but there are also many Africans – Kenyans, Tanzanians and Moroccans." A large number of the muhajiroon arriving in Mogadishu are Somalis with western passports, he says. Some of them went on to become suicide bombers.

"We take films of the shelling and the bombing by the government and the African Union, and we show to the young in the diaspora and they come here enraged and passionate," he says. "We have our supporters in America, Australia and in Europe. Their duty is to recruit men and bring them to Somalia."

Many things have changed in Mogadishu over the last year. Gone are the plastic chairs in the presidential office and in have come wooden chairs with leather padding. The air-conditioned office is by far the coldest place in Mogadishu; a sweater is needed to stop you from shivering, while outside the sweltering heat envelops everything and everyone.

Even the president looks happier. The trappings of power seem to suit him. He no longer carries the world-weary look I saw when he took office last year. His face slips easily into a confident smile. He wears a thin, gold watch encrusted with glittering gems.

But Ahmed, who was described by Hillary Clinton as "our best hope", now rules only over a hilltop compound, the Villa Somalia, and a few adjacent streets. His government is on the verge of collapse, the parliament is split and infighting and corruption are paralysing the administration. Officers in the army say that they haven't been paid for months, the soldiers say they have no food to eat, and a major arms dealer told me that senior officers sell him their newly supplied guns and ammunition.

"We have learned a lot in the past year," says Ahmed, his fingers flipping the turquoise stones of a prayer bead as he speaks. "We don't think just in terms of military offensives. We think about humanitarian services, of understanding the people and orienting them towards their sacred responsibility of their holy duty towards their government."

## RECRUITS

A few days after meeting him, I head back to the presidential compound to attend the army day ceremonies. On one side of the hall are dozens of newly trained recruits, all in uniforms and boots supplied by the foreign powers that trained them, from France to Sudan and Djibouti.

On the other side are officers – former officers from the army, militia commanders and warlords. In between are ministers, dignitaries and more warlords.

Thickset bodyguards in sunglasses lead the president into the room. A brass orchestra strikes up the national anthem and everyone stands. A thin and elderly officer, carrying a rusted ceremonial sword and wearing a peeling red helmet, goose-steps to the front of the hall, saluting the president and the flag with his sword.

After an hour of speeches and as the president takes the podium, I stand outside watching a scuffle break out among the newly trained soldiers over the scraps of leftover food from the dignitaries' lunch inside. The Ugandan soldiers standing guard at the gate attempt to keep order but soon give up.

Then a big explosion rocks the building. The insurgents have started shelling the Villa Somalia compound just as the president begins to speak. The soldiers keep fighting for the scraps of food but a Ugandan tank parked close to the hall starts firing back at the insurgents' positions in the crowded markets of the city underneath. Six shells whoosh from the tank.

Eighteen people were killed and 64 injured from the shelling, I was told the next day when I went to Madina hospital. The director and the staff had spent the night in the operation room. "We did 35 operations during the night," the director tells me.

Just another day in Mogadishu's very uncivil war.

16 JUNE 2010

# Return to Derry: Bloody Sunday's victims vindicated at last

### SIMON WINCHESTER

We first knew that something truly remarkable, something historic, was in the offing when the hands began to appear, squeezing through the window-grilles of the old Guildhall. First one, then three, then 10 – and as they eased their way painfully under the barely open Victorian stained glass, so all raised up their thumbs, pointing to the sky.

They were the hands of the victims' relatives, of men and women from the Creggan and the Bogside who had been allowed in early to read the long-awaited report. There was a brief moment of bewilderment below – then suddenly the crowds realised and, as one, they went wild in a paroxysm of uncontained joy: the Saville report had vindicated the victims. Lord Saville had pronounced his verdict: the dead and the injured were all innocent, the soldiers had done them a terrible wrong, and a foul crime had been committed on the streets of Derry, 38 years before.

Minutes later, in perhaps the most hauntingly memorable of all of Britain's post-imperial moments, the prime minister got to his feet in the Commons and publicly apologised for what his country's soldiers had done, all those years ago. It was impossible to defend the indefensible, he said.

Men of the support company of the 1st Battalion Parachute Regiment had shot without justification. Victims had been shot in the back, or while they were crawling away. Soldiers had lied under oath. The episode would never be forgotten, could never be forgotten.

There was a roar of cheering at the high points of Cameron's speech – and barely no jeering, even during the obligatory utterances of praise, destined for the shires, for other soldiers in other places. But when it was over, the square was filled with a vast silence. It was as though they could scarcely believe what they had just heard, a British prime minister, a Tory at that, offering a formal and sincerely meant apology for what his soldiers had done nearly four decades ago to men and women who were guilty only of protesting at the excesses and longevity of British colonial rule of Ireland. It was a speech unprecedented in its tone, its scope and its content.

For the 30 minutes following, and in an episode for which one can forgive the slick choreography, the victims' closest surviving relatives spoke, one by one, quoting from the report and then ending with one cry: innocent!

There were fists punched in the air, whoops of joy – and tears. Many, many tears. I met an elderly lady, white-haired, cardiganned and dignified, spilling out of the square, weeping uncontrollably. I smiled at her, and she grinned back. "We did it!" was all she said, dabbing at her cheeks.

And someone had the good sense and taste publicly to tear up the blue-backed copy of the Widgery report, the 1972 travesty, a document giving politically motivated credence to the soldiers' now proven lies, and produced by the Lord Chief Justice of England, a man of shameful memory. The woman who tore it into shreds then tossed it into the air like confetti. It drifted down in front of the Guildhall doorway, allowing us to see the motto carved on the lintel a century and a half ago: *Vita. Victoria. Veritas*, it read. Life. Victory. Truth.

While yesterday's crowds formed on a day of warm Irish sunshine, on that Sunday 38 years ago, it was cold and clear, and the road over the Glenshane Pass from Belfast was slick with ice. I was driving fast and nearly lost control of the car, even before I reached Derry.

The political auguries were similarly bad. It had already been a dreadful month in Ulster, grim with killings. A foul mood had settled on Ulster's nationalists, following a deeply unpleasant incident a week earlier when the Civil Rights Association, having discovered the existence of a secret internment camp at Magilligan strand, on the shore of Lough Foyle 10 miles from Derry city, had organised a march – despite a province-wide ban on demonstrations – to bring its otherwise clandestine existence to popular attention.

There, they were surprised to be met by an elite company of Paras and given a most horrible thrashing: rubber bullets fired in faces, heads broken with nail-studded batons, with dozens of battered and bleeding protesters being hauled out of the water before they drowned. I watched and was horrified. My children were there – it was, after all, the seaside.

Reaction was swift; on Tuesday the CRA announced that a protest would take place in Derry the following weekend. "This latest act of violence," a statement from the Bogside said, "strengthens the will of the people of Derry to march in peaceful protest on Sunday next."

I was up early on Sunday morning for what we all knew would be a very big story. Police and army roadblocks were everywhere; on the radio the more rabid loyalists were predicting civil war. But

I had been told by my contacts among the Provisional IRA that they were moving their weapons away from the Bogside for the weekend: their brigade commander told me he assumed that British army snatch squads would use the occasion to search for guns, and they didn't want theirs found. So there would be an almighty riot that afternoon, that was certain. But I doubted if much firepower would be deployed, by anyone.

I told the news desk in Manchester to expect a probable candidate for page one. And then I sauntered in to the Bogside and the Creggan estate, past the barbed-wire barricades that the Royal Green Jackets were rolling into place. Inside, the crowds were assembling, and the speakers warming up at the microphones, mounted on the back of McGlinchey's coal lorry.

At one point, I thought I might get a better vantage point from where the troops were milling. But when I tried to go back outside the perimeter at the notorious flash point known as Aggro Corner, flashing my press card, the soldiers refused to let me through. "You stay and take what's coming, you!" one snarled, and pushed me back into the crowd of young Bogsiders.

The shuddering unfolding of that next 90 minutes will stay with me for as long as I live. The first shot that I noted was fired at 4.05pm, I believed from within the crowd; Saville, however, concluded yesterday that it was the paratroopers who opened fire first.

But there is no doubt about what happened next. Just a few moments after the shot, and as I was making my way towards where the speeches were starting, there came a sudden rising howl of screams, and then shouts and running and hysteria. "The soldiers, the soldiers!" people started shouting – and then, screeching into the lanes came lines of armoured cars and lorries, and I could see paratroopers, the same men from Magilligan, throwing themselves to the ground. And then, incredibly, they started firing,

firing, firing in our direction. I was too stunned to wonder why: all I knew was that I had to get out of the lines of fire, and quickly.

I ran and then, as bullets whizzed above me, dropped face down into a puddle of broken glass. A man fell beside me, blood gushing from his leg. I could see the soldiers taking up new firing positions, moving in a fan towards the crowd. I got up, raced toward a row of rubbish bins and dropped behind them, heart pounding. There was more firing. People were sobbing, cursing. I crawled, crab-like, into an alleyway; then with others I got up and ran again, stopped, breathing heavily, in a doorway. Two men lay motionless on the ground. A priest was moving past the blocks of flats with a small gaggle of men, carrying a wounded figure. He was waving a blood-stained white handkerchief.

A youngster of 16 or so was with me, terrified. At one point, the two of us managed to crawl on hands and knees up a slight rise, to a point below the city walls. I remain convinced that at this point a soldier fired at the two of us: I saw a soldier on the ground suddenly point his rifle at me, and his arms jerked, twice. I dived, and skittered up the laneway to a church, dived through the doorway, to be greeted by the keening wails of scores of men and women, sheltering in the pews, white-faced and terror-struck by what was happening outside.

And then, at around 4.20pm, the gunfire stopped, more or less. I left the church and walked down towards where they were now loading bodies and the wounded into cars. "Look at what they've done to us," said one demonstrator to me, in tears.

Maybe four or five had died, I thought. It was a terrible, terrible thing. There seemed no good reason for it. If the Paras had blazed in, even as a reaction to a single shot, their sudden spasm of shooting was surely out of all proportion. Was there perhaps a more sinister reaction? Was it planned? In the end I doubted it. I thought what had happened was simply, awfully, a needless loss of discipline, by soldiers made angry by the grind of their Ulster duties.

Nothing prepared me for the moment, at around 6pm, when I called the Altnagelvin hospital to check on the final numbers, so I could write my piece. I can still remember standing shivering in the telephone box outside the City hotel and being put through to a Mr Thompson, the hospital secretary.

"I have seen 12 bodies in here that have all most probably been killed by gunfire," he said. "There are 16 people in the wards. Fifteen of these have gunshot wounds, and one of them is a woman." He paused, spoke to someone in muffled tones. "I am sorry. There are 13 dead now. I have just been told."

I rang the news desk in Manchester, staffed that Sunday by a laconic, seen-everything old-timer. I told him the number of casualties. "My God!" he said, over and over. "My God!"

The repercussions we know about. In the short term, the burning of the British embassy in Dublin, the fall of Stormont eight weeks later, the effective displacement of the reasonable men of the CRA by the stony-faced zealots of the IRA.

And there was Lord Widgery, author of the contemptible first report on the shootings: it still rankles when I think of how the London press officers banned me from attending the briefing on his infamous report, reserving it only for accredited defence correspondents.

And then there were the longer-term consequences, of which the Good Friday agreement must necessarily be one – to the same degree that Brigadier Dyer's excesses at Amritsar were bombing a crucial step on the road to India's independence, and the bombing of the King David hotel part of the pathway to Israeli sovereignty.

Nine hundred witnesses came to Lord Saville's inquiry; I was one. How would I possibly remember the colour of a coat that had been worn by a dead man, 30 years before? Or whether I stood in the doorway to the left side or the right; or how easily I could identify the difference between the sound of an SLR and a heavy machine gun?

But for all the inadequacies of my own testimony, Saville, with his astonishing care and attention to detail, seemed to me at the time, and still seems today, a profoundly good idea: a proper full stop and colophon to Britain's unlovely and untidy colonial experience in Ireland.

For this now has been a true imperial moment, part of a colonial endgame, in its own way as symbolically important as all those lowering-of-flag ceremonies and the doffings of goose-feather helmets in tropic climes.

It was only tragic that such a moment should be required in the first place – serving as it does as a reminder of the lines from Auden:

*Acts of injustice done,*
*Between the rising and the setting sun,*
*In history lie like bones, each one.*

17 JUNE 2010

# Kyrgyzstan killings are attempted genocide, say ethnic Uzbeks

## LUKE HARDING

It was early afternoon when the mob surged down an alley of neat rose bushes and halted outside Zarifa's house. The Kyrgyz men broke into her courtyard and sat Zarifa down next to a cherry tree. They asked her a couple of questions. After confirming she was an ethnic Uzbek, they stripped her, raped her and cut off her fingers. After that they killed her and her small son, throwing their bodies into the street. They then moved on to the next house.

"They were like beasts," Zarifa's neighbour, Bakhtir Irgayshon, said yesterday, pointing to the gutted bed frame where she had been assaulted. A few pots and pans remained; the rest of the family home was a charred ruin. Zarifa's husband, Ilham, was missing, Irgayshon said, probably dead. Only his mother, Adina, survived the Kyrgyz-instigated conflagration that engulfed the neighbourhood of Cheremushki last Friday.

The scale of the ethnic killing that took place in Osh – as well as in other towns and villages in southern Kyrgyzstan – was grimly obvious. In the next street were the remains of another victim. He burned to death in his bed. Not much was left, only a jigsaw-like spine and hip. Nearby, Uzbek survivors were retrieving the bodies of seven small children. They had been incinerated, together with their mother, while cowering in a dark cellar.

Witnesses said the attacks by the Kyrgyz population on the Uzbek minority were attempted genocide.

The violence erupted in Osh last Thursday evening, possibly ignited by a row in a casino. But much of it appeared co-ordinated and planned, Uzbeks said. The attacks took the prosperous outlying Uzbek areas of town unawares.

"It started on Friday lunchtime," said Rustam, an Uzbek lawyer. "It came in three distinct waves. The Kyrgyz entered Cheremushki district driving an armoured personnel carrier. This paved the way. Several of them were wearing army uniforms. At first we felt relieved. Someone had come to rescue us, we thought! Then the BKR opened fire and started shooting people randomly.

"Behind them was the second wave. This was a mob of about 300 Kyrgyz youths armed with automatic weapons. Most were very young – between 15 and 20 years old. The third wave was made up of looters and included women and young boys. They stole everything of value, piling it into cars. Then they set our houses on fire."

According to Rustam the official toll from the riots – 178 dead and 1,800 injured – is a woeful underestimate. In reality, around 2,000 Uzbeks were slaughtered, he said, as the pogroms quickly spread from Osh to Jalal-Abad, 25 miles away, and other Uzbek villages in the south. Rustam said: "I carried 27 bodies myself. They were just bones. We are talking here about genocide."

With the violence largely now spent, and only the occasional gunshot disturbing Osh's evening curfew, survivors debated who was to blame. Some suggested Kyrgyzstan's ousted president, Kurmanbek Bakiyev, was behind them – describing the violence as a premeditated attempt by him to take revenge on the new leadership. Bakiyev fled the country in April after bloody protests in the capital, Bishkek. His supporters remain in control in much of the south. They dominate Osh's monoethnic Kyrgyz police and power structures, and also control the local mayor's office.

Few believe the riots could have taken place without the local administration's connivance. But it is clear that other grievances are at play. Ethnic Uzbeks make up 15% of Kyrgyzstan's 5.6 million population, and dominate the towns of Osh and Jalal-Abad. These settlements near the Fergana valley ended up in Kyrgyzstan by accident – when Lenin dumped them there in 1924.

"We're hard-working people. We were never nomadic like the Kyrgyz. We never lived in yurts. For the past 2,000 years we've built stone houses," Rustam said. He acknowledged that the town's Uzbeks were usually better off than their Kyrgyz neighbours. "Since the Silk Road, we've been involved in commerce and trade. We are successful. The Kyrgyz are jealous and resent this."

In the centre of Osh, Uzbek enterprises were in ruins. Shops marked with "KG" for Kyrgyz had been spared. Oktam Ismailova managed to save her home from the flames by sloshing water on her roof. A brick thrown through the window hit her father on the head. He survived. "We can't believe what happened. We are in shock," she said.

When the trouble started, thousands of Uzbeks fled to the Uzbekistan border, just three miles from Osh. Not everyone made it: one witness described how two Uzbek youths drove into a Kyrgyz mob in the centre of town. "They pulled the two Uzbek boys out of the car, and killed them in less than five minutes using sticks and knives. Then they dumped them in the Ak-Bura river," said Maya Tashbolotova, who watched, peering over the fence of her guesthouse.

So far, tens of thousands of refugees have crossed into Uzbekistan. According to Unicef, 90% of them are women, children and the elderly.

Yesterday, Uzbek guards sealed the border, a 5ft barbed wire fence. Nearby, Uzbek refugee children were washing in a stream while an old lady beaten in the face was being treated. The mood was one of anger, disbelief and betrayal. Many of the girls arriving at the border had been raped, witnesses said.

"Why did I train to be a surgeon? Was it for this?" said a 35-year-old Uzbek doctor, who declined to be named, crying quietly in the corner of his temporary surgery. The doctor said that many victims had been shot in the face and head. A nurse showed footage on a mobile phone of an Uzbek man who had been doused in kerosene and set alight. His head and arms were blackened stumps. He had no eyes. But he lived for several days, dying two days ago in agony.

"We have been discriminated against for 20 years," the doctor said, referring to the ethnic riots that took place near Osh in 1990, just after the breakup of the Soviet Union. Recently, he said, Kyrgyz chauvinism had grown, fuelled by the weakness of the government, and by a fear that the Uzbek minority was becoming too strong and was prone to secessionist-minded leaders.

There was not much sign of humanitarian relief yesterday, with Kyrgyz drivers too scared to enter Uzbek neighbourhoods. Uzbeks had demarcated their territory by felling maple trees and building makeshift barricades with burned-out cars. Nearby, Kyrgyz soldiers had set up checkpoints in a post-facto show of strength. Some Kyrgyz locals blamed the riots on Uzbek youths, who they said ransacked a local casino.

Back in Cheremushki, Rustam said the events of the last week heralded a return to barbarism in an age seemingly governed by international rules and institutions. Asked who was to blame, he said: "It was the state against us. It was the whole system. It was everything."

23 JUNE 2010

# Wimbledon live blog: John Isner v Nicolas Mahut

## XAN BROOKS

3.45PM: The drama has now moved, lock, stock and barrel, to Court 18. There John Isner and Nicolas Mahut are locked in a deadlock that shows no sign of ending. The pair are tied at 15 games all in the final set of a mountainous struggle.

4.05PM: The Isner-Mahut battle is a bizarre mix of the gripping and the deadly dull. It's tennis's equivalent of *Waiting for Godot*, in which two lowly journeymen comedians are forced to remain on an outside court until hell freezes over and the sun falls from the sky. Isner and Mahut are dying a thousand deaths out there on Court 18 and yet nobody cares, because they're watching the football. So the players stand out on their baseline and belt aces past each other in a fifth set that has already crawled past two hours. They are now tied at 18-games apiece.

Ooh, I can see the football out of the corner of my eye. England still 1-0 up!

4.25PM: John Isner's serving arm has fallen off. Nicolas Mahut's head is loose and rolling bonelessly on his neck. And yet still they play on. The score is now 21-21 in the fifth and final set. This is now, officially, the longest final set in Wimbledon history.

4.50PM: It's over. It's finally over. It was a long, hard match and it took its toll on the players. But finally, at long last, we have a result.

I'm actually talking about the football here. England win 1-0 against Slovenia to go through to the knock-out stage. The Isner-Mahut match is still ongoing: 24-24 in the final set. Isner's leg has just dropped off.

5.05PM: Under the feet of John Isner and Nicolas Mahut, the grass is growing. Before long they will be playing in a jungle and when they sit down at the change of ends, a crocodile will come to menace them. They are poised at 25 games apiece in a deciding set that is now nudging three hours.

5.55PM: Is it a dream, a lie, or is John Isner really about to triumph in the longest match in tennis history? The American flicks a back-hand return up the line to reach 15-40, with two match points. But then Mahut finds the line with a forehand and hastens in to tap away a terrified volley. Incredibly, he saves the second match point too and then pulls level once more: 33-33 in the final set. So yes, it was a dream, it was a lie. The Amazing Zombie Tennis Pros are not through with us yet. Ha ha ha ha! Ha ha ha!

6PM: The score stands at 34-34. In order to stay upright and keep their strength, Isner and Mahut have now started eating members of the audience. They trudge back to the baseline, gnawing on thigh-bones and sucking intestines. They have decided that they will stay on Court 18 until every spectator is eaten. Only then, they say, will they consider ending their contest.

6.25PM: The scoreboard is barely visible through the grass and weeds and trails of Spanish moss. It shows that John Isner and Nicolas Mahut are locked at 37 games each in the final set.

I'm wondering if maybe an angel will come and set them free. Is this too much to ask? Just one slender angel, with white wings and a wise smile, to tell them that's it's all right, they have suffered enough and that they are now being recalled. The angel could hug them and kiss their brows and invite them to lay their rackets gently on the grass. And then they could all ascend to heaven together. John Isner, Nicolas Mahut and the kind angel that saved them.

7PM: The umpire climbs down from his chair and starts mildly slapping the net cord with his right hand. No one knows why. John Isner winds up for a backhand and misses the ball entirely. No one knows why. What's going on here? Once, long ago, I think that this was a tennis match. It's not that any more and hasn't been for a few hours now. I'm not quite sure what it is, but it is long and it's horrifying and it's very long to boot. Is it death? I think it might be death.

7.30PM: Let it end, let it end, it's 46-all. It was funny when it was 16-all and it was creepy when it was 26-all. But this is pure purgatory and there is still no end in sight.

7.45PM: What happens if we steal their rackets? If we steal their rackets, the zombies can no longer hit their aces and thump their backhands and keep us all prisoner on Court 18. I'm shocked that this is only occurring to me now. Who's with me? Steal their rackets and then run for the tube. It's 48-48. What further incentive do you need?

8.40PM: It's 56 games all and darkness is falling. This, needless to say, is not a good development, because everybody knows that zombies like the dark. So far in this match they've been comparatively puny and manageable, only eating a few of the spectators in between bashing their serves. But come nightfall the world is their oyster. They will play on, play on, right through until dawn. Perhaps they will even leave the court during the changeovers to munch on other people.

9.10PM: Is it over? It is not over. For a brief moment back then, I thought it was over. Isner clambers to match point on Mahut's serve. Mahut steps forward and saves it with his 95th ace. It's 59-59. Mahut wants to come off now; the light is almost gone. But the official orders the pair to play two more games. "We want more! We want more!" chant the survivors on Court 18. I'm taking this as proof that they have gone insane.

9.12PM: Mahut prevails! Mahut wins! This is not to say he wins the match, of course. Nobody is winning this match; not now and not ever. But he prevails in his complaint and his wish is granted. Play is suspended. They will come back tomorrow and pick it up where they left off, at 59-59 in the final set. Apparently the last set of this match has now lasted longer than any match in tennis history. Can this really be true? Nothing would surprise me any more.

9.25PM: If you're going to watch a pair of zombies go at each other for eleventy-billion hours, far into the night, it might as well be these zombies. They were incredible, astonishing, indefatigable. They fell over frequently but they never stayed down. My hat goes off to these zombies. Possibly my head goes off to them too.

Thanks so much for sticking with me; for your comments and tweets and your emails too. It was very much appreciated. If you're going to live blog a tennis match in Necropolis, it's reassuring to have someone there to hold your hand.

I'm off tomorrow, possibly lying in a ditch somewhere. I'm back on Friday, by which time this contest will probably be into quadruple figures in the final set. We'll simply pick it up and take it from there.

*John Isner won the match the following day, 6-4, 3-6, 6-7, 7-6, 70-68. The above is an edited selection of the (very long) Wimbledon live blog*

28 JUNE 2010

# World Cup 2010: England re-enact the drama of failure

## PAUL HAYWARD

The men of 1966 can pack their diaries with yet more heroes' dinners and brand-ambassador spin-offs because 44 years of waiting could be just the start.

England have still not beaten a top-flight nation in a World Cup knockout round since the Bobby Moore-Geoff Hurst generation exploited home advantage in the country's one and only appearance in the final of an international tournament. A brutal pattern reasserted itself in the Free State as German youth flourished and English maturity tipped over into obsolescence. Mesut Özil and Thomas Müller – flag-bearers for a more thrilling German style of play – pushed a whole crop of English household names into permanent shadow.

The Frank Lampard-Steven Gerrard generation have had failure's nail banged into them and it shows. Deep in their minds a voice must cry out that success at World Cup and European Championship level is simply beyond imagining. The temptation across the English game must be to retreat to the sanctuary of the

Premier League, with its Super Sunday clashes between empires of debt. These expeditions in the Three Lions livery are only a trail of tears.

Five of England's starting XI in this second-round match had played in Champions League finals. Pressure and expectation are written into their daily lives. With England, though, their talent evaporates, their sense of self collapses. They look tight and ponderous and tactically illiterate.

Germany played dazzling football in bursts and adjusted their pace and pattern of play to suit the circumstances. They worked out how to win the game and reach a quarter-final. Two counter-attacking goals in four minutes showed up England's defensive naivety and wooden pursuit of an equaliser after the goal-that-never-was: the best indictment yet of Fifa's neanderthal prejudice against goal-line technology.

In the Wimbledon fortnight a simple machine can say whether a tennis ball has crossed a white line. Here in football's biggest competition Fifa tells men their lives will be defined by what happens on the World Cup stage and then denies them the equipment that would make those definitions fair. But this legitimate gripe will not conceal England's ineptitude in allowing Germany to counterattack their way to a crushing victory and so extend the hurt inflicted in 1970 and 1990.

Germany have advanced further than England in every World Cup the two nations have contested since 1966. Capello's team didn't lose to a history book, however, they folded in the here and now against a side with an average age four years lower. On a shallow, Premier League-warped reading of the team-sheets they would have feared the gifted Özil, 21, and Müller, 20, and known all about Lukas Podolski's fierce shot and Miroslav Klose's exceptional international goalscoring pedigree (50, now, which is one more than Sir Bobby Charlton's England record).

Yet English players who have faced Barcelona and Real Madrid in Champions League combat cannot have felt that Germany were an unstoppable historical force. They will have played the names in front of them, which makes their demise all the more frightening. Germany brought zest and zip and cunning to their attacking play. England advanced in lumpen 4-4-2 formation without any of Germany's geometrical cleverness.

A recurring truth is that the way football is played in England (or by English players) is not conducive to international success. In Africa's first World Cup, specifically, they won one of their four fixtures – 1-0, against Slovenia – scored three and conceded five. Insiders say the campaign hit psychological turbulence when Robert Green committed a pub keeper's error in fumbling Clint Dempsey's shot in the USA game. There was, by all accounts, a collapse of faith that the win over Slovenia only partially restored.

In the 21st century alone England have seen the ball sail over David Seaman's head in Japan (2002), successive penalty shoot-out defeats to Portugal (2004 and 2006) the non-qualification debacle of Euro 2008 and a promising qualifying campaign unravel here in South Africa. Regression is the tale of Capello's first World Cup as a manager. Quarter-finalists in 2002 and 2006, England stumbled out of Group C in second place and lost to the first big-name team they came across.

Wayne Rooney's sole imprint on this great competition remains the stud marks he left on the groin of Portugal's Ricardo Carvalho four years ago. Given his precocity, Brazil in 2014 will be his last chance to impress the judges in an England shirt. Rooney improved against Germany: his first touch and link play were sharper, more aware. But over the four games he was a phantom of his real self. The English culture managed to deliver its best player to a tournament hollow and semi-detached.

In the calamity catalogue we file Rio Ferdinand's knee injury in the first training session, Ledley King's breakdown inside 45 minutes of the USA game, the Green goalkeeping howler and John Terry's failed insurrection. It was fashionable to say at least England were not like France. In retrospect it would have been more fun to go out like the French, with eruptions everywhere, than concede two goals on the counter-attack when the score was still 2-1. Can England not press for an equaliser more intelligently?

Over the three weeks Ashley Cole, John Terry and Glen Johnson performed creditably (though Johnson left his rear-view mirror back at base again yesterday), Lampard was mostly innocuous, Gerrard was wasted on the left and Joe Cole under-used. Aaron Lennon and Shaun Wright-Phillips were passengers. Michael Dawson, Stephen Warnock, Joe Hart and Michael Carrick were all denied a kick. All will flee the Royal Bafokeng complex glad to have escaped this eternal wheel of fire.

Capello toured the shires in search of fresh talent and found none. Ashley Young, Gabriel Agbonlahor and even Theo Walcott were discarded. The manager was surely right to conclude that English football's nursery is not producing fruit. National coaching programmes and strategic planning are not the English way. Feeding the Premier League monster is the only show in town. The Football Association, where a vast power void now prevails, throws money at 44 years of frustration by importing first Swedish then Italian expertise and locking itself into expensive long contracts.

Feel better now? Each time the mantra is that we need to be honest about the true state and standing of the England football team and we never are.

19 July 2010

# Baldrick would applaud Osborne's cunning slash-and-burn plan

## LARRY ELLIOTT

Like Baldrick, George Osborne has a cunning plan. It involves growing the economy through cuts. And not just any old cuts either: the cuts the chancellor has in mind are the biggest and most sustained cuts in public spending since the second world war. Plus some tax rises and benefit changes that will hit the poorest families in Britain hardest.

Ministers do not doubt for a moment that the austerity measures will cause pain but argue that Britain, according to Osborne, is so deeply in hock to its creditors following the recession that a whole parliament of retrenchment is both unavoidable and beneficial. It will be good for us in the end, because the financial markets will be impressed by the pain that the government is prepared to inflict on voters.

Investors will flock to the City of London and buy UK bonds (known as gilts) as if they are going out of fashion. The stronger the demand for gilts, the lower the interest rate the government has to pay to service its debts. And it is that interest rate that helps determine the cost of overdrafts, long-term mortgages and business loans. Lower interest rates mean stronger growth. Excessive public spending leads to higher interest rates and hence lower growth, so cutting public spending is good for us because it enables interest rates to fall. That, in essence, is the cunning plan.

It's fair to say that some private-sector beneficiaries of the plan have yet to realise just how cunning it is. Construction firms kept going during the recession by the Building Schools for the Future programme have responded to the news that 750 projects are to be canned by laying off staff.

The International Monetary Fund doesn't seem to "get it" either, since it has cut its growth forecast for the UK this year and next in the light of Osborne's budget. The rating agency Standard & Poor's has expressed doubts about whether the government has the stomach for the austerity in prospect.

What concerns the IMF is that almost every western nation, barring the United States, has its own version of Osborne's cunning plan. Domestic demand is to be squeezed in Germany, Italy, France, Britain and Spain but all will be well because every country is going to export more. US policymakers think this is nonsense, and are clearly worried by the relapse in the property market, the persistently high level of unemployment and the depressed level of activity among small firms.

In the past week or so, the cunning plan has come under more scrutiny. The penny has dropped that Osborne is embarking on his fiscal squeeze at the moment when the eurozone has locked itself into deflation and the US is facing an economic slowdown and perhaps a double-dip recession. It has been noted that despite the 25% fall in the exchange rate over the past three years, Britain has not received any boost from trade.

What's the plan B if the cunning plan goes wrong? The answer is simple: there is no plan B because the Treasury believes the need for one will not arise. There may be some slowdown in the recovery, both here and elsewhere, but there will be no second leg to the recession.

Ministers, though, would be well advised to keep a wary eye on what is happening in the US, because in 2007 and 2008 what happened across the Atlantic happened here after a six-month time lag. Equally, they should be concerned about the fragility of the labour market, where total hours worked are still falling although the number employed is going up as a result of an increase in part-time jobs. And that is before the public-sector job cuts start to bite.

Imagine that it is the summer of 2011 and the austerity measures are starting to bite. Higher VAT is squeezing consumer spending, the axe is falling on the public sector, and exports are being stifled by sluggish growth in Europe and North America. Unemployment is heading rapidly towards three million among the under-25 age group, where the jobless rate is already more than 17%, one in four are out of work. On the 30th anniversary of the Brixton riots, trouble erupts in the inner cities.

So what does the coalition do in those circumstances? The bank rate is already at 0.5% and can go no lower, while to water down the public spending cuts or abandon the tax increases would be to invite the wrath of the bond markets that the draconian fiscal policy is there to avert.

Despite the spin coming out of the Treasury, the financial markets have taken a relatively relaxed view of Britain's deficit, even during the months leading up to the election when the result was uncertain. Bond yields certainly did not suggest that the economy was in crisis or needed the sort of indiscriminate cuts that have been seen in the past two months.

One example of the slash-and-burn approach was the scrapping of the Future Jobs Fund, an attempt to provide guaranteed work for long-term unemployed young people. It was part of an activist approach to the labour market by the last government that prevented job losses during the recession from approaching the levels seen during the slumps of the early 1980s and early 1990s.

The Organisation for Economic Co-operation and Development in Paris has expressed concern about the abolition of the fund, warning that deficit reduction should not come at the expense of dealing with the employment legacy of the recession. That is precisely what is happening, with the coalition's macho language, as well as its policy decisions, eerily redolent of early Thatcherism. Yet even Margaret Thatcher had a plan B, which involved lower interest rates, a falling exchange rate, financial deregulation and a North Sea oil bonanza.

Osborne has said that if growth disappoints, the Bank of England could announce a new round of quantitative easing, pumping electronic money into the banking system through the purchase of bonds. To the extent that there is a plan B, this is it.

But the Bank admits it does not know how to assess fully the impact of QE; it says the £200bn of asset purchases in the year to February 2010 helped reduce long-term interest rates by a percentage point but cannot really quantify what the impact was on the wider economy as opposed to asset prices.

Moreover, fresh asset purchases will only be triggered if the Bank's monetary policy committee believes that more QE is consistent with hitting the government's 2% inflation target. There is no evidence that a resumption of QE is in prospect and – if the experience of 2008 is anything to go by – the Bank will only act when it is too late.

A proper plan B would involve an approach to deficit reduction that helps rather than hinders growth and a QE2 programme that would finance a green investment bank, with the proceeds channelled into retro-fitting homes and low-carbon technologies. That would have the effect of finding work for construction workers and boosting the growth of the environmental industries.

This, though, is a government that has the finesse of an 18th-century sawbones operating in the days before anaesthetic. The operation is not considered a success unless unnecessary pain is involved. Medical science has moved on since those days. The dismal science, it seems, has not.

26 JULY 2010

# Massive leak of secret files exposes true Afghan war

## NICK DAVIES AND DAVID LEIGH

A huge cache of secret US military files today provides a devastating portrait of the failing war in Afghanistan, revealing how coalition forces have killed hundreds of civilians in unreported incidents, Taliban attacks have soared and Nato commanders fear neighbouring Pakistan and Iran are fuelling the insurgency.

The disclosures come from more than 90,000 records of incidents and intelligence reports about the conflict obtained by the whistleblowers' website Wikileaks in one of the biggest leaks in US military history. The files, which were made available to the *Guardian*, the *New York Times* and the German weekly *Der Spiegel*, give a blow-by-blow account of the fighting over the last six years, which has so far cost the lives of more than 320 British and more than 1,000 US troops.

The war logs also detail:

- How a secret "black" unit of special forces hunts down Taliban leaders for "kill or capture" without trial.
- How the US covered up evidence that the Taliban have acquired deadly surface-to-air missiles.

- How the coalition is increasingly using deadly Reaper drones to hunt and kill Taliban targets by remote control from a base in Nevada.
- How the Taliban have caused growing carnage with a massive escalation of their roadside bombing campaign, which has killed more than 2,000 civilians to date.

In a statement yesterday, the White House said the chaotic picture painted by the logs was the result of "under-resourcing" under Obama's predecessor, saying: "It is important to note that the time period reflected in the documents is January 2004 to December 2009."

The White House also criticised the publication of the files by Wikileaks: "We strongly condemn the disclosure of classified information by individuals and organisations, which puts the lives of the US and partner service members at risk and threatens our national security. Wikileaks made no effort to contact the US government about these documents, which may contain information that endangers the lives of Americans, our partners, and local populations who co-operate with us."

The logs detail, in sometimes harrowing vignettes, the toll on civilians exacted by coalition forces: events termed "blue on white" in military jargon. The logs reveal 144 such incidents.

Some of these casualties come from the controversial air strikes that have led to Afghan government protests, but a large number of previously unknown incidents also appear to be the result of troops shooting unarmed drivers or motorcyclists out of a determination to protect themselves.

At least 195 civilians are admitted to have been killed and 174 wounded in total, but this is likely to be an underestimate as many disputed incidents are omitted from the daily snapshots reported by troops on the ground and then collated, sometimes erratically, by intelligence analysts.

Bloody errors at civilians' expense, as recorded in the logs, include the day French troops strafed a bus full of children in 2008, wounding eight. A US patrol similarly machine-gunned a bus, wounding or killing 15 of its passengers, and in 2007 Polish troops mortared a village, killing a wedding party, including a pregnant woman, in an apparent revenge attack.

Questionable shootings of civilians by UK troops also figure. The US compilers detail an unusual cluster of four British shootings in Kabul in the space of barely a month, in October/November 2007, culminating in the death of the son of an Afghan general. Of one shooting, they wrote: "Investigation controlled by the British. We are not able to get [sic] complete story."

A second cluster of similar shootings, all involving Royal Marine commandos in Helmand province, took place in a six-month period at the end of 2008, according to the log entries. Asked by the *Guardian* about these allegations, the Ministry of Defence said: "We have been unable to corroborate these claims in the short time available and it would be inappropriate to speculate on specific cases without further verification of the alleged actions."

Rachel Reid, who investigates civilian casualty incidents in Afghanistan for Human Rights Watch, said: "These files bring to light what's been a consistent trend by US and Nato forces: the concealment of civilian casualties. Despite numerous tactical directives ordering transparent investigations when civilians are killed, there have been incidents I've investigated in recent months where this is still not happening. Accountability is not just something you do when you are caught. It should be part of the way the US and Nato do business in Afghanistan every time they kill or harm civilians."

The reports, many of which the *Guardian* is publishing in full online today, present an unvarnished and often compelling account of the reality of modern war.

Most of the material, though classified "secret" at the time, is no longer militarily sensitive. A small amount of information has been withheld from publication because it might endanger local informants or give away genuine military secrets. Wikileaks, whose founder, Julian Assange, obtained the material in circumstances he will not discuss, said it would redact harmful material before posting the bulk of the data on its "uncensorable" servers.

Assange allowed the *Guardian* to examine the logs at the newspaper's request several weeks ago. No fee was involved and Wikileaks was not involved in the preparation of the *Guardian*'s articles.

26 July 2010

# Grim toll of small tragedies at hands of jittery troops

DAVID LEIGH

Shum Khan was a deaf and dumb man who lived in the remote border hamlet of Malekshay, 7,000ft up in the mountains. When a heavily armed squad from the CIA barrelled into his village in March 2007, the war logs record that he "ran at the sight of the approaching coalition forces ... out of fear and confusion".

The secret CIA paramilitaries (the euphemism here is OGA, for "other government agency") shouted at him to stop. Khan could not hear them. He carried on running. So they shot him, saying they were entitled to do so under the carefully graded "escalation of force" provisions of the US rules of engagement.

Khan was wounded but survived. The Americans' error was explained to them by village elders, so they fetched out what they term "solatia", or compensation. The classified intelligence report ends briskly: "Solatia was made in the form of supplies and the Element mission progressed."

Behind the military jargon, the war logs are littered with accounts of civilian tragedies. The 144 entries in the logs recording some of these so-called "blue on white" events cover a wide spectrum of day-by-day assaults on Afghans, with hundreds of casualties.

They range from the shootings of individual innocents to the often massive loss of life from air strikes, which eventually led President Hamid Karzai to protest publicly that the US was treating Afghan lives as "cheap". When civilian family members are actually killed in Afghanistan, their relatives do, in fairness, get greater solatia payments than cans of beans and Hershey bars. The logs refer to sums paid of 100,000 Afghani per corpse, equivalent to about £1,500.

US and allied commanders frequently deny allegations of mass civilian casualties, claiming they are Taliban propaganda or ploys to get compensation, which are contradicted by facts known to the military. But the logs demonstrate how much of the contemporaneous US internal reporting of air strikes is simply false.

Last September there was a major scandal at Kunduz in the north of Afghanistan when a German commander ordered the bombing of a crowd looting two hijacked fuel tankers. The contemporaneous archive circulated to Nato allies records him authorising the air strike by a US F-15 jet "after ensuring that no civilians were in the vicinity". The "battle damage assessment" confirmed, it claims, that 56 purely "enemy insurgents" had died.

Media reports followed by official inquiries, however, established something closer to the real death toll. It included 30 to 70 civilians.

In another case the logs show that on the night of 30 August 2008, a US special forces squad called Scorpion 26 blasted Helmand positions with multiple rockets, and called in an air strike to drop a 500lb bomb. All that was officially logged was that 24 Taliban had been killed.

But writer Patrick Bishop was embedded in the valley nearby with British paratroops at their Sangin bases. He recorded independently: "Overnight, the question of civilian casualties took on an extra urgency. An American team had been inserted on to Black Mountain ... From there, they launched a series of offensive operations. On 30 August, wounded civilians, some of them badly injured, turned up at Sangin and FOB Inkerman saying they had been attacked by foreign troops. Such incidents gave a hollow ring to Isaf [the occupying forces] claims that their presence would bring security to the local population."

Some of the more notorious civilian calamities did become public at the time. The logs confirm that an entirely truthful official announcement was made regretting the guidance system failure of one "smart bomb". On 9 September 2008 it unintentionally landed on a village causing 26 civilian casualties.

The US also realised very quickly that a Polish squad had committed what appeared to have been a possible war crime. On 16 August 2007 the Poles mortared a wedding party in the village of Nangar Khel in an apparent revenge attack shortly after experiencing an IED explosion.

It is recorded under the heading: "Any incident that may cause negative media". The report disclosed that three women victims had "numerous shrapnel wounds ... One was pregnant and an emergency C-section was performed but the baby died." In all, six were killed. The Polish troops were shipped home and some eventually put on trial for the atrocity. After protests in their support from a Polish general, the trial has apparently so far failed to reach a conclusion.

But most of the assaults on civilians recorded here do not appear to have been investigated. French troops "opened fire on a bus that came too close to convoy" near the village of Tangi Kalay outside Kabul on 2 October 2008, according to the logs. They wounded eight children who were in the bus.

Two months later, US troops gunned down a group of bus passengers even more peremptorily, as the logs record.

Patrolling on foot, a Kentucky-based squad from 1st Battalion, 506th Infantry Regiment, known as "Red Currahee", decided to flag down the approaching bus, so their patrol could cross the road. Before sunrise, a soldier stepped out on to Afghanistan's main highway and raised both hands in the air.

When the bus failed to slow – travellers are often wary of being flagged down in Afghanistan's bandit lands – a trooper raked it with machine-gun fire. They killed four passengers and wounded 11 others.

Some of the civilian deaths in the list stem from violent actions by US special forces attempting to hunt down Taliban leaders or al-Qaida incomers. In a typical case, last November, the army files record a demonstration by 80 angry villagers who broke an armoured car window in the village of Lewani. A woman from the village had been killed in an assault by the shadowy Task Force 373.

The influence of the then new commander, General Stanley McChrystal, can be seen, however. Brought in last year with a mission to try to cut the number of civilian casualties, he clearly demanded more detailed reporting of such incidents.

The Lewani file is marked with a new "information requirement" to record each "credible allegation of Isaf ... causing non-combatant injury/death".

McChrystal was replaced last month, however, by General David Petraeus, amid reports that restraints aimed at cutting civilian deaths would be loosened once again.

The bulk of the "blue-white" file consists of a relentless catalogue of civilian shootings on nearly 100 occasions by jumpy troops at checkpoints, near bases or on convoys. Unco-operative drivers and motorcyclists are frequent targets.

Each incident almost without exception is described as a meticulous "escalation of force" conducted strictly by the book, against a threatening vehicle.

US and UK rules require shouts, waves, flares, warning shots and shots into the engine block, before using lethal force. Each time it is claimed that this procedure is followed. Yet "warning shots" often seem to cause death or injury, generally ascribed to ricochets.

27 JULY 2010

# People's say I'm fixated on faeces. But it's politics I love

STEVE BELL

Sometimes life at the cartoon face can be tough, but not that tough. Nobody's shooting at you, though some of the comments on our website can feel like that. It is important to take a break, though, from the relentlessness of daily double deadlines so when I asked Martin Rowson if he could cover for me this summer and he said he was busy working on his new version of *Gulliver's Travels*, a problem arose.

Martin came up with an elegant solution. We are both constantly badgered by young cartoonists waiting for us to die (as indeed Martin himself once urged me to), as well as editors complaining about how difficult it is to find fresh talent. He suggested using our longer than normal holiday period of six weeks to showcase some of the talent we know full well to be out there.

Political cartooning has no strict career path and no particular age or gender limit, in spite of the obvious fact that all the leading newspaper practitioners are white, male, middle class and getting on a bit. The six we chose are the best we know of. They range between 19 and 48 – three women and three men and with an uncanny ability to think, draw, make a point and even have a laugh. Doing all these things simultaneously and hitting a deadline is more than a little challenging.

I was very fortunate when I first approached the *Guardian*, way back in the mists of time in 1981. They happened to be looking for a homegrown strip to run alongside Doonesbury. I'd been doing strips in children's comics, in lefty magazines and latterly a weekly strip for *Time Out* called Maggie's Farm. But a daily cartoon is a much more difficult proposition. When I went to meet the then editor, Peter Preston, and he invited me to do a month's trial, I was thrilled to bits, then terrified. The deal was that they would pay me to do the strip for four weeks, and if they liked them, they would use me. My first faltering efforts at the If... strip were never actually published, and I'd been doing a strip six days a week for nine years before I ever got to do a "big one" on the Comment page in November 1990.

For me, cartooning in this position in this paper is the best job in the world. Not only does it mean I get to draw and paint every day, but it also presents a perfect opportunity to shout back at the torrent of preposterous rubbish issuing from radio, television and any other media yet to be devised every single minute of every day. There is nothing quite so satisfying as turning politicians into cartoon characters and then, capriciously, insolently, toying with their fate.

It does require a certain arrogance to sit in judgment over the great and good, as well as the not so good and the less great who rule our lives, but I've had a political agenda as long as my arm since I was in flared trousers, and have never been expected to express any point of view other than my own. The fact that I've been trusted by the *Guardian* to do it for so long is something for which I am eternally grateful. Yet the very nature of what I do compels me to not only bite but despise the hand that feeds me.

I've worked for the paper from the days when I regarded it as a bourgeois, SDP-loving crapsheet. In some ways nothing has changed, except that nowadays the SDP-lovers would be considered far too leftwing. There is a kind of innate unruliness in a cartoon that disrupts the carefully laid-out and authoritative design lines of the modern newspaper. It has to be autonomous and speak for itself, floating on a sea of text, but more often than not directly contradicting that which surrounds it. It can be read in an instant or digested at length. It can cause paroxysms of laughter, love and loathing – or comment simply and eloquently without any words at all.

Yet the cartoon is often thought of as trivialising issues and contributing to a growing cynicism about politics and politicians. It is also resented because of its licence to be the very antithesis of responsible journalism. This is in part a result of prejudice. Cartoons and comics are regarded by some as irredeemably vulgar, the humour coarse and imagery frequently scatological. Cartoonists, it would seem, are not fully developed psychologically, and remain fixated on faeces and bodily fluids. I would maintain that – while fully understanding that people don't wish to be put off their breakfast – if you are unable to laugh at your own waste products you may be the one with the psychological problem.

I would also assert that it is politics itself that makes people cynical. When manifest drivel like the "big society" goes through a whole election campaign largely unchallenged, cynicism is the only healthy response. Far from being a growing irrelevance within the dying medium of printed newspapers, there never has been a greater need for cartooning. While politics is so obsessed with image control, cartoonists are uniquely placed to take such imagery apart and reassemble it in whatever ludicrous or intriguing manner they think fit.

This is not only taking the piss; it is a vital and necessary part of our democracy.

Nonetheless, the way cartoons work is still a mystery to me, though I've been doing them professionally for more than 30 years. What I do know is that a cartoon can hinge on the slightest detail, and discovering whether a drawing works or not (which you can only judge on seeing it, in cold print, the day after you've drawn it) is a constant source of delight. You have to try things out, and you do have to take some risks. Strangely, there are times when you need to dare to be bleeding obvious (as happened with the first big one I ever did for the paper, after Geoffrey Howe's resignation speech put paid to Margaret Thatcher). Quite often those turn out to be the best and most effective of all.

This is something of a baptism of fire for our posse of cartoonists, but over the next six weeks you will see something very special in development. Their styles are all very strong and distinctive. It may turn out to be professionally suicidal for Martin and I to encourage such talent, rather than break its fingers, but we think you will agree that the future of political cartooning in this paper is assured for some time to come.

30 July 2010

# Afghanistan journal: on the ground with US forces

## SEAN SMITH

26/6/2010 Kandahar air base is the main military operational hub for southern Afghanistan. There are thousands of French, Canadian, Italian, British, Romanians and Americans here. But it's clear the Americans are running the show. There's a big contrast between here and the smaller bases. Everyone is in clean uniform. There is a dress code; in some areas you have to salute, and others you don't – it's quite surreal. There is a German army shop here that's selling all sorts of expensive penknives, muscle-builders' magazines and combat clothing. There's Columbia outdoor clothing and chequered shirts for contractors. All the restaurants are awful; we are better catered for in the army canteen – except that every soup there, no matter what flavour, tastes of cream of chicken.

27/6/2010 All the journalists here are starting to act like they want to be soldiers. They're talking about "L-shaped attacks" and speaking military speak. I hear one saying, "Right, now we're being drawn into L-shaped attacks, so they're planting IEDs in front of them." They're all getting very enthusiastic, going into the military shops and buying contractor-type trousers and getting military haircuts.

29/6/2010 I arrive around 1.30am at Camp Bastion, then I have an early flight to the US Marine Corps' HQ at Camp Dwyer. No one is expecting me. I find that I am not going to Marjah in Helmand province, but I am instead going south. The long journey has begun.

30/6/2010 Checked in for the helicopter flight to Forward Operating Base Delhi in southern Afghanistan. I'm joining the 1st Battalion, 3rd US Marines. I don't spend any time there. I've had about three hours' sleep. I'm trying to find out where I'm going – I'm told there is a convoy next morning going south, so I'm getting on that. I overhear on a radio in the background that there is a helicopter under fire where I am going. They've got injured.

2/7/2010 Joining the route-clearance convoy driving even further south. It is all by road now. These clearance guys are trying to keep the main roads going south clear for supplies and stuff like that. There are 10 trucks in the convoy.

They drive down the road and if something blows up under the first truck, then that is one more IED cleared from the road. The first truck is supposed to be IED-resistant, but still there is only one guy in it in case it is blown up. They've got rollers in front of it to try to blow up the IED before the truck itself gets there.

No one is talking much. The engine is very noisy. They have air conditioning in most of the trucks, but sometimes it doesn't work because it gets clogged up by all the dust. We're reading magazines, everything from porn to *National Geographic*. We drive for about eight hours.

03/07/2010 Still with the 1st Battalion, I join a convoy pushing further south to PB Karma – Patrol Base Karma. No one knew why it was called that. Probably a joke. It's almost the furthest point south that the Americans have reached.

The gunner up on top is watching everything, trying to see if there are kids about. If there are no kids and it looks as if people have cleared away, then you might be expecting an IED. So kids can be a good sign. We left at seven in the morning and it is now getting dark but we have probably moved less than 20km. It has taken eight hours.

I'm now in Karma base. It's an old hospital with sandbagged compound walls. Sleeping on a fold-out bed in the corridor trying to get a bit cooler. There are probably 30 people based here. I later find out the company has lost three people in the last two weeks.

The area is completely littered with IEDs. This is the front line.

The idea of the foot patrols here is to talk to any locals, to visit a few houses about a kilometre from the base on the edge of the desert. People are pretty polite but guarded. Nobody says: "We hate you, we don't want you here." We get back around six or seven in the evening.

4/7/2010 Take "contact" heading south. Our patrol is on foot. We are trying to keep on owning ground, keeping the Taliban away from the patrol base. We are about 20 people, maybe less, walking, carrying water, body armour, grenades, helmets. It's sweaty, but you forget about it after a while. It's a short patrol, maybe three hours. A long patrol would be about 10 hours. The temperature will get up to 55C. The combination of the heat, the weight, the uneven ground – you just have to try to look where you're going, try to keep aware of your surroundings, all the while trying to film. It is difficult because you have to keep walking. We are spreading out in case one of us steps on an IED – best to keep about 50 metres apart. So, we are spread over half a kilometre.

It's so hot. A little jump over an irrigation ditch becomes a huge effort, even though it would normally be a small step.

Then the attack comes. It went like this. The radio operator got news that an attack was imminent. The message that came over the radio was: "We don't know if it is your position or not, but there is a possible imminent attack."

The lieutenant says, "You are using a double negative, dickhead. 'Possible' and 'imminent' are two different words – what is it going to be? Possible? Or is there an attack about to happen?"

Over the radio: "This is Top Three. We have a marine hit. We've got a gunshot wound in the back."

They're now getting shot at. All I can hear is: "Fuck. He's over here. Ah fuck, oh shit, fuck. It was right over our heads. Which way are we going?"

Something incoherent comes from the radio. Radio again: "I say we have got an RPG hit. Rocket-propelled grenade. Two casualties."

The helicopter then comes in and picks up the two casualties. They survive. The marines then walk 1.5km back to their base.

Afterwards, everyone is pretty hyper, joking, a great release of tension. One guy has been grazed by a bullet. Their uniforms are shredded from lying around on the ground.

I'm worried that I haven't got it all on film.

5/7/2010 A recruiting sergeant turns up to see if he can re-enlist people for another four years. He sits around for a few days, but isn't busy. Only a couple of people re-enlist. That night, the guys are sitting playing Risk. I also play a bit of poker with them – the marines are pretty standoffish in the beginning. But if you are prepared to do what they do, go out on patrol with them, then you are all right.

6/7/2010 We go out on 11-hour foot patrol at about 6am. The temperature is up to 55C again. There are about 10 of us. No one speaks. We are just putting one foot in front of the other, plodding along in the heat, walking over rough ground. There aren't many roads and you try to keep off them. As well as full battle-dress, each marine must carry five litres of water.

7/7/2010 The next day, I move to another US marine patrol base nearby, a small base in an old vineyard, about 800 metres south of the Karma base. This is the southernmost base of the US and British – the last frontier. The vineyard has been bulldozed and the base is surrounded by giant sandbags. The soldiers live in tents inside. It is called Patrol Base May – named after a marine killed a few weeks earlier. Base Johnston – about 400 metres from Karma – is named after another dead marine. A third base is about to be built, another 400 metres away. It will be called Harris; he was killed just last week.

All three were killed by IEDs. Corporal Harris was trying to help an injured marine during a firefight. While he was moving him, he stepped on an IED that took his leg and arm off.

I talk to Staff Sergeant Jeremy Wilton. "It's steady progress. We're trying to move south down to the border of Pakistan. It's taken a year to move 20km. It's work in progress."

8/7/2010 The next day we go out with engineers to sweep the road in front of our base. There are 10 of us. They keep finding more IEDs just opposite the base. They blow them up as the easiest way of getting rid of them. After one, Wilton chuckles: "I love the smell of cordite in the morning."

9/7/2010 At 3am we head south to check out deserted family compounds to see if any people have come back. We find one man walking along the road. The lieutenant stops him to tell them that we are here to bring security. While we are talking, it appears that a group of armed Taliban are about 800 metres away – we watch them and they watch us.

They are waiting for the marines to attack but they don't. We get back to the base at about 9pm. There is a bit of a debrief from the lieutenant explaining why the marines weren't allowed to attack. The Taliban, he says, cannot dictate the terms of the engagement. A couple of the marines are disappointed, but mostly everyone is just knackered and beyond the gung-ho stage.

10/07/2010 There are five Afghans based with the marines – but not much talking. It's polite enough. A supply truck arrives with a big box of T-bone steaks that someone has "liberated" from the main base. The marines make a barbecue and cook the steaks, and the Afghans make rice in return.

11/7/2010 Everyone is ordered to get their hair cut because today we are going to walk back up to Karma base for the memorial service for Corporal Harris. The marines have taken a few casualties over the last couple of weeks so the colonels and bigwigs are coming down for the memorial service.

A couple of Harris's friends speak and pay their respects in front of his boots, rifle and dog tag. The preacher does the "Why did God take this man from us?" stuff, and then it's back to the fray.

After the memorial, Harris's friends are back on guard duty. One starts talking about the day Harris died: "I felt hopeless. There was nothing I could do. I was only 50 metres away. We couldn't go there because we didn't have any metal detectors. We heard Corporal Harris had had his legs blown off. I thought he'd be fine.

"I remember hearing he was gone. I just didn't want to believe it. I was like, 'Yeah, there's no way he's gone. He'll make it.' But I heard he'd stopped breathing. I didn't want to believe it for a couple of days."

**14/7/2010** Hanging around. It's a quiet day. We are told there will be no patrolling because a big suicide bomb hit a bazaar 20km behind the front line and all the hospital space is full. So they don't want us going out on patrols and getting injured.

**15/7/2010** Eight of us go out on a very short patrol along the little canal near the base. We go less than 100 metres. We see a couple of people down at the canal. They look like Taliban who appear to be planting IEDs. They are watching us and we are watching them.

Then we retrace our steps back to base. When we get back there is a massive explosion from the canal, big enough to blow up a bus, a huge column of dust and smoke about a kilometre away. Looks like they blew themselves up planting the IED.

**16/7/2010** London is pulling me out. I hitch a lift on a truck heading back up north. It is like being in a huge metal coffin. But the mood is light because we are moving back from the front. A couple of kids start chucking rocks at us. They are always chucking rocks at us. The gunner on top gets hit.

*Sean Smith's film from Afghanistan can be viewed at http://gu.com/p/2tyh9*

31 JULY 2010

# How the BP spill spelt the death of my community

## TIM GAUTREAUX

Those who live in Louisiana all their lives develop an understanding of disaster. We know a hurricane can turn over hundreds of offshore oil rigs in one pass and then come to land and do the same to our homes. Refineries explode, rigs blow up, pipelines burst, well pressures cause accidents that take fingers, feet, arms, legs and life itself.

There's hardly a family in the Gulf region that does not have a member involved in the oil industry. My father was a tugboat captain who handled barges of crude oil for the sprawling refineries, my brother sells oilfield equipment and technology, my nephew captains offshore supply vessels, my great-nephew operates a giant crane currently picking Katrina-smashed equipment from the Gulf floor. Cousins manage oil leases.

So, even though I am not an oil worker, the industry is part of my environment, my history, and when I saw images of the April Deepwater Horizon explosion and fire, I thought at once, "Wait a minute. Something's wrong. That rig is state-of-the-art, the size of a small factory, loaded with technology that rivals the space programme in complexity. Why is the fire so enormous?" And later, when the labyrinth of pipes and valves keeled over in a rumbling, hissing nimbus of flame, I was astounded, thinking, "Why didn't the blowout preventer shut down the well?" And days later, when it was revealed that the device was not functioning, a dark spill began to spread in my soul, a burgeoning realisation that nothing could stop a runaway well 5,000ft below the Gulf's surface. Nothing. A wide open fire hydrant blasting a plume of water out of a four-inch opening operates on a pressure of 50 pounds per square inch. The oil and gas venting from the rig's seven-inch pipe is propelled by at least 3,000 psi. Or more. And if the pipe beneath the blowout preventer fails? The reservoir pressures, I understand, are 11,000 psi. Unchecked, the subterranean caverns of oil would roar to the surface for years. BP has made a number of attempts to stop the fountain of oil and all have failed, except for the latest cap. But even this success poses many dangers, including a well rupture far below the ocean floor, initiated by the high pressure caused by the cap. No one knows what the result of such a failure would be, and this highlights the most frightening facet of the catastrophe: its unpredictability. The final solution is supposed to be the relief wells BP is drilling, and on the day I realised even these might not arrest the blowout, I decided to stop thinking about it all.

I drove into my south-east Louisiana town of Hammond to get something good to eat. At a seafood cafe I ordered Oysters Scampi. The TV was on above the bar, showing miles-long strands of red oil streaming across the face of the Gulf. I thought of the men killed in the explosion, how they spent their lives trying to avoid something like this. My oysters were large and plump. I ate the first fellow, then looked up at the oil. Locally, it's well known that 60% of the US's oysters come from Louisiana's coastal regions. The oyster beds would be killed by the oil and take years to regenerate. Longer, if the oil kept coming next year. And the next. The spill inside me widened as I realised that the shrimp fisheries would soon be closed, the commercial taking of red snapper, grouper and all their delectable cousins banned. I remembered that Louisiana supplies 73% of the nation's shrimp. My God, what about the charter boat industry and sport fishermen from Texas to Florida?

The nightly news told of oil coming ashore. Unlike its neigh-bour states, Louisiana has no shore, no sand beach except for a small spit called Grand Isle, no dunes, hills, cliffs. The entire Gulf border and its wide attendant marshes are exactly at sea level. The shore is mostly gritty mud held in place by tall, dense marsh grass. What is not water is grass, thousands of square miles of it. When the oil kills the grass, the shore will begin to melt away. This coastal marsh is home to millions of birds – pelicans, terns, egrets, great herons – and a rich variety of mammals and reptiles. It is threaded through by countless miles of narrow bayous, inlets and lagoons, all spawning areas for shrimp and succulent blue-claw crabs, nesting grounds for vast flocks of migratory geese and ducks – a hot and humid greenhouse teeming with life.

Louisiana is a relatively small state, but it contains 40-45% of the nation's coastal wetlands. The neighbour states of Texas, Alabama, Mississippi and Florida have similar fertile and produc-tive marshes, though such areas are much smaller.

The oil that began to show up, the so-called tar balls, were really reddish pancakes of axle grease; they began to appear on Grand Isle, then east, on the Alabama beaches, followed by a nasty inva-sion of the lovely green water and white sand shores of Pensacola and Santa Rosa Island. Heavy dark oil began to pool against the Louisiana marshes, coating wildlife with a greasy, glue-like batter – no one can ever know how many thousands of animals have died, how many carcasses are at the bottom of the quarter million square miles of the Gulf.

Next, every fisherman's greatest fear happened. The govern-ment had to close over 80,000 square miles of the Gulf to all fishing, and suddenly tens of thousands of fishermen were out of work, losing their identity and a way of life they and their ances-tors have pursued for generations. The Cajuns have fished since they arrived in the 1700s; the Vietnamese, Croatians, African

Americans, Native Americans, Islenos and plain American country boys who trawl and fish and process are all on the bank watching their livelihoods drown in oil. How much oil? Who will ever know? As of now, a safe final estimate, if the cap holds and the relief wells work, is 200 million gallons. The oil washing up in July might have leaked in April. Locals are losing sleep about how much oil is looming underwater to bedevil us next year or for 10 years. Calls to counselling and crisis lines are through the roof. Fourteen million people depend on fishing and oilfield work for a living in the Gulf region. The fishermen can't pay rents and mortgages, utility bills, insurance, buy fuel for their boats, save for any kind of future; they stand in charity food lines on 100-degree days.

The oilfield people are facing cutbacks because of the new ban on deepwater drilling. This is affecting shipbuilding, crewboat, supply and helicopter fleets, machine shops, pipe yards, supply houses, foundries and a hundred other businesses. The fishermen are hurting acutely at the moment, but the oil workers are worried for their futures as well, as the industry is facing a wind-down that could last for years. The news keeps getting more uncertain and, yes, things can get worse because hurricane season is now upon us and no one knows what havoc a big storm in the Gulf could cause. It could do anything from pushing a bow wave of killing oil over the estuaries to painting New Orleans with black rain.

I don't think people living outside the region understand what is happening. One so-called environmentalist suggested Gulf fishermen and oil workers should just get educated in green technology and work in solar panel factories. What are they supposed to do for 20 years until the technology is perfected and the factories built? Fishermen want to work as fishermen; the Gulf is 1,000 miles wide and they are independent members of a huge culture, not employees.

By the end of June I tried to limit my news intake. It was now clear the enormous Gulf tourism industry was on shaky ground because all the beaches from Panama City, Florida to Grand Isle, Louisiana were fouled or soon to be fouled, and the result was a freefall in hotel, condo and restaurant bookings, and trade in the thousands of gift shops, filling stations, convenience stores, bait-and-tackle shops. Each type of business was firing workers, cutting orders, falling into debt.

After a charter boat captain shot himself in the head, I turned off the television. But everywhere I went, neighbours, bank tellers, waitresses, university professors all fretted about the spill. Last year, one billion pounds of fish was harvested from the Gulf; now only a tiny fraction of that is being caught in the small areas still open, and chances are even that clean catch will be distrusted by buyers outside the region. How many years will it take for Gulf seafood's reputation for quality to return?

This disaster rides like a tumour on the back of the monster Katrina, a storm that in 2005 killed more than 1,800 people in the New Orleans area. Many residents of the region were finally getting their homes rebuilt, their boats and docks restored.

It is true a few hundred men have been hired by BP at low wages to shovel muck off the shores. Several motels have been rented to house workers and BP has been leaking out cheques to fishing families and charter boat operators (though there are tales of cheques never arriving). Hundreds of boats have been hired to go after the oil, but not a man in a thousand miles is glad about any of it.

Everyone has a sense of why the accident happened. Weeks before the explosion, it seems BP knew the blowout preventer was leaking and missing a crucial seal. About 10 hours before 11 men were burned up, employees report an argument broke out between the rig's BP manager, who wanted a speedy and cheap sealing of the well, and the driller and cementer, who demanded traditional, safe plugging methods. The company man overruled the experts. He wanted to save money, ignoring the first rule of industry economics: safety is never more expensive than an accident.

The clean-up bill is complex and will extend for years. In Florida, workers clean a beach at dusk; at sunrise it's covered again. The spill is slathering four states now. It could be blown over to Texas. It could show up in the marinas of Key West, or even Wilmington, North Carolina on the Atlantic, wherever the Gulf Stream carries it. The coming expense is not to be imagined. Lawsuits are spilling out with no judicial blowout preventer to slow them down. Injury and loss of livelihood suits, suits from hotels for loss of bookings, suits from restaurants, bars, stores, suits for mental anguish, even claims from municipalities for loss of taxes.

The future? There is a large, years-old black spot in my driveway where my old Jeep once leaked a quart of transmission oil. It's not fading away. The BP spill is likewise staining the coast's soil, and sinking into the psychological fabric of the Gulf. Beneath the sorrow lies suspicion and anger based on the notion that if this spill had occurred near a place like Boston harbour where a lot of wealthy, well-connected people live, every oil-skimmer in the hemisphere would have been brought in and every offer of foreign help accepted immediately, instead of 71 days after the spill began.

The locals have watched with disbelief some of BP's lunatic and expensive clean-up methods, such as wiping down each blade of marsh grass with paper towels. They have watched their own, more effective, home-grown efforts ridiculed and crushed by irrelevant Coast Guard regulations and "experts" who have never seen Louisiana's coast except perhaps through the windows of a plane.

In three to 10 years, maybe the lawsuits will be settled, maybe the sea grasses will grow back to hold the marshlands together, maybe the fish now trying to breathe clouds of undersea oil will somehow propagate, maybe trust in the world's best seafood will return. But a person's life is composed of minutes and is most fulfilled by working and bringing one's earnings to the family table. And who can give back even one ruined minute?

2 August 2010

# I wouldn't wish this illness on my worst enemy

## MARK RICE-OXLEY

I can't say exactly when it started. Maybe the day in July last year when a headache in the shape of a question mark curled itself around my right eye and made itself at home. Or a month later, when a liquid fatigue poured into my legs and set. The autumn, perhaps, when short, surreal episodes would come and go, like I was seeing the world through the bottom of a highball glass.

But the moment when I really knew something was wrong was the night of my 40th birthday party in October. We were motoring up the Thames with a boatful of my closest friends all dressed in 1969 fancy dress and Woodstock wigs. I felt overwhelmed. From under my Jimi Hendrix hair I whispered to my mother, "Stay close." I gripped her hand as if it were the first day at school. I couldn't look anyone in the face for more than three seconds without a tide of screaming panic rising up. I tried to circulate but needed to sit. When I sat, I needed to stand. I tried eating, then threw my dinner in the bin. At last midnight came and we all went home. That night, for the first of many dark nights, I lay awake, small and frightened, and utterly unable to keep still through the dreadful hours.

It got worse. For two weeks I felt neither ill nor well. Then, during a weekend at my parents' home – the house I was born in, the place I still love – I disintegrated. It was the weekend the clocks went back, and as we arrived I rippled with a sense of unease. I couldn't watch television or read. I started cups of tea but couldn't finish them, sat down to dinner but couldn't eat. The first night I roamed around, twitchy and unable to settle, heart hammering in my throat, ears full of white noise, a buzz in my stomach. At 5am, I couldn't take any more.

I knocked on my parents' door and soon found myself wedged between them in bed, for the first time since I was born. The next night was worse.

I was rocking back and forward, ranging, pacing, terrifying everyone. When I blurted out something about how it was all finished for me, my dad jumped into the car to find an out-of-hours NHS dispensary. "At least we're making the most of the extra hour," he said.

They used to call it a nervous breakdown. Now it's depression. Neither term is helpful. The former doesn't come close to expressing the long list of symptoms that apply (insomnia, anxiety, dismal mood, panic, thoughts of suicide, loss of energy/weight/joy/libido/love). The latter is, if anything, worse, conjuring up misleading images of people staring through windows at drizzle. But depressive illness isn't like that Monday-morning feeling, or getting back from holiday to find the cold water tank has burst. It's a medical fact, like breaking an arm, only the broken bit is in the chemical circuitry of the brain. It's delicate stuff in there. It takes a long time to fix. Usually, I am told, you get better.

If there was one consolation it was that I was not alone. My decline from unremarkable working dad of three to stranded depressive sitting on the floor doing simple jigsaws certainly felt unique. In fact, it's universal.

The chances of the average adult getting it are perhaps higher than they have ever been.

According to Graham Thornicroft, a professor of community psychiatry at the Institute of Psychiatrists, between 20% and 25% of adults will have an episode of mental illness in any given year. Over a lifetime, the risk rises to around 40%. In Britain, antidepressant prescriptions have doubled in the last decade. The World Health Organisation warns that by 2030 depression will be second only to HIV/Aids in the toll it exacts on society.

"Life has become more stressful and there is more alienation than there used to be. People who meet disadvantage meet it very much alone," says Tim Cantopher, a psychiatrist and author of *Depressive Illness: Curse of the Strong.*

Who's most at risk? "Women and poor people," says Thornicroft. "General rates of depression among women are up to twice as high as among men. And in lowest socio-economic groups it is up to twice as much as in higher groups."

I fit neither category, so why me? Depression is often triggered by sudden life events such as bereavement, loss of job or change of house. But again, none of these apply. Far more common, however, is a stress-induced condition that may build over a number of years.

"If you try to do the undoable, you're going to get this," Cantopher says. "Stress doesn't make you ill. You do – by trying to do the undoable."

And, if I'm honest, I have been trying to do the undoable for years. I have realised I am essentially an idle soul inhabiting a very busy person's life. Years of late-night shifts and early mornings with small children asking tricky questions such as, "Daddy, if you had to break one of your legs, which one would you break?" I was a "portfolio parent", part-time work, part-time homedad, part-time freelancer. On paper, it looked marvellous. In reality, it made for long years of chaotic breakfasts, a messy school run, some exercise, a dash into London, 10 hours on a pinball newsdesk, back to release my wife for a school governors' meeting or a conference call or to move the house slightly to the left. Late for everything.

I understand that this is the lot that many working women have had to bear for decades. I find it unsurprising that so many are succumbing to depressive illness. But since I "came out", I found a startling number of do-it-all fathers who are suffering too.

And yet not many of us find it easy to be forthcoming about our illness. Thornicroft's real killer stat is this: that 75% of us know someone with mental illness. But we may not know they are mentally ill. Because, of course, mental illness is a taboo. And few people talk about it or let on – unless they are so ill that they can't help it.

Sue Baker, director of the Time to Change programme set up to change negative attitudes towards mental illness, says nine out of 10 people with mental illness say they have experienced stigma and discrimination. "Yet, paradoxically, 'coming out' can be the best thing for someone with a mental illness. It can have a powerful influence," says Baker. "If you don't disclose, then people who might help you aren't going to be able to."

I tried to be honest and, in return, people did well at asking all the right questions. How has it been? What's it like? Why did it happen to you? In the interests of brevity, I usually just said: "Pretty tough" or "I'm on the mend" or "not out of the woods yet". What I really wanted to say is: there were days when I just sat on the bed and stared at the wall and wondered if I was losing my mind, when even trying to do a child's jigsaw puzzle would wear me out. Days – long joined-up hours when I thought I would never work, write, parent, play or love again. Days when

I agonised at the enormous burden my wife was under; when I resented the impact on my children, two of whom seemed to develop mild sympathetic symptoms; when I wondered how much further there was to the bottom. But the days weren't the problem. Nights were worse. Sleeplessness became both symptom and cause of the illness, a wicked loop of empty hours and catastrophic thoughts. By 4am I'd be desperate for dawn. But morning brought no relief, just more empty hours, with another threatening night thereafter.

Christmas was the lowest ebb. All that snow, all the lovely children with faces shiny like apples. I couldn't be near them, but couldn't be alone. I trailed around the house after my poor wife like a small dog with internal bleeding. I slept eight hours in four nights. On 23 December, I went for an emergency meeting with my psychiatrist who shook his head and said, "I'm sorry it's turned out this way." Afterwards, in the thickening twilight and with the first vapours of sedation gathering, I felt my wretchedness in the joy of others: the shoppers and their gift bags; the lovers giggling; the young man on the tube engrossed in a book. I wish I was him, I thought. I wish I was engrossed in a book on the tube.

How do you get better? Like wars and love affairs, depression is a thing that is easy to get started but difficult to bring to a close. Somehow, time passed. Days dragged by so slowly, but weeks seemed to mount up quickly. The lost time began to unsettle me, so I found different units to measure the duration of my illness: in haircuts, porridge boxes, *Countdown*. Any kind of stress was insupportable. But also any kind of excitement. Television could overwhelm me.

I couldn't watch sport, felt seasick at the motion and envious of the energy of the participants. Small social events helped, but only for about half an hour. Thereafter diminishing returns set in, and they diminished pretty rapidly: if you overexert in any way, very bad days follow. I spent hours and hours with a deck of cards, and camomile tea, and got pretty bored by both.

The four things that really helped: meditation, love, time and therapy.

I discovered the first through a colleague who sent me some CDs. At first, meditation feels hard and slightly odd. In time, it's a valuable technique. Love – in a child's Halloween face, or a friend's casual invitation to lunch – boosted morale. Time worked away on the broken bits. Therapy taught me that I'm not who I think I am, that some of my reflexes and instincts are unhealthy.

But it wasn't a smooth ride. Some days, exercise would help. Some days, it was too much and I'd suffer for two or three days. Some days, odd jobs felt wholesome, sometimes they felt depleting. Some days, just making dinner would be too much. Other days, I would feel like doing nothing, but know that doing nothing was the worst thing I could do. Some days, most painfully of all, being with the children was just too much. At other times, just to sit and watch them climb or paint was a blessed relief. I could still parent, after all.

"Be a scientist, not a manager," says Cantopher. "Look at the evidence that your body gives you. If you are overdoing it, your body will tell you. You've got to pace it in the early stages. To begin with, do a little – leave tasks half done, don't try to complete things at the beginning. Be kind and gentle to yourself. Once you are better, then it's about recognising that if you keep putting 18 amps through a 13 amp fuse, it will keep blowing."

Spring helped. I got stronger. I finished reading a novel for the first time since September. I put on all the weight I'd lost and more. I planted potatoes, cooked, sifted compost, borrowed a neighbour's bike. I kept a nerdy graph of how I was feeling, and took comfort in a general upward trend behind the violent peaks and troughs. Good friends brought lunch and we walked and talked. The office sent a box set of *The Wire*. Pretty soon I was up to watching it. I began to notice things more, things I had taken for granted for years – beauty, seasons, people.

I bought birthday presents on time.

I rediscovered gentle ways to spend the time – chess, libraries, yoga.

I learned how to let time pass without trying to fill it.

It wasn't straightforward. I relapsed six weeks after going back to work and needed another month to build up from the bottom again. Even now, a year on from that first, dark question mark, I still feel the sharp edge of something. But, happily, it does little more than prod me, remind me that I need to tread carefully.

I wouldn't wish this illness on my worst enemy; it's the most terrifying thing that has ever happened to me. But, in a strange way, I am glad of the lessons it taught me. "A lot of patients are grateful," says Cantopher. "They say that without the illness they wouldn't have been able to make the changes they made to become happy."

It has been strange writing this story. Almost like I am writing about another person. A friend died the other day at 44. My story seems trivial by comparison. But it is a story I really wanted to tell because it is a story I wanted to read 12 months ago, when I was desperate for reassurance. Yes, it's tough; yes, it'll turn your life upside down. But it does get better. You do recover. I've nearly made it. You can make it, too.

5 August 2010

# The US isn't leaving Iraq, it's rebranding the occupation

## SEUMAS MILNE

For most people in Britain and the US, Iraq is already history. Afghanistan has long since taken the lion's share of media attention, as the death toll of Nato troops rises inexorably. Controversy about Iraq is now almost entirely focused on the original decision to invade: what's happening there in 2010 barely registers.

That will have been reinforced by Barack Obama's declaration this week that US combat troops are to be withdrawn from Iraq at the end of the month "as promised and on schedule". For much of the British and American press, this was the real thing: headlines hailed the "end" of the war and reported "US troops to leave Iraq".

Nothing could be further from the truth. The US isn't withdrawing from Iraq at all – it's rebranding the occupation. Just as George Bush's war on terror was retitled "overseas contingency operations" when Obama became president, US "combat operations" will be rebadged from next month as "stability operations".

But as Major General Stephen Lanza, the US military spokesman in Iraq, told the *New York Times*: "In practical terms, nothing will change." After this month's withdrawal, there will still be 50,000 US troops in 94 military bases, "advising" and training the Iraqi army, "providing security" and carrying out "counter-terrorism" missions. In US military speak, that covers pretty well everything they might want to do.

Granted, 50,000 is a major reduction on the numbers in Iraq a year ago. But what Obama once called "the dumb war" goes remorselessly on. In fact, violence has been increasing as the Iraqi political factions remain deadlocked for the fifth month in a row in the Green Zone. More civilians are being killed in Iraq than in Afghanistan: 535 last month alone, according to the Iraqi government – the worst figure for two years.

And even though US troops are rarely seen on the streets, they are still dying at a rate of six a month, their bases regularly shelled by resistance groups, while Iraqi troops and US-backed militias are being killed in far greater numbers and al-Qaida – Bush's gift to Iraq – is back in business across swathes of the country. Although hardly noticed in Britain, there are still 150 British troops in Iraq supporting US forces.

Meanwhile, the US government isn't just rebranding the occupation, it's also privatising it. There are around 100,000 private contractors working for the occupying forces, of whom more than 11,000 are armed mercenaries, mostly "third country nationals", typically from the developing world. One Peruvian and two Ugandan security contractors were killed in a rocket attack on the Green Zone only a fortnight ago.

The US now wants to expand their numbers sharply in what Jeremy Scahill, who helped expose the role of the notorious US security firm Blackwater, calls the "coming surge" of contractors in Iraq. Hillary Clinton wants to increase the number of military contractors working for the state department alone from 2,700 to 7,000, to be based in five "enduring presence posts" across Iraq.

The advantage of an outsourced occupation is clearly that someone other than US soldiers can do the dying to maintain control of Iraq. It also helps get round the commitment, made just before Bush left office, to pull all American troops out by the end of 2011. The other getout, widely expected on all sides, is a new Iraqi request for US troops to stay on – just as soon as a suitable government can be stitched together to make it.

What is abundantly clear is that the US, whose embassy in Baghdad is now the size of Vatican City, has no intention of letting go of Iraq any time soon. One reason for that can be found in the dozen 20-year contracts to run Iraq's biggest oil fields that were handed out last year to foreign companies, including three of the Anglo-American oil majors that exploited Iraqi oil under British control before 1958.

The dubious legality of these deals has held back some US companies, but as Greg Muttitt, author of a forthcoming book on the subject, argues, the prize for the US is bigger than the contracts themselves, which put 60% of Iraq's reserves under long-term foreign corporate control. If output can be boosted as sharply as planned, the global oil price could be slashed and the grip of recalcitrant Opec states broken.

The horrific cost of the war to the Iraqi people, on the other hand, and the continuing fear and misery of daily life make a mockery of claims that the US surge of 2007 "worked" and that Iraq has come good after all.

It's not only the hundreds of thousands of dead and 4 million refugees. After seven years of US (and British) occupation, tens of thousands are still tortured and imprisoned without trial, health and education has dramatically deteriorated, the position of women has gone horrifically backwards, trade unions are in effect banned, Baghdad is divided by 1,500 checkpoints and blast walls, electricity supplies have all but broken down and people pay with their lives for speaking out.

Even without the farce of the March elections, the banning and killing of candidates and activists and subsequent political breakdown, to claim – as the *Times* did yesterday – that "Iraq is a democracy" is grotesque. The Green Zone administration would collapse in short order without the protection of US troops and security contractors. No wonder the speculation among Iraqis and some US officials is of an eventual military takeover.

The Iraq war has been a historic political and strategic failure for the US. It was unable to impose a military solution, let alone turn the country into a beacon of western values or regional policeman. But by playing the sectarian and ethnic cards, it also prevented the emergence of a national resistance movement and a humiliating Vietnam-style pullout. The signs are it wants to create a new form of outsourced semi-colonial regime to maintain its grip on the country and region. The struggle to regain Iraq's independence has only just begun.

11 AUGUST 2010

# The milkman who learned to speak Gujarati

### HUGH MUIR

There came a moment, "Jimmy" Mather tells me, when he realised that the world as he knew it was changing and that he would have to change with it. He encountered a housewife on her doorstep. Nothing unusual about that. He is a milkman.

But when she tried to place an order, he didn't really know what she was talking about. There wasn't much call for Gujarati when Jimmy grew up in Oswaldtwistle, Lancashire, or in his early days guiding a horse and cart around Blackburn. But he could see the area was changing fast, and anyway, it seemed more sensible to engage, for the business and for his own curiosity. Gujarati, thought Jimmy. I'd better learn.

That was almost half a century ago and now, riding beside Jimmy in his timeworn delivery van, what is immediately noticeable is that when people approach, no one greets him in English. "They tell me I speak the language better than some of them," he says, writing an order in his ledger book. "You listen, talk and soon pick it up. I have a good brain for remembering these things."

In days past, Jimmy hauled the crates and skipped from house to house, shop to shop, handing over milk, eggs, yoghurt, butter. But at 69, he isn't as strong or healthy as he was. He is still out there, seven days a week, including Christmas, driving down the narrow streets, passing the time through a wound-down window in Gujarati, sometimes Bengali. But others do the running about. Today it's a lean, smiling young man, Usman Yakub. "I've worked with him on and off since I was a kid," he says. "He has had a lot of us working with him."

"Best way to keep them out of trouble; get them to do something with their lives," interjects the milkman, staring straight ahead.

He should pack it in now, really. He's done his bit, seen families arrive, watched their children grow, received invites to quite a few weddings. But he won't. Once you have a place in a community it's probably hard to imagine life without it. "I'd miss the people," he says, voice reduced to a gentle whisper. "I'd come back anyway to speak to the people. May as well stay put."

# The late, great Jimmy Reid
# left a legacy for our times

## MARTIN KETTLE

It is not often in leftwing politics that one comes across someone who really appears to have it all. But that was how Jimmy Reid, the Scottish trade unionist who died on Tuesday, seemed once. Reid had the background, the brains, the ability, the vision, the charisma to have been one of the great leftwing political leaders of modern Britain. In some ways, this is what he actually was, especially in the early 1970s.

My goodness, you should have heard him back then. He was the most authentic, radical, working-class political orator north or south of the border. There is no one like him today, least of all in the Labour leadership contest. But Reid could have been so much more. The *Daily Telegraph* columnist Alan Cochrane – yes, the *Telegraph* – wrote this week that it was a tragedy of public life that Reid never made it to the House of Commons. The place might have been made for him, he said. But Reid could have been a party leader too. Like the bonnie Earl of Moray, he might have been a king.

That he was not can be principally explained by one thing. For much of his life Reid was a communist. For people like me, growing up in the communist hothouse of the 1960s, this impediment was hard to grasp. Reid was British communism's golden boy in those years. He offered the illusion that the party had not in fact stalled as an industrial and political force. I remember writing a school essay about "Britain in 20 years' time", in which I said

Jimmy Reid would be prime minister in 1985. This tells you quite a lot about me at 15 but also something about Reid, too. My teacher, however, had never heard of him.

By 1971, when Reid led the work-in at Upper Clyde Shipbuilders, he became a national figure after all. The UCS work-in, along with internment in Northern Ireland, were the two political events of 1970s Britain that were reported worldwide. Reid's rectorial speech at Glasgow University, declaring that "the rat race is for rats", was printed in the *New York Times*, and comparisons were drawn with the Gettysburg Address. Communists thought he might be the party's first MP for a generation when he ran in Dunbartonshire Central in the deeply polarised February 1974 general election. But Reid came a poor third.

Though his star occasionally shone brightly in later years, his political career lost its way. He joined Labour, then supported the Scottish Socialist party, and finally, appalled at New Labour, fell in with the Scottish National party. He remained a master of devastating repartee. "If kamikaze pilots were to form their own union, Arthur [Scargill] would be an ideal choice for leader," he once said, illustrating the difference between the cavalier and roundhead strands in the revolutionary tradition of which Reid and Scargill were respectively the last leaders. But industrial Britain and industrial politics were in epochal transition, and Reid, like Scargill, was from deep roots, which made it hard and unpleasant to keep up with the change.

Reid was a man of parts with plenty of flaws. But at his best he was an absolutely formidable and supremely talented political leader. As the decades pass, however, it is tempting to romanticise such careers as Reid's and, in a very different part of the leftwing forest, that of the writer Tony Judt, who died last week. Their finest hours seem so splendid, their finest utterances so magnificently apposite to the demands of compelling times – in Reid's case against employers who see workforces as simply expendable costs, in Judt's against politicians and writers who are carried far from the principles of social democracy on the fast-running tide of least resistance – that it is hard not to sigh that those who remain are not worthy of the example that they set.

In some respects, no doubt, that is true. Yet the fact remains that Reid's own career, like that of the larger movements of which he was at times such a dazzling tribune, was marked at best by isolated successes amid wider failure. The industrial Britain and industrial Clydeside in which Reid flourished no longer exist. The shop stewards' movement and the trade union movement itself are, except in the public services, shadows of their past. Communism has collapsed. Socialism and even social democracy are minority political movements with, at best, uncertain futures. Holding on has proved difficult enough, never mind building a New Jerusalem. The future of the left as a political force lies in alliances, not purity.

There is at least one living idea, however, that Reid has handed on to the 21st-century left and deserves to be nurtured even in difficult and seemingly unpropitious times. In the finest moment of his finest hour, Reid insisted that the UCS workforce should respond to the prospective closure of their plant not by striking but by working. The workers, Reid said, knew more about the viability of their trade and their business than the managers, financiers and, not to be forgotten, the Treasury officials too, who all insisted there was no alternative but to bow to the markets and padlock the shipyard gates. Reid was right. Nearly 40 years on, two of the three yards that once formed part of UCS are still building ships today. And the Treasury is still wrong.

The living lesson of UCS is not that closures have to be blindly resisted in every circumstance. It is that the workforce is frequently at least as good a judge of the needs of their business as the management. Sometimes, as on the Clyde, it is a much better one. But the great late-20th-century failure of the British trade union movement was that it never embraced the idea of industrial democracy when it was on offer. Unions saw the works councils and worker representation on boards envisaged by Alan Bullock's 1977 report as a threat to their own bargaining position. To which, in far too many industries in the 33 years since Bullock, one can now only bleakly retort: "What industries? What unions?"

In the aftermath of the financial crisis of 2008 there is much talk in all parties of the need to create a new and more balanced capitalist economy, better able to withstand the kind of collapse that overtook the financial sector two years ago. It is hard to see how that can be achieved without the decisive hand of government. But it is also hard to see how it can be sustained without the kind of industrial partnership – co-determination as the much more successful Germans call it – that Bullock offered long ago. Jimmy Reid in his revolutionary days might not have agreed. But it is his legacy nevertheless.

13 AUGUST 2010

# How Capello fluffed Beckham's farewell

RICHARD WILLIAMS

This is getting to be beyond a joke. Whatever one's feelings about David Beckham's England career, it is saddening to see it come to an end – if indeed it has – in a welter of misunderstandings and accusations that illustrate the state of disorganisation into which the England camp has fallen under Fabio Capello.

The latest twist in the series of public relations calamities that began in May with the launch of the Capello Index says two things about England's Italian manager. First, his £6m salary is clearly not enough to persuade him to make his own phone calls, even to a man who captained the national side from November 2000 to June 2006. Second, if Don Fabio is unable to convey a simple but important message in a straightforward manner during the space between matches, then what hope does he have of communicating tactical instructions in the heat of battle?

In asserting that there will be no more caps to add to the 115 already collected by Beckham, Capello was trying to thrust a gold watch into the player's hands. Beckham, who already has more than enough expensive timepieces, would rather feel that his career is open-ended, in the sense that although the manager determines if and when he will play, Beckham will decide when he wants to announce the termination of his availability.

This is an honourable stance, as well as a sensible one. On past evidence, you would not bet the house against that 115 becoming 116. Discarded in 2006, Beckham forced his way back into the squad through the strength of his will and his ambition. He is 35 now, but that ambition seems to be undimmed. And, after all, stranger things have happened. There are plenty of people convinced that Paul Scholes, who is six months older than Beckham, should still be an automatic choice (and might have been, had Capello not deputed Franco Baldini to make that call, as well as the one to Beckham).

Capello, of all people, ought to be aware of the danger of trying to write Beckham off. When the Italian arrived at Real Madrid for his second spell in 2006, he made it clear that he viewed the Englishman as the most overindulged and dispensable of *galácticos*. Beckham would not be making any further appearances and would be well advised, indeed, to seek another club. In the second half of the season, however, Capello was forced to revise his opinion, and Beckham's unselfish energy became a significant factor in the late run that gave Madrid the title and helped to cement the manager's reputation as a serial winner.

After Sven-Göran Eriksson and Steve McClaren, England believed that they needed a hard man. What they got was a head coach whose self-belief is sometimes indistinguishable from an unhelpful inflexibility.

Capello's poor command of English has undoubtedly limited his ability to operate and to explain his actions both to his inner circle (the players) and to the world. It has also made his manners seem worse than they probably are, although that air of autocratic disdain cannot be wholly dismissed as a professional facade.

Nor is he entirely straightforward. Given his statement, when accepting the England appointment in December 2007, that this would be his last job in football, he was being more than a little disingenuous the other day when he dangled before the media and the public the news that he had been offered the head coach's role with three big clubs this summer.

For the amount of money it pays him and his retinue of stooges, and given the lack of an end product in South Africa, the Football Association should feel entitled to demand harder work and higher standards of behaviour. At the moment it is defending his lapses (and the association's investment), but one day it may be forced to conclude that enough is enough.

18 AUGUST 2010

# One hundred days
# of the coalition

## JONATHAN FREEDLAND

Barring yet another comeback, Peter Mandelson's last act of political stage management was a decision to accelerate events on Tuesday 11 May 2010 so that Gordon Brown would not leave Downing Street in the dark – slouching away like a guilty man – but in the bright light of day. The victim of this piece of theatrics was David Cameron, who made his debut outside No 10 in the twilight. That deprived him of any dream he might have nurtured of launching his premiership in the manner of his role model, Tony Blair. Cameron could not declare a "new dawn".

That seemed cruelly appropriate for a man who had not stormed so much as limped across the finishing line into No 10. Denied a majority by a wary electorate, he was obliged to stage two photo-ops before that famous black door. After the night-time shots with his wife, Samantha, he stood the next morning with his new partner, Nick Clegg. Indeed in those first evening hours Cameron's fate lay in the hands of Liberal Democrat MPs and peers: without their votes he could not become prime minister.

It was an inauspicious start, one that suggested the new government would be a fragile creature, a hybrid grafted together from two parties that had each failed to win a mandate. Surely the divisions would be constant, the frailty of the arrangement so pronounced that its very survival – in a country whose last experience of coalition was 65 years ago – would forever be in doubt. Even if it somehow managed to survive, such a novel, two-headed beast would surely be unable to do very much. A coalition would be weak, its ambitions limited. Any bold act of policy or legislation risked splitting the new government in two. Coalition governments were inherently weak: David Cameron himself had said so, again and again, during the election campaign, when he warned against victory for what he called "the hung parliament party". This new bird was surely born with its wings clipped.

That was 100 days ago today. Just three months later, the picture already looks very different. It will doubtless change in another three months and change some more in another three years. But as the Con-Lib or Lib-Con or Con-Dem coalition – one thing this government has not yet achieved is a settled name for itself – passes the milestone made significant by Franklin Roosevelt, each one of those early assumptions has been confounded.

The most striking change is the fading of novelty. This is not to be confused with the end of the coalition's honeymoon, which – if lukewarm approval ratings are any guide – has also come astonishingly fast. It is instead the speed with which a political arrangement once confined to the dreams of nerdish games of fantasy politics, has become entirely unremarkable. There was some gasping at the "firsts": Lib Dems strolling up Downing Street for their first cabinet meeting since 1945; Vince Cable clambering into a ministerial car; Lib Dems sitting alongside Tories on the government benches; Clegg deputising at prime minister's questions. But after each first time, the second lost its frisson. Now the sight of Chris Huhne at the dispatch box is no more unexpected than the sight of, say, Jeremy Hunt: they're just the government. Coalition politics is the new normal.

The passing of novelty has helped feed a sense of stability and assumed longevity. There's a downside to that, one felt particularly by Lib Dems: "We've gone from the new politics to business as usual very fast," says one close-up observer. But the upside is that few now express the coalition's life expectancy in months or short years, as some once did. The working assumption is that the government will serve out its term in full, right up to its own deadline of 7 May 2015 (the adoption of fixed-term parliaments was one of the coalition's earliest innovations). Indeed, the summer speculation was of a longer lifespan, with Conservatives and Lib Dems entering some kind of electoral pact. Michael Portillo suggested they fight the next election as "the Coalition". Conservative MP Mark Field has urged Tories to "hold their fire" in seats where Lib Dems risk defeat by Labour: that could mean putting up a nominal Tory candidacy or no candidacy at all. While such talk has been swiftly dismissed by the Lib Dems' left-leaning deputy, Simon Hughes, more excitable Conservatives foresee an outright merger – if not a takeover – of the Lib Dems.

Labour leadership candidate David Miliband, meanwhile, warns the Lib Dems they are about to get gobbled up: "If you go to tea with an alligator, don't be surprised if you get eaten." But even if these musings on the five- or 10-year horizon come to nothing, they are confirmation that the more fevered initial expectations – of a coalition coming apart at the seams before Christmas – have melted away.

Instead, these have been 100 days of relative amity and harmony, especially when compared with the government that went before. While Brown and Blair fast became notorious for hurling crockery, the blue-yellow alliance is a story told, at least by those involved, in the language of Mills & Boon. It started at the top and at the beginning, with that sun-drenched joint press conference by Clegg and Cameron in the Downing Street garden. Instantly the sketch-writers hailed it as a civil partnership, with gay innuendo the framing metaphor of the last three months. Lord Ashcroft was said, via David Davis, to refer to the administration as the "Brokeback coalition".

The rapport between the two men at the top is indeed agreed to be extremely good. But others are working closely alongside each other, too: when David Laws quit as chief secretary to the treasury not much more than a fortnight into the government's life, George Osborne paid a farewell tribute that suggested the two had rapidly become the closest of comrades. Lower-level aides and communication staffers operate as a single team inside No 10. Nick Clegg's holiday reading this summer includes *The Pinch*, an essay in sociology and public policy by the Conservative minister David Willetts. The smart money now says the real faultlines in this government do not run along the obvious party divide, but are found in subtler places. A crucial gulf, says one coalition insider, is between the urban, metropolitan Conservative Osborne and the old-school, shire Tory Cameron. (How to define the difference? Imagine, offers one *Guardian* colleague, that an out-of-town supermarket wants to build on the edge of a country town: Osborne would be for it, Cameron against.)

Both sides say they like the new arrangement. The advantages are obvious: the Lib Dems get to look like a serious party of government, rather than of the permanent, sandal-clad fringe, while the Tories gain a legion of Lib Dem human lightning rods, constantly at their side taking heat that would otherwise be convulsing the Conservatives alone.

There is, say those in the loop, another merit to multiparty government: they just don't know each other that well. Normally colleagues in a political party have worked together for years, carrying decades of baggage, filled with rivalries, snubs and betrayals. The loathing has usually had a long time to ferment. Today's government ministries, by contrast, are populated by men and women who, in many cases, barely knew each other before 11 May. Rick Nye, former head of the Conservative Research Department and now director of the Populus polling organisation, says: "It's like inviting your fiancée's brother to your stag weekend: it's inherently civilising. You're not going to have the strippers, you're not going to get blind drunk." To Nye, the Lib Dems are the fiancée's brother, forcing the Tories to be polite and behave themselves.

Of course there are disagreements and tensions. Cable opposes the severity of Cameron's plan to cap immigration, and the business secretary found no support from Downing Street for his proposed graduate tax. When Clegg used his PMQs debut to condemn the Iraq war as illegal, No 10 was happy for the statement to be described as a gaffe. And several Lib Dem backbenchers swallowed hard before they could vote for 20% VAT. But those expecting the first months of this shotgun marriage to be shaken by loud rows between the newlyweds have been disappointed.

Some predicted that the only way the government would achieve domestic tranquillity was by not doing very much. Those expectations have also been confounded. Indeed, the scale of this administration's ambition has been its biggest surprise. Not content with a plan to wrestle the deficit to the ground and then transform it into a surplus within five years – a goal that would count as challenge enough to most governments – the Cleggerons have launched one grand scheme after another. Michael Gove says he aims to transform education in England; Andrew Lansley has embarked on the largest reorganisation of the health service since the NHS's founding in 1948; Iain Duncan Smith wants a full upheaval of the entire system of welfare and benefits. Every one of those grand projects taken on their own would be enough to keep a government busy. But to do all these at once – along with big shake-ups in policing and criminal justice – is either a mark of supreme confidence or outright recklessness. Or, perhaps, the latter fed by the former.

This radicalism does not aim entirely in the same direction. One reason why Labour has struggled to craft a simple message of opposition, besides the party's introspective absorption in a leadership contest, is that the government it confronts is Janus-faced. Liberal enough to scrap ID cards, call for the abolition of custodial sentences for lesser crimes and to establish an inquiry into intelligence agency complicity with torture – yet Thatcherite enough to open the door yet further to the private sector in health and education as well as scything through public services with planned cuts of 25% to 40%, more brutal than anything dared by the lady herself.

It is the ideological temper of the government's ambition that is the surprise within a surprise. There was, for example, no mention of Lansley's NHS reorganisation – which will put GPs in charge of an £80bn budget, with private companies likely to be taking on much of that workload – in the Conservative election manifesto nor even in the coalition agreement, the seven-page document that serves as the holy, foundational text of this government. Voters knew that the Conservatives wanted to cut spending earlier and deeper than Labour, in order to get a head start on taming the deficit – but Osborne gave little clue that he aimed to eradicate the deficit entirely by 2015, an objective beyond the dreams of even the most hard-core deficit hawks. Instead of a Conservative-led administration governing in a shade of light-blue, reined in by the social democratic instincts of their Lib Dem partners, the coalition is emerging as full-bloodedly neoliberal on economics and beyond, with a dash of permissive liberalism in the realm of civil liberties.

How to explain this break from a script that foresaw caution if not moderation? The first answer is pure politics. "You might as well be hanged for a sheep as a lamb," says one coalitionista: even if you were less bold, you'd still be attacked and become unpopular with those destined to lose out under the cuts. So why be timid?

The second explanation lies in the preparatory work undertaken by the Conservatives prior to the election. They studied a variety of examples, from Sweden to the 1990s shredding of the deficit in Canada and the first term of Tony Blair. The one large lesson they learned is that it's better to "front-load the pain". Get all the cuts out of the way now, so that they have become a distant memory replaced by success and prosperity, come election day. At least that's the theory.

Blair's example especially has taught them to get on with it: he wasted too much of his first term, they believe, by being uncertain of what exactly he wanted to do with power. They intend to suffer no such hesitation. Witness Gove's rushing of his academies bill through parliament using emergency procedures usually associated with anti-terror legislation. He is part of a government in a hurry.

Lastly, the Lib Dems have refused to play the role assigned to them, that of moderating influence on economic or spending policy. The official narrative on this is that previously pinko Lib Dems took one look at the Treasury books, realised the depth of the black hole and became instant converts to deficit hawkery. The more credible explanation is that many Lib Dems had been on an intellectual journey over the last five or more years to which insufficient attention (including by the media) had been paid. The likes of Clegg and Laws and even the sainted Cable share more common ground with the Tories on fiscal policy than had previously been understood. Put simply, that this coalition is able to advance at full steam ahead is partly because the Liberal Democrats are perfectly happy to be on board.

If the stability, ambition and ideological colour of this government have all come as something of a surprise, one aspect of these last 100 days was both predictable and predicted. David Cameron has made a great personal start in the job of prime minister.

One doesn't have to like his programme to admire his perform-ance. Sure, he has benefited from the contrast with his immediate predecessor: it's easier to look at ease in a job after Gordon Brown made such an obvious show of his discomfort doing it. The bar was set low. But Cameron has cleared it twice over.

The moment when that became undeniable was his parliamen-tary statement on the publication of the Saville report into Bloody Sunday. The register was pitch perfect: statesmanlike but also plain speaking and emotionally intelligent. Where Blair would have sounded actorly, even melodramatic, Cameron came across as sincere. His performances in parliament have been relaxed and assured; he is, for now, fully in control of his party.

Apparently Cameron enjoys those duties Brown would have regarded as irritating obligations of the job: hosting garden parties, meeting the Queen, chairing cabinet meetings. "It's not that power suits him, it's that the office suits him."

Some Conservative colleagues have noted a lack of attention to detail, as if Cameron regards himself as a non-executive chairman rather than a chief executive. One coalition insider sees Cameron as more of a head of state than a head of government. (Some Lib Dem observers see this comfort with the establishment as a faultline between them and the Conservatives: "Cameron's born to rule," one told me, "Clegg's born to reform.")

There have been definite missteps, three of them coming while travelling abroad: insulting Pakistan while in India and Israel while in Turkey, and suggesting Britain was the "junior partner" to the US in 1940, when that was the year the country stood famously alone against the Nazis. He erred again this month, breezily telling an audience in Sussex that Iran "has got a nuclear weapon": that came as news to those capitals hellbent on prevent-ing just that outcome. Some in his own party regard with equal fury his early, and unsuccessful, attempt to defang the backbench

1922 committee of Conservative MPs. These errors may yet come to loom larger, even to form a pattern that defines David Cameron: "foreign policy klutz" is Labour's phrase. But right now the coalition is headed by a man most professionals would describe as good political horseflesh.

Will the story of these first three months match the eventual story of this government? Few would bet on it, especially those who remember that Gordon Brown also marked his 100 days with good reviews. The test that matters, says one senior operative, is "the 100 weeks test". There is so much that can go wrong. Will the big macro-economic gamble of rapid and radical deficit cutting have paid off – or will the country be languishing in the depths of a double-dip recession? Will the NHS be improved – or sunk by Lansley's reforms? Will more than a handful of parents be setting up Gove's "free" schools? How will voters react to huge cuts in public services when their full force is felt? Will the referendum on the alternative-vote system for the Commons bring a "Yes"or loud "No" from the British public?

On the answer to those questions will hang the fate of this government. No one can know whether the marriage of Cameron and Clegg will end with a realignment of the centre-right of British politics, shutting out Labour for a generation – or in an economic calamity that disqualifies the Tories and Lib Dems from power for just as long. All we can know now is that the coalition has surprised those who thought it would be a novelty characterised by weakness, division and timidity. It has started strong and bold. And it will surely surprise us again.

# Acknowledgments

The rather wonderful job of editing *The Bedside Guardian* came after 10 years toiling as a managing editor. It has been a real pleasure to dive back into the deep pool of *Guardian* journalism and for that I must thank Alan Rusbridger, the editor of the *Guardian*. Lisa Darnell was a wise and very supportive publisher to this first-time anthologist. Aster Greenhill, well above and beyond the call of duty, prepared folders and folders of cuttings for me to read, and two previous "Bedsiders", Hugh Muir and Martin Kettle, gave me terrific advice. Harriet Lake calmly and with great aplomb took all my ers and ums and endless panicky changes of mind as I was forced to choose between pieces that I loved but wouldn't fit, and turned them into clear and concise lists, containing every last bit of information that Toby Manhire, a wonderful colleague and text editor, needed to actually put the book together. Finally I have to thank Sue, Beth and Kate who were forced to holiday each day with me as I sat poring over cuttings, muttering to myself. They have had a lot up with which to put.

*Chris Elliott, September 2010*